INTERNATIONAL PUBLIC RELATIONS

INTERNATIONAL
PUBLIC
RELATIONS

Negotiating Culture, Identity, and Power

Patricia A. Curtin
University of Oregon

T. Kenn Gaither
Elon University

SAGE Publications
Thousand Oaks ▪ London ▪ New Delhi

For information:

Sage Publications, Inc.
2455 Teller Road
Thousand Oaks, California 91320
E-mail: order@sagepub.com

Sage Publications Ltd.
1 Oliver's Yard
55 City Road
London EC1Y 1SP
United Kingdom

Sage Publications India Pvt. Ltd.
B-42, Panchsheel Enclave
Post Box 4109
New Delhi 110 017 India

Printed in the United States of America

Library of Congress Cataloging-in-Publication Data

Curtin, Patricia A. (Patricia Ann), 1955–
International public relations: Negotiating culture, identity, and power / Patricia A. Curtin, T. Kenn Gaither.
    p. cm.
Includes bibliographical references and index.
ISBN-13: 978-1-4129-1414-7 (cloth)
ISBN-13: 978-1-4129-1415-4 (pbk.)
    1. Public relations. 2. Public relations—Cross-cultural studies.
3. Intercultural communication. 4. Culture and globalization.
I. Gaither, Thomas Kenneth. II. Title.

HM1221.C87 2007
659.2—dc22   2006025768

This book is printed on acid-free paper.

07   08   09   10   11   10   9   8   7   6   5   4   3   2   1

Acquisitions Editor:	Todd R. Armstrong
Editorial Assistant:	Sarah K. Quesenberry
Production Editor:	Diane S. Foster
Copy Editor:	Carol Anne Peschke
Typesetter:	C&M Digitals (P) Ltd.
Proofreader:	Scott Oney
Indexer:	Molly Hall
Cover Designer:	Candice Harman

Contents

Preface

When we sat down to write a 300-page book, we asked ourselves, "Do we really need to spend 2 years of our lives producing yet another book on international public relations?" Obviously, we answered in the affirmative.

We need another book on international public relations for two reasons: to produce a text inclusive of all types of practice found around the world and to provide a new foundation that embraces cultural nuances, environmental changes, and the ongoing process of how people make sense of their world. Our belief in the need for a critical and cultural approach stems from our years of agency and corporate practice and was reinforced by our participation in the spring 2005 voyage of the Semester at Sea study abroad program. The shipboard-based university program incorporates classroom material with experiential learning in ports around the world, presenting a comparative culture perspective. For one author it was the seventh Semester at Sea experience; for the other, the first. But for both, the global voyage to developing countries, which contain the majority of the world's population, firmed our resolve that too much public relations activity is taking place around the world that current theoretical approaches to international public relations don't recognize, don't support, and can't explain.

In this volume we attempt to capture the richness of the field and its variety by not privileging one organization, region, or form of practice over another. We examine not just multinational corporations but also nongovernment organizations, militaries, governments, activist groups, and others originating in a multitude of global locales and performing myriad functions. But this is not a book of case studies. Although informative, case studies are limited in their heuristic value and often in practical guidance as well—unless, of course, you're faced with the same situation in the same place at the same time. And many case studies of "international" practice simply describe practice in a country other than the United States in comparison to U.S. theory and practice, providing an inherently ethnocentric perspective.

Instead, we use a variety of examples to build support for a cultural studies perspective that addresses issues of cross-national or cross-cultural public relations. We approach international public relations as a synergistic, holistic process, building a broad theoretical framework that informs the wide variety of global practice while supporting a flexible practice matrix that takes into account situational particulars.

We don't claim the resulting theory to be a normative one. Consistent with the cultural studies paradigm we embrace, readers will find that the theory presented is more descriptive than prescriptive. But considerations of ethical practice in the face of global challenges form an underlying thread in each chapter, threads we pull together in chapter 11.

If we've succeeded in our task, readers will find that the theoretical base and practice matrix outlined are applicable to any public relations practice, not just an international one. Culture clashes happen in the domestic workplace, technology compresses time and space to create new interfaces between the global and local in even the most rural areas, and power remains a constant in any relationship, in any region of the world.

This book is far from the last word on public relations practice, international or otherwise. We hope it serves as a foundation and catalyst for future scholarship that increases our understanding of the field while strengthening our ability to practice public relations in a manner respectful of those with whom we are communicating, no matter our nationality, culture, class, ethnicity, or gender. As an ongoing update and research aid to students and researchers, a supporting Web site can be found at http://jcomm.uoregon.edu/~pcurtin.

One caveat: We have tried to avoid U.S. centrism, but we are both U.S. citizens. We apologize up front for any ethnocentrism that may have crept in, despite our best efforts to keep it firmly at bay.

❖ ACKNOWLEDGMENTS

We would like to acknowledge the many people who helped see this project to fruition. Our reviewers made many valuable suggestions and increased the international scope of the text. We thank Carolina

Acosta-Alzura, The University of Georgia; Lowell Frazier, Zayed University; Shirley Leitch, University of Waikato, New Zealand; Jacquie L'Etang, Stirling Media Research Institute, University of Stirling, Scotland; Judy Motion, University of Waikato, New Zealand; Usha Raman, L. V. Prasad Eye Institute; Ming-Yi Wu, Western Illinois University; and R. S. Zaharna, American University.

The editorial staff at Sage—first Margaret Seawell, then Todd Armstrong and Sarah Quesenberry—lent us unflagging confidence and assistance throughout the project, as did Helen Allrich, who went well beyond the call of her research assistant duties to ensure that this book saw the light of day.

The first author would like to thank her children, Chandra and Dara, for their continuous, boundless support. She also owes a debt of gratitude to her coauthor, Kenn Gaither, for introducing her to the incredible experience that is Semester at Sea and, as always, making the project both intellectually challenging and incredibly fun. The result is a true collaboration; it wouldn't have been possible alone.

1

The Challenges of International Public Relations

❖   ❖   ❖

Public relations is coming of age around the world. In the 20th century, the United States took the lead in defining its practice and formalizing its structure. But in the new millennium, public relations is blossoming from a U.S.-based industry into a global industrial phenomenon spanning countries with vastly different cultures, economic and political systems, and levels of development. The number of public relations agencies and organizations that have sprung up around the world in the past few years are proof that public relations is recognized and formalized around the world, from the United States to sub-Saharan Africa to Asia.

Consider, for example, Ireland, Romania, Russia, and Italy, which are among the more than 20 different European nations with public relations associations. Public relations in Italy has grown so much that T. M. Falconi, president of the Italian Federation of Public Relations, claims 1 of every 1,000 Italians is a "public relations operator" (2003, p. 15). In Bulgaria, the public relations field is "developing too fast and it will be not overstated if we say that most of the public relations agencies and departments are as good as they [sic] colleagues from West Europe" (Boshnakova & Zareva, 2005, p. 12). In 1992, there was only one public relations agency in Bucharest, Romania; now there are 20 (GAPR, 2004).

According to a 2004 poll, China has more than 1,500 public relations firms, and public relations is one of the top five professions in the country. The growth of the profession in China has caused a shortage of qualified public relations professionals (Wood, 2005). In Russia, Mikhail Margelov, head of the Russian Information Centre, said, "The Russian experience since 1996 is one of rapid and steady growth of public relations work practically in all spheres of the life of the country" (in Fish, 2000, ¶ 53). The Middle East Public Relations Association anticipated a 30% surge in membership in 2005 (MEPRA, 2004).

To maintain the crown, Hatshepsut ruled as a man to fit patriarchal Egyptian society.

Photo 1.1   Hatshepsut, Known for Her Skillful Ability to Curry Public Favor and Strong Leadership Qualities

SOURCE: Metropolitan Museum of Art.

But this talk of the growth of public relations is really about the increasing presence of institutional structures to define its practice and to legitimize it. Although public relations has been studied as a social science and formalized only in the 20th century, evidence of its practice can be traced back to ancient civilizations in Egypt, Babylon, China, Greece, and Rome, to name but a few. In medieval India, *sutradhars*, or traveling storytellers, spread rulers' messages, serving a common public relations function. Egyptian leader Hatshepsut, the first woman Pharaoh, might not have been able to hire a public relations agency to help improve her image, but she was surrounded by advisors who guided her using public relations techniques (Photo 1.1). The elements of public relations are as old as ancient Egypt and older, and they have developed over the years around the globe in various ways.

Because of the varying forms of public relations in much of the world, the field is fraught with inconsistency and varied international views of its purpose and practice. There is still no overarching definition of public relations, and there is little consistency among practitioners for describing their profession. In Asia, public relations professionals commonly see their work as tantamount to sales and marketing, in Latin America event planning might be viewed as public relations, and in the United States it is often called a strategic management function. The gap between these forms of public relations is evident in the lack of a truly international public relations theory that addresses disparate nations, varying economic and sociopolitical systems, and different cultures. Recent scholarship has made progress toward addressing some of these needs. Still, the practice of public relations is far more progressive than its scholarship.

This book addresses these issues by using a cultural studies approach to develop international public relations theory that is culturally sensitive, reflexive, and dynamic. Its purpose is to provide a comprehensive theoretical base to inform the wide array of global public relations practices and to demonstrate its applicability in formulating and executing campaigns around the globe. As a caveat, you'll find that public relations resists easy categorizations. It's too new and its practice too uneven to generate a uniform and logical narrative. Instead, you might find the discussion of international public relations in this book unpredictable, complex, and even illogical at times. This is the peril of studying public relations around the globe; it rarely makes sense, even less so when terms such as *international* and *culture* are applied.

This chapter centers on fundamental issues in public relations by attempting to define it and summarizing how it's practiced around the world. We begin by examining various definitions of public relations as a foundation for what it means to do and to study international public relations. The next section illustrates some types of public relations practice around the world to demonstrate the breadth and diversity of the field. The final part of the chapter brings this information together to provide a context for the remainder of the book, which informs international public relations theory development. A logical starting point is an issue that has puzzled scholars for decades and continues to divide practitioners around the world: What is public relations?

❖ IN SEARCH OF AN IDENTITY: DEFINING PUBLIC RELATIONS

Pick up any textbook on public relations from anywhere in the world, and chances are it begins with a chapter devoted to defining public relations. The practice of public relations is most formalized in the

United States, which has the greatest global concentration of public relations education programs and degrees, public relations agencies, and associations and generates a disproportionate amount of public relations scholarship. Many U.S. textbooks present their own definition of public relations, often citing researcher Rex Harlow, who compiled more than 470 definitions of public relations before creating his own 87-word definition. The Public Relations Society of America (PRSA) promulgated a shorter, widely accepted definition in 1988: "Public relations helps an organization and its publics adapt mutually to each other."

More recently, scholars have sought to develop more parsimonious definitions and, rather than providing a definition per se, identify key words that describe the practice of public relations. A study of U.S. public relations educators and practitioners (Reber & Harriss, 2003) identified four words linked to the profession: *strategy, managerial, tactical,* and *responsive.* The researchers found public relations too complex to fit into a single definition. Hutton (1999) and Bruning and Ledingham (1999) offered relational definitions that emphasize the management of strategic relationships. Other descriptive definitions commonly include words such as *reputation* and *credibility,* which describe general concerns of public relations that shape its form.

Another approach is to develop a composite definition of public relations from the Web sites of international public relations agencies, including Burson-Marsteller, Weber Shandwick Worldwide, Fleishman-Hillard, Porter Novelli, and Edelman. Such a definition might be as follows: A form of strategic communication directed primarily toward gaining public understanding and acceptance and the process of creating a good relationship between an organization and the public, especially with regard to reputation and to communication of information.

The individual definitions public relations agencies use to describe their field reflect the collective definitions espoused by public relations associations worldwide. Consider those of the Middle East Public Relations Association ("the discipline that looks after reputation with the aim of earning understanding and support, and influencing opinion and behavior") and the Chartered Institute of Public Relations (CIPR) in the United Kingdom ("the discipline which looks after reputation, with the aim of earning understanding and support and influencing opinion and behavior. It is the planned and sustained effort to establish and maintain goodwill and mutual understanding between an organisation and its publics."). In the Netherlands, a professional public relations organization met for the express purpose of defining public relations and eventually gave up, concluding that such an endeavor was fruitless (van Ruler, 2003).

These functional definitions of public relations are balanced by **normative approaches** to defining the field, which *describe what public relations should be and give us guidelines for practicing public relations*. In the United States, the dominant definition among scholars is that of Grunig and Hunt (1984, p. 6): "management of communication between an organization and its publics, best accomplished using two-way symmetric communication." This definition illustrates the sweeping scope of public relations practice; an organization could be a few individuals rallying around a cause or a multi-billion-dollar corporation. Publics could include internal publics, such as employees, or external audiences, such as other governments, nongovernment organizations (NGOs), stockholders, strategic alliances, and citizens.

The range of publics in the public relations arena is one of the factors that complicate efforts to provide a functional definition of the field, tilting it toward normative approaches. Skeptics of normative approaches and theories contend that there is a difference between how things should be and how things are, and that's where normative theories fall short. This book focuses on describing rather than prescribing to complement the strengths of normative stances while recognizing the key role ethics plays in any practical communicative endeavor.

Normative theories are based on empirical research, so they are likewise grounded on observation and data. That research is then extended to make inferences about public relations under given circumstances. The problem is whether those theories apply in circumstances that differ from the research that developed them. In international public relations, it is especially important to reflect critically on theory and whether it effectively translates across borders and socioeconomic and political systems different from its country of origin. Western European countries and the United States are the countries of origin for many public relations theories. These same regions have led the way for defining public relations. We'll examine the implications of the Grunig and Hunt definition, including how it privileges a certain perspective and its relevance to international public relations, in more detail in chapter 3.

Defining public relations is even more complex when semantics are considered internationally, that is, in different countries and languages. The term *public relations* was coined in the United States. Where the term has been adopted around the world, the functions associated with it in the United States have also tended to be adopted. The Japanese language has no word for public relations, and many

European languages such as German similarly don't have a commensurate term (Sriramesh, 2003; Valin, 2004). Public relations in Japan has meant "press relations" (Cooper-Chen, 1996). In South Korea, an idiomatic expression for public relations, *hong-bo,* is often used (Kim, 2003). Romania has a term for public relations, but it's often confused with *relations with the public,* which describes the customer and information service desk function (GAPR, 2004). Undermining the definitional complexities of public relations is the extent to which public relations practice varies by region of the world.

Regardless of the hundreds of definitions of public relations, there is one certainty: **Public relations** *is a communicative process; that is, it involves some form of communication, whether it be written, verbal, or neither, as a purposeful choice, and it is a process.* As such, it isn't static, fixed, or immutable; rather, public relations is largely about creating and recreating ideas and generating meaning. Such a nonlinear view of public relations defies strict parameters and complicates the quest for a single definition. Yet this view offers a rich vein for reanalyzing concepts that have blurred public relations internationally, such as propaganda and persuasion. These are just two contested meanings that merit some consideration in discussions of international public relations processes.

We believe that international public relations must be inclusive to accurately reflect the diversity of worldwide communication processes. In this light, a single definition of public relations may be less important than an informed worldview that embraces diverse meanings and the recognition that meaning in international public relations is a generated and iterative process.

❖ MYRIAD FORMS OF PUBLIC RELATIONS

A wide base of public relations research, generated mostly in the United States, holds that public relations exists only in certain conditions, which commonly include democracy, economic and press freedom, and civil liberty. Significant parts of the world fail these conditional criteria, and we believe those areas have much to offer the development of a theory that is truly international in scope. In those areas, public relations is practiced in some form or another, although that form might differ from the U.S. conception of public relations as an organizational function that precludes propaganda and persuasion. Most U.S. theories posit that two-way communication is needed, with an organization using research to initiate a dialogue with targeted publics. Through that research, traditional symmetric theory holds, it's possible to build meaningful relationships by adapting and remaining flexible. One-way concepts of communication, such as propaganda and persuasion, are subsequently rejected, cast into an ill-defined area other than legitimate public relations.

But what are we to make of some Eastern European countries, where propaganda is still seen as a tool of centralized governments? Or countries in Latin America, Africa, and Asia, where government control of information and media conflict with democratic principles? Or the many countries around the world that hardly differentiate between public relations, propaganda, and persuasion? Our position is that these questions must be explored to inform public relations as an international practice: Public relations is being practiced around the world, independent of Western theories and definitions, whether or not traditional theories have adequately accounted for that practice and its diversity.

Research suggests that propaganda can be either a phase in a process that leads to traditional public relations or synonymous with public relations, particularly in countries emerging from dictatorships and authoritarian governments. When propaganda is considered as a form or relative of public relations, it becomes part of a process of generating meaning, influenced by cultural norms and perceptions depending on region of the world. This idea explains why "public relations" in one country might be "propaganda" or "information" in another.

This section describes international public relations in the 21st century by examining some of the developing dominant forms of practice, including regional perceptions of public relations and the roles of government, economies, and politics, among others. Collectively, these considerations have shaped the global form and development of public relations. Note that organizing international public relations in this manner is a departure from many studies of international public relations that group its practice into regions through country-by-country case studies or continental overviews.

With increasing globalization, shared situations transcend national lines and contiguous boundaries as key factors. Globalization has dissolved national boundaries into a distinct set of situational particulars. The new chips on the international game board include governments shifting to democracy, nation building, multinational corporations (MNCs) envisioning expansion, NGOs trying to boost development and monitor global issues, and nations branding themselves to attract tourism and investment. Culture is the layer that doesn't lend itself to monolithic designs of national identity. In sum, by observing how shared situations and cultures clash and assimilate, we can identify common areas of practice.

Emerging Democracies, Developing Public Relations

We've already suggested that public relations is present to varying degrees in all countries and all sociopolitical systems. That supposition doesn't explain why the United States has emerged as the worldwide leader in codifying public relations. One reason is because it has an open communication environment bound by democratic systems and principles. The U.S. legacy of a free press and a marketplace of ideas has spurred the industry's rise in associations, conferences, and practices since the beginning of the 20th century. In the United States, the growth of public relations has corresponded with institutional structures, such as public relations agencies, that could define their work and value to society. Conversely, many countries don't have the same constituencies to define their work.

The plurality of voices and structures in the dialogue of what it means to define and practice public relations is limited in countries with centralized governments. Some scholars have pointed out that authoritarian governments abase Western notions of public relations by restricting media and squelching dialogue with target publics. In these countries, government is the preeminent voice and might be associated more with propaganda than public relations.

Many scholars have pointed out the historical association between public relations and propaganda. That link is still fresh in Latin American countries such as Chile, parts of Africa, Asian countries including China and the Philippines, and Eastern European countries such as Poland, Slovenia, Romania, and Russia. In these countries, public relations isn't a wholly separate concept from that of propaganda.

Reforming communication from the pejorative of propaganda to the accepted realm of traditional public relations is a slow process. In Russia, propaganda was associated with oligarchies until the launch of McDonald's in the country in the late 1980s. At that time, the Russian government was slowly divesting its power, giving way to privatization. This shift arguably created the need for public relations and redefined it. No longer was the emphasis on government communication and one-way messages pounded into powerless publics through propaganda. Now it could be used in new ways by private organizations. The contested definition of public relations changed as the political paradigm shifted in Russia, making it more varied, open, and flexible than ever before.

Nation Building

Many African nations gained independence from their colonial rulers in the 1960s. In the early 1990s, the Soviet Union dissolved into individual countries including Latvia, Belarus, and Georgia. The slow process toward democracy in the former Soviet Union centered on *perestroika,* which loosely translates as "restructuring" in English. The term became a symbol for change and signaled a branding of new republics as divorced from the old legacy of communism. More recently, East Timor became a nation in 2002.

Conversely, the United States has had more than 200 years of independence and more than 200 years to initiate and refine its nation-building strategies. The other countries just mentioned have had far less time to conduct nation-building activities; they are new to nationhood, not far removed from a colonial legacy. They're almost all developing countries with the challenge of building a national identity not inherent in the artificial geopolitical boundaries imposed by former colonial rulers. Many developing nations are working to build a national identity along these lines, which often cross traditional cultural boundaries.

Nation building *is a concentrated government effort to achieve domestic and international goals.* Domestically, governments might strive for national unity or consensus for a national cause or effort. Internationally, nation building is an effort to bring a country into a global stream of credibility and awareness, often for economic support from other governments or aid organizations. One trend is the number of developing countries worldwide, including Russia, the Philippines, and Nigeria, that have used Western public relations agencies to develop and execute nation-building public relations campaigns. Such countries dot the globe, bound only by their global status as developing countries.

As newly formed countries emerge from the ashes of colonialism or invasion, conditions often are ripe for terrorism, destruction, and power struggles as competing interests vie for control or try to undermine nascent government structures. In East Timor, for example, pro-Indonesia militias resisting East Timorese independence were blamed for killing approximately 1,400 Timorese (CIA, 2006). In such cases, building a new nation is punctuated by adversity and human rights concerns.

Among the challenges any communication apparatus faces in some developing countries are geographic size, ethnic and religious diversity, and linguistic barriers. The African continent comprises more than 50 countries and more than 1,000 different languages (African

Cultural Center, n.d.) and as uneven a level of development as one might imagine. In the Sudan alone, for example, there are an assumed 400 languages and dialects (Federal Research Division, n.d.). Ponder how a public relations practitioner might launch a public relations campaign to promote national unity in the Sudan, where the number of languages is overshadowed by development statistics that would preclude many Western public relations tactics.

According to the CIA (2006) *World Factbook* statistics for Sudan from 2003, 40% of the population was illiterate, 40% lived below the poverty line, 0.9% of its citizens had Internet access, and average income was 115,328.90 Sudan dinars (US$460). U.S. scholars have noted that "there is little opportunity for practicing public relations in the Western sense of the term" in African countries such as Sudan (Van Leuven & Pratt, 1996, p. 95). When Harare, Zimbabwe, embarked on a major public relations campaign to improve the city's image, one resident said, "No amount of public relations would stop sewer lines from blocking and roads from developing potholes" ("Harare Embarks," 2002, ¶ 8), demonstrating that public relations is far less important than basic human needs. The same holds true for many other parts of the world, where public relations faces a terrain vastly different from that of its practice epicenter, the United States.

Best Foot Forward Public Relations

The complexities of international public relations are also reflected by a cultural emphasis on social relations, notably in parts of the Middle East and Asia. In the former, it's important to take into account the historical and ideological context of the region, often based on the Qur'an in Islamic countries. Cultural differences give rise to distinctly different communication traditions between most Arabic nations and the United States.

In Arab nations, "a press release, for example, may read more like a political proclamation than a news announcement" (Zaharna, 1995, p. 255). United Arab Emirates practitioners view public relations not as a communication function but as a social relations one, placing a great deal of emphasis on receiving delegations (Creedon, Al-Khaja, & Kruckeberg, 1995). Most Egyptian universities don't differentiate between sales, marketing, and public relations, and practitioners consequently often view public relations as a hospitality-related function (Keenan, 2003). In the Middle East, hospitality functions for dignitaries have constituted public relations (Ayish & Kruckeberg, 1999). Guest relations and translation services were similarly early forms of public relations in China (Culbertson & Chen, 2003). In Singapore, public relations often is seen as a sales and marketing function and is used heavily by the government (Chay-Németh, 2003).

Business-Driven Public Relations

For economic titans such as the United States, the United Kingdom, and Germany, international public relations often consists of MNCs establishing presences abroad and large agencies branching into different countries. These examples place business and corporate interests at the forefront of international public relations. Harold Burson (2003a), co-founder of Burson-Marsteller, said the agency's efforts to become a truly global business hinged on opening offices in Europe, Australia, and Asia. Well-known public relations agencies in the United States almost all have exported their business around the world by opening offices or partnering with local firms. Edelman, which bills itself as the world's largest independent public relations firm, maintains 43 offices around the world, according to its Web site.

For every well-known corporate behemoth such as Nike or Coca-Cola, scores of other businesses are expanding abroad and recognizing public relations is a necessity, not an option. Gone are the days of riding roughshod into other countries, opening shop, and watching money pile up in the company safe. As technology has linked the world, public perceptions of corporations and concomitant practices are some of the indicators of effective business practice. Nike's corporate reputation has been scorched by charges of operating sweatshops in countries such as El Salvador and China. Web logs (blogs), maintained by cause-minded individuals and groups, and watchdog group Web sites have supplemented traditional news media to make Nike's public relations challenges truly global.

Growth in technology and the emergence of regional trading agreements such as the European Union (EU) and the North American Free Trade Agreement (NAFTA) have paved the way for international public relations to thrive. Hundreds of case studies chronicle the public relations pitfalls and successes of MNCs. These case studies have increased our understanding of the multitude of issues an MNC or any organization might face as it commences operations in a new country, including

- Negotiating language in culture and vice versa, where meaning often is not literal
- Understanding cultural practices that extend far beyond language

- Balancing short-term corporate demand for economic results with the time needed to build relationships
- Working through and within asymmetric relations of power on many different levels
- Clashing with local and national governments over legal issues
- Raising awareness in countries with many languages and media systems

These are just a few of the challenges any organization or cause might face, and this list doesn't begin to address all the other domains where international public relations is practiced. Consider, for example, how worldwide health organizations raise awareness of pressing international health concerns, how governments and tourism associations promote their countries abroad, or how sporting events and activities relate to international public relations. This is to say that international public relations is more than a corporate, organizational, or government undertaking; it operates at an inestimable number of points of contact, where actors on an international plane interact with each other through any form of exchange or communication. As Botan (1992, p. 153) reminds us, we need "a definition of practice not tied to any one set of assumptions, particularly the assumption that public relations is a management function. We need a view that focuses on the process at the center of public relations—using communication to adapt relationships between organizations and their publics."

❖ CULTURAL RELATIONSHIP CONSTRUCTS

Asia offers layers of cultural constructs essential to understanding Eastern forms of public relations. Cultural constructs don't affect public relations practice; they are the essence of public relations practice. Korea has *cheong*, for example, an idiomatic expression that loosely relates to respect between two individuals (Rhee, 2002). At a 2002 public relations conference, one author saw a Korean scholar spend more than 10 minutes trying to explain *cheong* in English before giving up, saying he couldn't give the term due justice in English. China similarly has *renqing*, a set of social norms one must be able to negotiate to function effectively in Chinese society (Huang, 2001). The different cultural practices in relation to gender and age in Eastern cultures are minefields for unsuspecting public relations efforts that fail to negotiate the Eastern landscape, where sophisticated and systematic social relations define society.

Other cultural relationship constructs aren't formalized through terminology. They often exist as invisible webs that link people through relationships. Nu Skin, a multi-billion-dollar company with more than 1,000 employees worldwide, encountered unexpected problems when it sent a manager in his thirties to head its operations in Malaysia. Nu Skin didn't take into account the status accorded to age in Malaysia. The manager was deemed too young to head such a large organization, creating a perception that Nu Skin wasn't wholly committed to its Malaysian operations (Wakefield, 1999).

Nu Skin's failure to recognize and negotiate this invisible web of culture isn't uncommon. In many African countries, for example, aunts and uncles are regarded as parents. The expatriate manager of CBG, Guinea's largest bauxite mining company, noted that absenteeism ran as high as 20% as employees traveled to remote villages to mourn deaths of parents, aunts, and uncles (Auclair, 1992). Imagine a multi-million-dollar business steeped in capitalism moving into a new country and having one fifth of its employees absent to attend to family matters.

To a native Guinean, this example is hardly noteworthy. To a non-native, however, it offers a lesson that all cultures are necessarily complex, and international public relations practitioners often are outsiders looking in, trying to access the web of spoken and unspoken norms that constitute culture. The complexity of these concealed webs varies by culture, and public relations has struggled to access those webs, raising questions such as these: Does a one-size-fits-all approach to public relations work? Who should develop and implement a public relations program abroad: a host individual or agency? One lesson learned is that language skills aren't enough to execute a public relations campaign abroad. The idiosyncrasies of culture are as important to providing an environment for effective communication as is the language itself.

❖ INTERNATIONAL PUBLIC RELATIONS TODAY

Clearly, culture matters in international public relations. Its practice varies greatly around the globe through competing definitions of public relations and semantic nuances that suggest links to propaganda and persuasion. On a larger level, it's the cultural subtleties that alter not only definitions of public relations but also what it means to do public relations internationally. Culture represents the layers public relations must contend with to get to shared situations at the core of international public relations, whether building nations, attracting tourism, spurring economic growth, or quelling discord from opposition groups or nations. The layers of culture extend across international lines, from developed to developing countries, from democratic nations to authoritarian regimes.

Although it's important to define public relations practice, such an endeavor can also limit theoretical scope. Definitions privilege worldviews, establish power relations, and affix names to communicative processes that are constantly in flux, shaped by global forces that include economic and cultural tides. Many ongoing efforts to grapple with definitions of public relations fail because they're limited by Western notions of democracy and capitalism, forcing a foreign frame onto indigenous cultural constructs.

At its most basic level, culture is manifest in the daily interactions many of us take for granted. Those interactions can mean the difference between failure and success in a media relations campaign. For example, according to the International Communications Consultancy Organisation (ICCO, 2004, p. 5),

> German journalists like small press briefings, but UK journalists prefer one to one interviews. The Italian press are OK with breakfast meetings (not too early though!) but don't like dinners or parties—evenings are for private, family time. Belgian press don't like breakfast meetings, but enjoy a lunch or dinner (including beer).

This chapter has sought to describe what international public relations looks like today, not how it ought to be practiced or why it should be practiced a certain way. Observing public relations on its own terms around the world is a critical component of this book. How it has progressed and come to mean so many things to so many people across so many different cultures provides the descriptive patterns generating the international public relations theory in this book.

In chapter 2 we take a closer look at international public relations by examining two cases: Coca-Cola in India and image cultivation campaigns in South Korea and Swaziland. These cases point to the need for a cultural studies approach as the theoretical framework for the book because of its emphasis on issues of culture, identity, and power. In chapter 3, we introduce the circuit of culture model, examining how it can inform global public relations theory and practice. The chapter introduces you to the moments that constitute the circuit: production, representation, consumption, identity, and regulation. Each moment—and how they relate synergistically—is framed within the launch of New Coke®.

The next five chapters examine each moment of the circuit in greater detail, again integrating theory and considering how the moments interrelate as a process. Chapter 4 studies the regulatory environments of global public relations practices by examining the role of political, economic, and technological infrastructures and cultural norms in shaping global public relations practices. Chapter 5 discusses the moment of representation, including the ways in which cultural meanings are encoded in the content and format of public relations campaigns and materials. Through examples in Russia, Asia, and the Galápagos Islands, we explicate the role of power at the basis of global public relations practice and demonstrate the role of public relations in building individual, media, organizational, and national agendas.

The constraints and conditions under which practitioners work and how meaning is imbued in their work is the theme of chapter 6, which focuses on the moment of production. Examples from around the world illustrate how the cultural process of production often is gendered and racialized, making globalization a site of competition for power in production. The circuit stresses that the moment of production cannot be isolated from the moment of consumption because meaning resides not in an object itself but in how that object is used.

That use is part of the moment of consumption, discussed in chapter 7. The chapter demonstrates that simply encoding a dominant meaning in public relations materials doesn't guarantee that consumers, particularly in other cultures, will decode those meanings in the same way. Chapter 8 rounds out the circuit by focusing on the moment of identity. Public relations campaigns create identities for publics and for products and services, organizations create brands to differentiate themselves from the competition, publics appropriate meanings to create new identities for themselves, and nations create identities to situate themselves within the power flow of world politics and economics. Identities are framed as continuously created, appropriated, defined, and redefined, as much a process as the circuit itself.

Chapter 9 is a macro-level discussion of the entire circuit of culture at work in a practical setting and proposes the cultural–economic model of practice. It identifies public relations practitioners as cultural intermediaries who can fulfill boundary-spanning roles by shaping and packaging issues at the nexus of culture, identity, and power. Those considerations provide the thrust behind chapter 10, which introduces a practice matrix to help you develop and apply a worldview. The move from theory to practice is manifest in the practice matrix, which provides a roadmap for the ongoing machinations of the circuit of culture.

Chapter 11 centers on ethical considerations in global practice. The circuit is used to establish a situation ethic in which moral decision making is grounded in the absolutes of each moment yet adaptable to various situational particulars. The final chapter looks to the future, providing new ways of thinking about how public relations practitioners serve as cultural intermediaries. It seeks to solidify the traits of practitioners and scholars with worldviews that enable them to grasp multiple viewpoints, recognize power issues, factor in exigent variables, and develop sound public relations campaigns.

CHAPTER SUMMARY

- Public relations is a process of communication, whether written, verbal, or neither, as a purposeful choice to create and recreate ideas and generate meaning.

- Public relations is practiced around the world, often without formalizing local structures to define its practice and role in indigenous society.

- Notions of public relations vary greatly around the world because of different cultures, languages, and socioeconomic and political conditions.

- The evolution of public relations has had a different path in all cultures, depending on historical, political, and economic development.

- Recognizing cultural diversity and nuances of culture are keys to understanding diverse public relations practices around the world.

2

Opening Global Gateways

❖   ❖   ❖

I was struck by the thought that although I was advising a banana company, I was actually fighting in the cold war.

—Edward L. Bernays, on his work for the United
Fruit Company in the early 1950s (1965, p. 766)

As a communicative process, public relations constitutes certain forms of representation. These forms of representation comprise innumerable texts, more commonly known as public relations tactics. Embedded in each tactic is a multitude of symbols that are both visual and verbal, spoken and unspoken, visible and invisible. How these texts are chosen and how the symbols are interpreted are influenced by culture, making it the glue in the process of meaning creation. When practitioners are formulating a public relations campaign, for example, they're ideally considering the strategic big picture to develop tactics that meet a desired goal. Traditionally, public relations has defined success by how well its target publics absorb those tactics.

Exactly what is being represented often is not easily determined in international public relations, however. U.S. public relations pioneer Edward Bernays realized this in his work for the United Fruit

Company (UFCO) in the 1950s. If we consider public relations as a text encompassing countless symbols, Bernays was a master at determining what text was needed and how its symbols should be arranged to meet a certain objective. In the case of the U.S.-owned UFCO, it was maintaining its stronghold over the Latin American country of Guatemala. UFCO relied heavily on countries such as Guatemala to import bananas into the lucrative U.S. market (Photo 2.1).

When a reformist government threatened to undermine UFCO's monopoly over banana production in Guatemala by nationalizing land, the company hired Bernays to protect its interests. Although there was little evidence the reformist government was communist, Bernays capitalized on the rampant fear of communism in the United States at the time by developing a campaign to discredit Guatemala's democratically elected president, Jacobo Arbenz Guzmán.

In this process, Bernays's efforts to represent UFCO were more than just representing a company in Guatemala. He was representing a cause by embedding it in the sweeping U.S. fear of communism. The campaign included staging events, writing leaflets and brochures, and flying U.S. reporters to Guatemala in carefully orchestrated junkets to see the communist evils of the Arbenz regime firsthand. The end result? By using public relations techniques for UFCO, Bernays helped overthrow the Arbenz government, thrusting Guatemala into decades of brutal dictatorships.

As Edward L. Bernays found in his work for UFCO, public relations work for multinational corporations often has larger political implications.

Photo 2.1   United Fruit Company Workers Pack Bananas for Shipment to the United States

SOURCE: Photo courtesy of Library of Congress Prints and Photographs Division.

We present this case not as a paragon of international public relations work but to demonstrate how Bernays was able to tap into a culture of fear, leading the U.S. government to view the Arbenz government as a regional threat to democracy. Culture is the context, or the stage, on which public relations activities play. Culture is also at the nucleus of the term *international public relations.*

International public relations is considered a top growth area by industry professionals and scholars alike (Sriramesh & Verĉiĉ, 2003; Tilson & Alozie, 2004; Van Hook, n.d.). Despite this elevated status, international public relations is still in its infancy, and much scholarly research identifies challenges to international public relations rather than extending theory or discussing effective practices. One of the difficulties in studying international public relations is the relative youth of its base, public relations, as a formalized profession and practice. Other oft-cited challenges include the lack of public relations education and training in some countries (Freitag, 2002) and the influence of public relations practitioners in an organization—and the resources, upper management respect, and power accorded to them—on efficacy (Grunig, Grunig, & Verĉiĉ, 1998). It's clear in almost all literature on public relations that culture plays an important role and merits much more research, particularly in developing countries, where local norms have led to development of public relations practices often not recognized as such by Western scholars and practitioners.

The research into these often understudied areas of the world has been called **international public relations,** *a title that denotes the practice and study of public relations across international boundaries and cultures.* Studies of international public relations often fall into general streams, such as

- Analyzing public relations practice in a country or region through a comparative case study
- Studying public relations practice in non-U.S. countries by determining whether those countries fit U.S. public relations models
- Focusing on multinational corporations and the relationship between the host culture and management style with the home norms, which often are Western based
- Examining government efforts to promote a cause, policy, or effort

The lens of international public relations is tainted by *difference.* In case studies, difference typically manifests itself through comparative studies. Comparisons allow us to see what something is by seeing what it is not. For instance, adding *international* to *public relations* must mean it's something other than public relations. In reality, it isn't. It's a form of public relations that indicates the primacy of culture and difference. In other words, *international public relations* signifies that the stage for public relations is different from that on which it's generally considered. Most case studies compare public relations in one country or region with that of the United States, which has dominated the practice and scholarship of public relations. What is important to note is that the United States is just one such forum for viewing public relations; there are many other stages that can be viewed on their own terms.

Culbertson (1996, p. 2) explores the link between public relations and international public relations as follows:

> International public relations focuses on the practice of public relations in an international or cross-cultural context. As an integral part of international or cross-cultural communication, it involves public relations practice in at least four different realms: international organizations (e.g., the United Nations, the World Bank, and the International Telecommunication Organization); intergovernmental relations (e.g., diplomatic recognition, alliance formation/disintegration, and sanctions/embargoes); transnational economic transactions (investment trading, financing of multinational corporations); and interactions among citizens of different nations (through tourism, arts, film/theater, sports).

This definition is useful for two reasons. It delineates the dimensionality of public relations practice and the many different actors involved in its production and consumption, from governments, to multinational corporations, to individuals, to grassroots organizations and activist groups, to name a few. It also stresses that public relations takes place across realms, not only geographically and organizationally but, more important, culturally. Public relations becomes a cultural artifact, bound by cultural beliefs, perceptions, and notions. This is why public relations in one country is propaganda or persuasion in another. It also explains why some communication activities traditionally have not been labeled as public relations activities in the West.

Public information campaigns in India, for example, have used folk media such as docudramas, dances, skits, and plays in rural areas (Sriramesh, 1992). In Ghana, dance, songs, and storytelling have been among the most important channels for public communication campaigns in towns (Riley, 1991). Poetry and public gatherings have been used as public relations tactics in Saudi Arabia (Alanazi, 1996). When a stream of media reports suggested that Islamists were winning the propaganda war after the September 11 attacks, the Pentagon hired a Washington, D.C.–based public relations firm. The agency organized an anti-Saddam propaganda effort that included two clandestine radio stations, Radio Freedom and the Iraqi Broadcasting Corp., and videos, skits, and comic books critical of the Iraqi leader ("Pentagon Hires," 2001).

Rarely would these tactics be part of Western public relations practice, but in many nations low literacy levels and underdevelopment necessitate different techniques than those traditionally used by Western practitioners. The term *international public relations* therefore denotes that public relations is not just a Western practice, and its definition, roles, and challenges are influenced by cultural factors. To help illustrate this point, we examine some of the main players in international public relations practice (i.e., business, government, travel and tourism, sports, nonprofits, and trade associations) and some of the issues that have arisen.

❖ MULTINATIONAL CORPORATIONS: GLOBAL OPPORTUNITIES AND PROBLEMS

One common domain of international public relations has been the challenges faced by multinational corporations (MNCs) and small and medium enterprises (SMEs) outside their host countries. Half of cross-border business ventures fail, largely because organizations routinely sacrifice cultural sensitivity and communication for adherence to business strategy and financial gain (Morosini, 2002). Ignoring cultural signs can be just as costly in the initial stages of an international business venture as they are to businesses with a longstanding presence, such as the Coca-Cola Company. Few companies are as globally minded as Coca-Cola, which *Brandweek* magazine and Interbrand Corp. have consistently ranked as the number-one global brand. That hard-earned brand credibility is increasingly under fire in some parts of the world, however.

In 1999, the French, Belgian, and Luxembourg governments banned Coke® sales after suspected cases of contamination. The case, called an "embarrassing public relations disaster" by the *Guardian* (Treanor, 1999, ¶ 1), caused mass hysteria in the affected countries. The company lost US$103 million and won no accolades for its public relations in the episode. A 2004 article in the *Guardian* called Coca-Cola's ill-fated attempt to launch Dasani® bottled water in Britain a full-scale public relations disaster (Lawrence, 2004). Scientific studies revealed that the water was merely tap water and might contain cancer-causing chemicals. A team of European branding experts called Coca-Cola's Dasani incident one of the worst marketing disasters of all time.

These examples contribute to the global perceptions of Coca-Cola. That perception—and how it is managed and maintained—are public relations issues of the highest importance to Coca-Cola. The company has splintered its name into country-specific Web sites that are fairly similar in design and appearance. What varies is the site content.

In India, home of numerous community protests against Coca-Cola for charges of water pollution and excessive water use, the company positions itself as a local company (see http://www.coca-colaindia.com):

> The Coca-Cola business in India is a local business. Our beverages in India are produced locally, we employ thousands of Indian citizens, our product range and marketing reflect Indian tastes and lifestyles, and we are deeply involved in the life of the local communities in which we operate.

Elsewhere on the site, the company describes its approach to water usage as follows:

> Allegations that The Coca-Cola Company is exploiting groundwater in India are without any scientific basis and are also not supported either by the Government authorities who regulate our water use in India, academics, or the local communities in which our plants are located.

On the surface, it sounds as if the company is doing all the right things; it appeals to its host country, proudly proclaiming its commitment to India and its citizens. Furthermore, it appears as if Coca-Cola is making a genuine attempt to understand the people of India through their "tastes and lifestyles."

Why, then, do third-party organizations and media sources excoriate the company for poor public relations? CorpWatch, a nonprofit global corporate watchdog organization, had this to say about Coca-Cola in India: "The emergence of local, grassroots struggles against the cola giant's operation in India should also serve as a reminder to Coca-Cola's bosses in Atlanta that this is not a public relations problem that one can just 'spin' and wish away" (Srivastava, 2003, ¶ 5). Another journalist wrote, "Coca-Cola certainly 'gave back' . . . in the form of profuse daily donations of foul wastewater and stinking toxic sludge from the plant's filtering and bottle-cleaning processes" (Cockburn, 2005, ¶ 9). Activist groups have formed in cities around India, including Bombay, to stage protests against Coke and its archrival Pepsi, which also faces allegations of contaminated soft drinks. The groups have staged "break bottle" campaigns, tramping on paper cups with Coke and Pepsi logos.

Many lessons from Coke's experience in India relate to our understanding of international public relations. First, we learn that integration into a host culture is an ongoing process with an indefinite end point. Coke has infused its operations in India with host nationals, but that does not shield the company from the perception of it as a corporate Goliath. Regardless of how Indianized Coca-Cola becomes, the playing field is asymmetric in the communities in which the company operates.

Second, we see that corporations bring with them perceptions of their national identity. Coca-Cola becomes more than just a soft drink company in its host countries; it's symbolically transferred into the national identity of the United States in the minds of Indians. As a BBC reporter noted, Indians attacked shops in southern India selling Coca-Cola to protest the U.S.-led war on Iraq (Farooq, 2003). For Indians who wouldn't otherwise have a direct forum for protest, an MNC becomes a contact point with the United States. This symbolic exchange is similar to Bernays's belief that he was fighting in the Cold War by representing the UFCO.

A final lesson is that MNCs can no longer isolate discord in far reaches of the globe. What happens in India—and how Coke responds—can affect its business thousands of miles away, a phenomenon known as **cross-national conflict shifting.** The term refers to the idea that *public relations challenges in one part of the world affect the operations of an international corporation elsewhere around the world.* In other words, the new global economy makes it impossible for an MNC to neutralize public relations challenges in one country without some effect on its global operations (Molleda, Connolly-Ahern, & Quinn, 2005).

For instance, the leaders of a 5.2-million-student union in the United Kingdom have threatened to boycott Coca-Cola for its questionable business practices in countries such as Colombia and India. The speed at which information and news travel has created a more informed citizenry and galvanized them behind issues and policies as never before. Key external publics for Coca-Cola are not only Indians, then; they also include governments that might want to encourage Coca-Cola to invest in their countries and worldwide activist groups that monitor corporate activity closely. Public relations can create communities that coalesce around issues and culture, sometimes not necessarily to the benefit of the organization. Thus, public relations is a cultural bridge that must change and cannot ignore economics, politics, or social issues on any level.

Any business that expands into a country other than its own is putting its name out for public inspection more than ever before. Opening global gateways can offer a business greater revenue and credibility, but it also comes with challenges that are far greater than those of doing business on home turf. Public relations activities for MNCs do not start at neutral. Before a company has initiated a single public relations tactic, it's generating messages by its very presence. How the host culture decodes those preliminary messages is the start of a process of creating meaning. This process is not linear and lacks an end point. This means that what worked back home might not work in the host country, and what worked yesterday might not work today. It calls for public relations practitioners to be agents of active involvement, recognizing the complexities of doing public relations in different environments and different cultures. Nations are encountering similar challenges when they engage in nation-branding campaigns.

❖ NATIONAL IMAGE CULTIVATION

Michael Kunczik (2004, ¶ 23), who has written extensively about the cultivation of national image, wrote, "The main objective of international PR is to establish (or maintain an already existing) positive image of one's own nation, that is, to appear trustworthy to other actors in the world system." Kunczik believes **national image** *is based on a construct of factors, including the mass media, stereotypes, and cultural beliefs.* **Image cultivation** *is a form of international public relations in which the target audiences are outside the country itself, such as other governments, MNCs, and international actors such as nongovernment organizations (NGOs).*

Image cultivation does not preclude the general public relations techniques a government might use to reach its own people, including those who, in this increasingly globalized world, are living and working in other countries. In fact, a strong argument can be made that internal and external public relations strategies are ingredients in a recipe for nation building. A positive national image is seen as an economic benefit that generates tourism, creates cordial relations with other governments, and increases the country's chances of receiving aid.

Dynamic South Korea

South Korea is one country that has invested heavily in public relations to enhance its international reputation. Many countries can make similar claims, but South Korea is different because this Asian nation of approximately 48 million makes its communication plan public on its official Web site. The Korean government has formed a national image committee for the stated purpose of advancing and improving the country's image. In 2004, the committee suggested internal strategies such as the development of a nationwide campaign to encourage Korean tourists to behave properly when abroad to avoid hurting Korea's reputation. It also recommended developing publicity messages, attending international conferences to promote Korea as a brand, developing Korean educational programs, identifying images and symbols that best represent Korea, and creating an "imagekorea" Web site.

Jae-woong Yoo (2005, ¶ 22), director of the Korean Overseas Information Service, linked the evolution of the public relations function in Korea to its change in government:

Under the past authoritarian administrations, PR activities were for the most part devoted to justifying the legitimacy of the regimes. But under the Participatory Government, which pursues the participation of the people, a market economy and liberal democracy, the core task of overseas publicity is how to enhance the national image.

Yoo talks of the Korean government's belief that a sustained public relations plan can help boost the country's international standing and support its "Dynamic Korea" brand. The government commissioned a study of citizens in the United States, Japan, and Germany to assess their attitudes of Korea and has made public some of those results to dovetail with its participatory government philosophy. Public relations also links to the country's efforts to introduce Korean culture to the Middle East and to form economic partnerships with Latin America.

Notably, the Korean government calls its communications public relations, signifying the government's willingness to participate in the continual loop of meanings that surround the term. As we have seen, public relations means different things to different people around the world; South Korea is a voice in the dialogue about what public relations means and how its practice varies globally.

Swaziland's Approach to Public Relations

Swaziland is another country with a stated commitment to public relations. The African country is almost completely encircled by South Africa and is slightly smaller than New Jersey (Figure 2.1). Its population of 1,173,900 makes it small by almost any standards; 254 cities worldwide are larger (Butler, 2005). Eighty-two percent of its population is illiterate, and the life expectancy in the country is 38 years. Because of its small size and relative stability in a region pockmarked with strife and civil unrest, Swaziland isn't a prominent media source worldwide. When it does make the news, it's for inauspicious reasons; it recently replaced Botswana as the country with the world's highest known rate of HIV infection. Also, various activist groups, including student organizations and labor unions, pressured the monarchy for democratic reform from the late 1980s into the early 1990s.

Figure 2.1   Swaziland Is on the Southern Tip of Africa, Embedded in South Africa

SOURCE: Map courtesy of the UK Foreign and Commonwealth Office and Department for International Development.

Recently the country has made news for the actions of its absolute monarch, King Mswati III. In 2004 Mswati bought a US$500,000 car with a television, DVD player, refrigerator, 21-speaker surround system, and sterling champagne glasses. BBC News contrasted Mswati's purchase with these facts: Swaziland's unemployment rate is 40%, about one third of the country's people rely on food aid for survival, and 70% of the people live on US$1 or less per day. Mswati's extravagance also made headlines earlier in 2004, when he held a US$600,000 birthday party for himself. Before that incident, the Swaziland parliament turned down Mswati's request for US$15 million to build palaces for each of his 11 wives. That figure was almost as much as the country's 2002 health budget ("King Seeks," 2004). In 2002, the parliament also turned down Mswati's request to purchase a US$45-million royal jet. Western media have also focused on the reed dance, an annual event during which the king adds a new wife.

What has Swaziland done to counter these images of rampant HIV and AIDS, occasional civil unrest, and the purchasing habits of its ruler? The prime minister's office released a statement in 2004 making public relations one of the government's main activities. The statement, as found on the government's Web site (see http://www.gov.sz), elaborated slightly:

> His Majesty's Government is committed to improve its public relations and the image of the country both within the country, the region and the world at large. Measures will be put in place to ensure that this is achieved to enhance tourism and Foreign Direct Investment in the country.

Unlike South Korea, which has actively incorporated public relations and communication into its policy statements, Swaziland has eschewed such transparency, possibly because its economic and national welfare are very different from those in Korea. Scant evidence supports the statement's claim that measures are being put in place to enhance tourism and foreign direct investment. A Southern African Tourism Consortium noted that it's nearly impossible to track tourism numbers for Swaziland because there's no formal means for capturing such information in the country. According to the Heritage Foundation/ Wall Street Journal Index of Economic Freedom, Swaziland's foreign investment continued to decline in 2005.

The governments of Swaziland and South Korea clearly are at separate poles regarding public relations activities. Much of that gap is attributable to the wide economic difference between the two countries and Swaziland's numerous other problems, including HIV and AIDS. It is difficult to make meaningful comparisons between the two countries because numerous other factors, including country size and differing colonial legacies, make them unique. The differences demonstrate that policy decisions are related to international perception and therefore are public relations concerns. It's one thing for a government to make public relations a priority; it's another thing altogether to actually practice it.

Swaziland is typical of African countries that struggle to project a positive image: "Africa's inability to attract and retain foreign investment has much to do with the negative public relations that surround its social institutions" (Fobanjong, 2004, p. 203). It would be a mistake to assume the government of Swaziland is not doing international public relations from its lack of formalized structures or activities that are labeled "public relations." For better or worse, the government's policies dance with public relations on a global platform.

MNC case studies and nation-branding campaigns are only two sites for international public relations practice. A brief discussion of other practice areas and their challenges follows, and many of these are discussed in more detail later in the book.

❖ TRAVEL AND TOURISM

According to the World Tourism Organisation and the World Travel and Tourism Council, travel and tourism make up the world's largest industry, generating billions of dollars annually. Tourism and public relations are inextricably linked under international public relations. International perceptions of a country are crucial in attracting tourism, which can provide an economic boon to countries and cultivate foreign investment. For example, to capitalize on the notorious ruler who inspired Bram Stoker's *Dracula*, Romania uses public relations to promote Dracula Land, a theme park intended to serve as a national economic engine (Doksoz, 2004). Likewise, if a tourist facility is run by an MNC, organizational perceptions of how they interact with the host country become crucial. The increasing specialization of tourism—from ecotourism to sustainable tourism to extreme tourism—challenges public relations practitioners to communicate to more niche-oriented, heterogeneous audiences.

Take, for example, the international scope of Disney theme parks. Whereas Euro Disney went bankrupt and is still heavily in debt amid complaints that the park was too American to appeal to Europeans, Tokyo Disneyland is one of the company's most successful theme parks. Oriental Land, the local parent company, made its original 180-billion-yen (US$1.5-billion) investment back in just 4 years, and the park continues to be profitable, even as other theme parks are being forced to close as the Japanese recession continues ("Welcome to," 2003; "Year of the Mouse," 2005).

Based on Tokyo Disneyland's success, Hong Kong's government entered a joint venture with Disney to open Hong Kong Disneyland in 2005, which includes creating the first train line in the world devoted to a theme park, with rail cars sporting mouse head–shaped windows. But the park has been plagued with controversy since construction began. Complaints of environmental damage surfaced during construction of the park on Lantau Island, also home to Po Lin monastery and its famous 85-foot-high Buddha statue. Disney ran afoul of animal welfare activists who alleged that park officials killed dogs that had been adopted by site workers. Workers have complained of short lunch breaks, long hours, and staff shortages ("Year of the Mouse," 2005; Wordsworth, 2005). On charity day, when the park was opened to a capacity crowd as a dress rehearsal for the grand opening, subways broke down and lines were painfully long for rides and food, causing the local parliament to demand that Disney decrease capacity by a third.

Even attempts to localize the Disney brand are proving problematic. A plan to appeal to Chinese tastes by putting shark fin soup on the menu was abandoned after Greenpeace launched an environmental campaign. And as Disney incorporated more photo ops with costumed characters for picture-loving Chinese tourists and ensured that the layout conformed to feng shui principles, opening day complaints centered on the fact that the park was too Chinese, lacking "American razzle" ("Year of the Mouse," 2005). As this case demonstrates, packaging a culture for consumption by another requires public relations practitioners to create cultural identities, which must change to meet changing challenges and expectations.

❖ SPORTS AND INTERNATIONAL GOODWILL

Sports often are overlooked in international public relations texts, yet sports can unify nations, promote social change, and affect the national psyche, making them a powerful cultural agent. The Beijing Organizing Committee has taken a remarkably transparent approach to public relations, devoting part of its Web site to its plan to promote China and the Olympics for the 2008 games. Great Britain similarly recognized the public relations value of its winning bid for the 2012 Olympic games. The day Britain won the Olympics, the *Guardian* reported, "the bonanza will have transformed the media, marketing, advertising and PR industries," reflecting the centrality of public relations to sport and vice versa (Brook & Tryhorn, 2005, ¶ 1).

The Olympics may be the most prominent international sporting event promoting international relations, and competition to secure the Olympics is high. Russia's 2014 Winter Games committee has hired

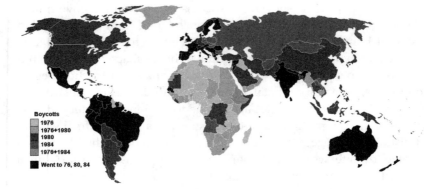

Boycotts
- 1976
- 1976+1980
- 1980
- 1984
- 1976+1984
- Went to 76, 80, 84

Although the Olympic Games can foster national pride and identity, they can also be sites of divisive political action. Boycotting the games is a common international relations tactic.

Figure 2.2   Boycotts at Olympic Games

Burson-Marsteller, with an estimated US$1 million budget, to help them secure the international attention that comes with a successful bid. But the high cost of bidding has put many nations out of the running, including most African nations, which cannot afford the estimated US$12 million needed for a creditable effort (Zinser, 2005). Nor can they afford the training facilities and support for world-class athletes that most developed nations can, making their participation in the games minimal in many sports. A possible exception is running, which involves little specialized equipment or training.

Although international sports provides a tool for diplomacy and improved relations, it is increasingly expensive, widening the gap between developed and developing nations. The cost of international public relations practitioners is another question that must be addressed in any approach to the field. Additionally, international sports can also become a focus of political protest and activism, providing an international stage and guaranteed media attention for a cause (Figure 2.2).

❖ NONPROFITS AND INTERNATIONAL NGOS

From the Red Cross to the YMCA to Oxfam, nonprofit organizations are considered synonymous with nongovernment organizations (NGOs) (Tkalac & Pavicic, 2003). Both place advocacy as central to their missions.

NGOs and *nonprofits with an international presence* (**INGOs**) have faced situation-specific public relations challenges, including conflicts of interest, bureaucracy, government interference, local indifference, and cultural misunderstandings.

These challenges, and many more like them, make effective public relations fundamental to any NGO or INGO. Freedom House has developed a media and public relations strategy document for NGOs because "it is important for NGOs to establish a proactive public relations program to help bring about positive recognition of the organization's work" (Sereg, n.d.).

But INGOs work with a host of publics, and creating positive relations with all of them may not always be possible given the organization's mission. Consider the case of Médecins Sans Frontières (Doctors Without Borders), which provides medical assistance to countries in need of humanitarian aid. Another part of its mission is to avert such crises by speaking out about government actions that may create problems. At times, this criticism has resulted in the group's expulsion from host countries, leaving people without much-needed aid. The group has refused to back down on its mission to address problems at their root. It believes doing so would implicitly support poor government practices, although it realizes that taking the moral high ground comes at the cost of human lives.

In turn, many people in developing nations are increasingly skeptical of INGOs, almost all of which are based in Western nations. They see INGOs as fostering a new form of dependency, or neocolonialism. This view is reinforced by the fact that these groups often represent developing nations as universally impoverished, incapable of action, and helpless, establishing a discourse of dependency. To raise support for their causes, they often use images of poverty-stricken children. Although these pictures may be the most effective fundraising tool in developed nations, critics have labeled them the *pornography of poverty* (Bell & Carens, 2004). Balancing a variety of constituents' interests and needs with organizational mission remains an ongoing challenge in this international practice arena.

❖ TRADE ASSOCIATIONS

Following the maxim that there's strength in numbers, **trade associations** *are corporate or cause-related groups that form to promote an industry or cause.* Pooling together resources and finances can give trade associations tremendous power, sometimes greater than the sum of their parts. Public relations is essential for trade associations, which must raise awareness of, educate people about, and promote their industry. Trade associations come in many forms. Some are government based, such as the European Free Trade Association; others are hybrids, tending toward corporate interests such as the Emerging Markets Traders Association or the International Reciprocal Trade Association. The Private Label Manufacturers Association is a good example of the strength-in-numbers philosophy. Its annual international trade show attracted visitors from about 90 nations in 2004.

Many trade associations base agreements on economic liberalism, often citing World Tourism Organisation criteria. But recent studies indicate that trade associations are most helpful when members have similar competitive advantages but can actually be harmful when inequities exist (Kono, 2002). The European Union, partly in response to complaints from smaller member nations over trade restrictions, has started decentralizing its US$100-million communication budget to make it more localized (Mahoney, 2004). By decentralizing, the EU hopes to help address such inequalities and empower smaller nations to take a key role in international trade.

If less empowered members do not receive the full benefits of group membership, they're likely to form splinter groups, and the advantage of association membership is lost to all. Maintaining balance and empowering minority members is crucial to successful cross-cultural communication.

❖ KEYS TO OPENING GLOBAL GATEWAYS

The key to opening the global gateways of public relations is to consider culture and the wider political implications inherent in a cultural approach. These are the adhesives that affect how governments operate; MNCs, trade associations, and INGOs function; and sports, the arts, and travel and tourism flourish. How these entities present themselves internationally becomes a matter of international public relations. Culture is a descriptor of complex variables, and to label a culture favorably or unfavorably is counterproductive. Recognizing its power and respecting it are the benchmarks for understanding culture.

For MNCs focused on the bottom line, ignoring those benchmarks can spell colossal failure. Governments across the world are judged by their policies and how those policies meet the needs of their peoples and stated goals. Issues such as economic plans, human rights, and press freedom contribute to national perception, which is often communicated without boundaries through the media and cyberspace. The very nature of governance becomes an exercise in generating meaning to and for various publics, creating a space where public relations can operate in more formal terms as a specialized function. At the heart of this logic is the idea that governance is about representing people and policies across vast distances and crossing international boundaries, cultures, and systems.

Because of the primacy of culture and politics in international practice and the recognition that relationships are always in flux, we turn to a critical cultural model of public relations practice to understand how international public relations operates and the concerns practitioners must address in any cross-cultural campaign. We depart from typical Western approaches that view public relations as a management function designed to serve organizational goals. Instead, we outline a cultural studies approach, examining public relations as a communicative cultural process that shapes and is shaped by the meanings and practices of everyday life. Chapter 3 outlines the particular definition of culture that informs our approach and introduces the circuit of culture model as a basis for sound international theory and practice.

CHAPTER SUMMARY

- Culture is at the nucleus of international public relations, which describes the practice and study of public relations across international boundaries and cultures.

- International public relations efforts never begin at a neutral starting point because mere organizational presence generates messages.

- Some industries and areas relevant to international public relations include the expansion and growth of MNCs, nation-branding campaigns, travel and tourism, international sporting events, nonprofits, and trade associations.

3

Global Public Relations and the Circuit of Culture

❖ ❖ ❖

The previous chapters have underscored the primacy of culture in any international public relations undertaking. Because of cultural differences, what works in Timbuktu (Mali) may be totally ineffective in Tuscaloosa (United States) and even offensive in Tijuana (Mexico). Used in this sense, we're referring to culture as the characteristics, norms, and practices of a society. Although we believe this sense of *culture* plays a crucial role in international public relations practice, we also embrace the broader definition that underlies the cultural studies tradition: **Culture** *is the process by which meaning is produced, circulated, consumed, commodified, and endlessly reproduced and renegotiated in society* (Williams, 1961, 1981; Hall, 1980). In this chapter we explore this larger notion of culture and demonstrate how it informs our understanding of public relations campaigns by applying it to the case of New Coke®.

❖ LANGUAGE, MEANING, AND CULTURE

Things and events don't make sense in and of themselves. We give things meaning by defining and presenting them; we socially construct meaning. Culture forms the basis of a society's shared meaning system. It provides the classification schema we use to make sense of our world, making culture, meaning, and language inextricably linked. Notice how we extend meanings by drawing on shared cultural experience, by defining anything new in terms of what we already know. Have you ever considered trying a new type of meat, such as alligator or frogs' legs, and been told by a friend who's already tried it that "it tastes kinda like chicken"? We define the new by relating it to the old, by what our shared experience has already classified, and then stating how it differs. Your friend probably continued with something along the lines of, "except it's [tougher] [sweeter] [less juicy]."

As meanings become widely disseminated, they change over time and through use. Competing meanings emerge, often within different social groups and with differing connotations. Take public relations, for example. We've already demonstrated how hard it is to define the concept. That's because the term takes on a variety of meanings, even within a culture. In the United States, scholars commonly use the Grunig and Hunt (1984) definition given in chapter 1: management of communication between an organization and its publics. As a result, supporting terms have emerged, such as *dominant coalition* and *two-way symmetric communication*. This definition elevates public relations to a management function and emphasizes accommodation between equally empowered players.

These assumptions concerning public relations practice form the U.S. **dominant discourse,** *language signifying a particular cultural meaning, certain unstated assumptions, that color how we think and act.* Scholars from other nations claim they have difficulty getting their work published in U.S. journals unless they adopt this viewpoint, even though it doesn't necessarily represent public relations as studied and practiced in other countries.

Contrast the U.S. academic discourse surrounding public relations with that of U.S. practitioners, who often don't read scholarly journals or belong to professional associations. They say public relations as discussed in scholarship bears little relationship to what they actually do, which they often define in terms of image or impression management, persuasion, and dissemination of information. Journalists use a different discourse yet, which may stem from historical circumstance. The majority of early U.S. practitioners were former journalists, who defined public relations by what it wasn't: journalism. If journalism was objective and had news value, then public relations was free advertising, was one-sided, and lacked news value. Public relations was the dark side of the journalistic fence.

Most journalists claim they don't use material from public relations practitioners, and relations between members of the two occupations have been notoriously poor. Because the two professions originally were closely related, however, many U.S. public relations programs remain situated in schools of journalism, which stress media writing skills and journalistic norms and values.

The average U.S. citizen believes public relations constitutes hype or spin and isn't a credible information source. As a result, the U.S. public historically has ranked public relations practitioners as less trustworthy than car salespeople and real estate agents (Newport, 2003). Of course, not every academic, practitioner, journalist, or citizen in the United States subscribes to the meanings just outlined. In each group you'll find a number of competing meanings as well. The positions outlined are broad generalizations, but they're coherent generalizations precisely because they form a dominant narrative, or discourse, within each group, with repercussions for how public relations is studied, practiced, and viewed in the United States.

This example demonstrates how language, meaning, and culture intertwine to create competing discourses or "truths." This notion owes much to British scholar Raymond Williams (1961, 1981), who proposed that culture actually constitutes meaning; it doesn't just define it. This conception of culture formed the basis of a new theoretical stream, cultural studies, and the establishment of the Centre for Contemporary Cultural Studies at the University of Birmingham, England, in 1964. As Stuart Hall, the center's director from 1969 to 1979, noted, culture isn't just the rules and traditions of a culture as commonly described in anthropology; culture is "threaded through *all* social practices, and the sum of their interrelationships" (Hall, 1980, p. 58). Based on this broad notion of culture, a group of scholars at Britain's Open University, including Hall, created the circuit of culture model (du Gay, Hall, Janes, Mackay, & Negus, 1997), which outlines how and where culture and power intertwine to create meaning.

❖ THE CIRCUIT OF CULTURE MODEL

The **circuit of culture** (Figure 3.1) consists of five moments in a process—regulation, production, consumption, representation, and identity—that work in concert to provide a shared cultural space in which meaning is created, shaped, modified, and recreated. There's no beginning or end on the circuit; the moments work synergistically to create meaning. However, each moment contributes a particular piece to the whole.

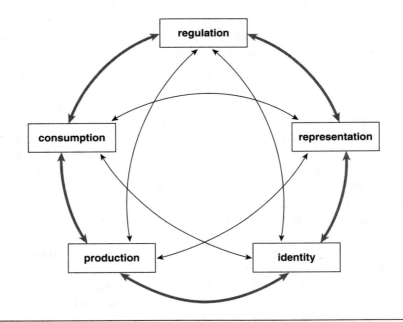

Figure 3.1   The Circuit of Culture, Showing the Interrelationships of the Five Moments

SOURCE: Graphic courtesy of Dara Curtin.

The Five Moments

The moment of **regulation** *comprises controls on cultural activity,* ranging from formal and legal controls, such as regulations, laws, and institutionalized systems, to the informal and local controls of cultural norms and expectations that form culture in the more commonly used sense of the term. It's in the moment of regulation that meanings arise governing what's acceptable, what's correct. In simplistic terms, it helps form the context in which public relations activities take place.

For example, in many of the former British colonies in Africa, protocol is stressed, with much formality guiding interaction between groups. One author was surprised to find when leading a series of service visits in Kenya that she was expected to make a lengthy formal speech at each stop to the assembled group, often young schoolchildren. It didn't matter that many of these children didn't understand English or that the author didn't speak Kiswahili. What mattered was the act of making the speech itself.

But constructing meaning is an ongoing process, and meanings do not go unchanged or unchallenged. What's allowable or expected in a culture often is determined by groups with economic or political power in a given situation. Specific circumstances and determined action can create competing discourses or narratives that resonate among wider social networks.

Activist groups provide a good example. When a small group of concerned citizens formed Greenpeace in Canada in 1971, they were at the forefront of the environmental movement, which hadn't yet been embraced by the majority. The media identified members as radical "tree huggers"—liberal environmental idealists—which made it difficult for them to establish themselves as credible media sources (Hansen, 1993). Environmentalism has since come to dominate many national and organizational agendas, and today Greenpeace is an international not-for-profit organization based in Amsterdam, with offices in 41 countries and 2.8 million supporters. It has influenced environmental regulation in a number of nations and constitutes an important source for international media on environmental issues. Meanings arising within a moment, then, are not predetermined but are part of an ongoing process in which the dominant narrative can shift over time.

The moment of **production** *outlines the process by which creators of cultural products imbue them with meaning,* a process often called **encoding** (Hall, 1993). In public relations terms, we can think of this as the process of planning and executing a campaign. Technological constraints play a role in the process because what's produced is partially dependent on available technology. Organizational culture provides the environment in which production takes place, such as departmental organization, management strategies, and expectations of employees or members.

For example, multinational corporations typically invest heavily in communication campaigns, but the organizational culture of each determines where public relations ranks in the organizational structure, particularly in relation to marketing and the amount of input public relations has into communication efforts. In most military organizations, a marked hierarchical structure and concerns for national security mean that information for public release must be cleared through several levels of command, slowing the communication process and restricting the scope of information released. Nonprofit organizations must fulfill their missions in cost-effective ways. Médecins Sans Frontières, for example, raises awareness of emergency medical issues around the world through an extensive network of global Web sites loaded with information for the media and the public. Production, then, creates meaning arising from organizational values, structure, and logistics.

Representation *is the form an object takes and the meanings encoded in that form.* Remember that meaning isn't inherent in the object itself but is socially constructed. Producers encode meaning into a cultural artifact, often with a specific target audience in mind. They hope to convey a certain meaning through all aspects of how they present the artifact. The content, the format, and even the method of distribution communicate an intended meaning.

In public relations terms, practitioners encode meaning into campaign materials by delineating certain target publics, scripting key messages, picking certain channels of communication, and so on. For example, when Yassir Arafat was head of Palestine, his official Web site was available in Arabic, Hebrew, and English, indicative of the target publics he wanted to reach and the global outreach of his communications. The home page contained a daily update on the number of Palestinians killed by Israelis, conveying a grim notion of the Palestinian situation and arguably designed to engender sympathy for the Palestinian cause.

In contrast, the Web site of Vaira Vike-Freiberga, the president of Latvia, is available in Latvian, English, French, German, and Russian, suggestive of a different sphere of intended influence. A link on the home page takes you to "Riga Castle," an area for children featuring pictures and a game, conveying a lighthearted side of the normally stern head of state and to the issues of national import addressed on the rest of the site.

Although practitioners try to shape discourse during production by encoding materials with meaning, some campaigns fail to achieve their objectives. Not all production efforts are successful. Failures often are attributable to meanings that arise during the moment of **consumption,** *when messages are decoded by audiences.* Consumers, more commonly spoken of as target publics in public relations, bring their own semantic networks of meaning to any communicative exchange. They are active creators of meaning, putting issues and products to use in their everyday lives in their own ways.

The creators of the circuit of culture note that although production provides a series of possibilities, they can become actualized only in and through consumption (du Gay et al., 1997), making consumption as important as production to ascribing meaning. Consumption, then, isn't the end of the line but another point on the circuit of culture. Consumption itself becomes a form of production as new meanings accrue to an artifact as a consequence of use.

Identities *are meanings that accrue to all social networks, from nations to organizations to publics.* A common role of a public relations practitioner within an organization is to establish and maintain an organizational identity. During production, practitioners encode organizational texts with the dominant identity they want to convey, around which they attempt to structure subsequent discourse. The U.S. Marines has created an elite identity, embodied in its advertising slogan, "The Few, the Proud, the Marines," and in its recruiting materials, which stress a yearning to belong (e.g., "Maybe you can be one of us") and the uniqueness of the "very special organization" (see http://www.usmc.mil).

In addition to maintaining organizational identities, practitioners often begin campaigns by segmenting publics, which creates identities for various target audiences. As we've already demonstrated when speaking about consumption, however, these groups must be understood as active constructors of meaning. Consumers also create their own identities and memberships, which may be multiple, fluid, and conflicting. And in turn, different consumer groups create and assign their own identities to organizations.

Take, for example, People for the Ethical Treatment of Animals (PETA). Some view this activist group as the leader in a righteous cause to protect basic rights, consistent with the dominant identity the organization encodes in its communication materials. But given the general lack of cultural currency for animal rights issues in the United States, others view the same organization as the lunatic fringe, criminals with no respect for property, and obstructionists who stand in the way of scientific research. Identities, then, are never fixed entities but are multiple, culturally constructed meanings that evolve and change.

The challenge for practitioners when designing a campaign is to create an identity that a product or issue and publics can share. For example, the elite identity constructed by and for the U.S. Marines is designed to appeal to young adults who want to "take control of [their] future" and "become part of the family." In Pierre Bourdieu's (1979/ 1984) terms, public relations practitioners function as **cultural intermediaries,** *mediators between producers and consumers who actively create meanings by establishing an identification between products or issues and publics.*

Balancing Determinism and Relativism

The five moments—regulation, production, representation, consumption, and identity—form an interconnected whole with no beginning or end. *At any particular spot on the circuit the moments overlap in what are called* **articulations,** a term chosen for its dual meaning: To articulate is both to express and to join together. Imagine taking the illustration of the circuit shown in Figure 3.1 and setting it spinning so fast the moments blurred together. If you threw a dart at the figure, the spot where it landed would be an articulation, one of an almost infinite number of points of overlap between the moments. Each articulation signals a particular situation or instance, a particular confluence of the five moments.

The circuit, then, doesn't determine meaning in any particular situation but indicates how it will arise and that it's always subject to change. In this manner the circuit embraces a degree of cultural relativism, but it does so within a structured framework provided by the five moments, which constrain the range of possible meanings. *Meanings may be socially constructed, but they're constructed within the range allowed by institutional frameworks and based on past meanings and formulations,* a concept known as **historicity.** Meanings are then reconstructed as consumers use them in their particular social situations, which arise in the articulations.

From different articulations, different dominant and competing discourses arise. Discourse prescribes how a cultural artifact can be meaningfully discussed and used. It "facilitates cultural communication while always recognizing the persistence of difference and power between different 'speakers' within the same cultural circuit" (Hall, 1997b, p. 11). Within the confines of historicity, then, articulations put relationships and power firmly at the forefront of what meanings will arise in any given situation. As Foucault (1975/1995) proposed, power is **micropolitical,** *inherent in all relationships but lacking absolute value: Power can be productive as well as controlling, positive as well as negative, enabling as well as constraining.* However, relative power leads to a particular discourse becoming dominant in any given articulation; it prescribes whose voice will be heard. The meaning inscribed by the dominant discourse becomes the "truth" that shapes subsequent actions.

To see how this works in practice, consider the earlier discussion of competing discourses surrounding the term *public relations.* How public relations is defined in different semantic networks helps determine what will be published in U.S. scholarly journals, what types of practice will be culturally sanctioned, and how and where public relations will be taught. However, it's important to remember that discourses arise from continuous processes within the circuit and are subject to the contingencies of articulations. Today's marginal meaning may be tomorrow's dominant meaning, and the dominant discourse of a producer may be adopted, changed, or spurned by a consumer.

❖ APPLYING THE CIRCUIT OF CULTURE TO PRACTICE

To better understand the theory underlying the circuit and how it can be used to guide public relations practice, it helps to examine it in the context of a case. As Hall himself said, "Theory is always a detour on the way to something more interesting" (in Morley & Chen, 1996, p. 19). We use the introduction of New Coke® to illustrate each moment of the circuit in action. Although the case is based in the United States, it has international ramifications that we discuss in this and subsequent chapters.[1]

Production

For years, Coca-Cola was the dominant soft drink brand, so much so that people commonly used *Coke* as a generic term for any cola beverage. In the 1970s, however, the Coca-Cola Company began steadily losing market share to Pepsi, particularly among the growing market of younger drinkers, who were targeted as the "Pepsi Generation." In 1981, Roberto C. Goizueta became CEO of Coca-Cola, and he instigated a culture of change in the company, telling his managers that everything about the company was open to challenge, including product formulation (Hollie, 1985a).

With support from Harold Burson (2003b), a close friend, and his international public relations firm Burson-Marsteller, Goizueta worked to create a climate of "intelligent risk taking" in the company. He added new product lines, including Diet Coke and Cherry Coke, and he expanded the business vertically, buying Columbia Pictures and starting a line of branded clothing. He also vowed to get the original flagship brand rolling again by the company's 100-year anniversary in 1986.

The top-secret "Project Kansas" was born to reformulate Coke and recapture market share within this new culture of change and innovation. The company had plenty of resources, and it threw them behind the 3-year development and $4-million U.S. consumer testing of the new formulation. Blind taste tests with 190,000 consumers demonstrated a significant statistical preference for the new formula, although focus group results indicated that a backlash could develop if the formula was changed. But conventional marketing wisdom held that statistics had a scientific power and veracity that the "soft" data of focus groups lacked. Continuing to produce both the original and New Coke wasn't a consideration at the time because of technological constraints. Bottlers could not easily accommodate another product line.

Although this is only a brief overview, it points to a number of regulatory issues that informed how meaning was encoded into the process of producing New Coke. Company officials instigated change based on a felt need to retain a majority of market share. Cultural norms both within the organization and within the wider, national culture encompassed the predictive power of science, denying any truth to "nonscientific" methods. And although financial resources weren't lacking, technological constraints contributed to the belief that only one Coke could be produced for market. We turn now to how these meanings take shape in the production of cultural texts.

Representation

Coca-Cola didn't lightly set out to take on an expensive retooling of its product line and subsequent marketing campaign. But with hard scientific evidence in hand, the management team agreed to take the huge step of reformulating the company's flagship brand. The company's media advisory for the introduction billed it as the most significant marketing move in the company's history (Hollie, 1985c). Although CEO Goizueta wasn't comfortable with media, he presided at the news conference, conveying the import of the announcement. Using a key message that "the best had just gotten better," he announced that the formula for "old" Coke would stay locked in a bank vault, symbolically placing the old out of reach and out of mind. The event conveyed a message of a progressive company putting the past behind it and still holding on to the #1 spot in the soft drink market.

Because Coke's slip in market share was attributed largely to the growth market of young drinkers, New Coke was designed to appeal to a younger audience. The taste was sweeter, and a stylish can design was unveiled in silver and red, rather than Coke's traditional white and red, which introduced the wavy line design we've come to associate with Coke. Marketing materials stressed both the new taste and the youth aspects, with slogans such as "Catch the Wave" and a new advertising jingle: "Coke Is It."

Everything from the product itself to the can to the campaign name was designed to convey a progressive image of a company on the move, a company and a product with which upbeat youth could identify. How could you not when Coke was "It"? If you wanted to be out front, if you wanted to catch the leading edge of the wave, as symbolized by the can design and in the promotional materials, you had to drink New Coke.

So what happened? Why did the company announce barely 3 months later that it was bringing back the previous Coke formula? The answer lies in the discursive nature of meaning, in the ways in which meaning circulates and is renegotiated in the process. It lies in the moment of consumption.

Consumption

The novelty factor led to an original spike in sales as customers tried out the new product. During this early period media adopted the company's message of innovation, reporting Coca-Cola's move as aggressive and bold. But it didn't take long for the company to realize that trouble was brewing. Its toll-free customer line, which had averaged about 400 calls a day, was receiving more than 1,500 calls a day. And the feedback wasn't positive, nor were the more than 40,000 letters of complaint received. One woman lamented, "There are only two things in my life: God and Coca-Cola. Now you have taken one of those things away from me" (in Greenwald, 1985, p. 49). Another wrote, "Changing Coke is like God making the grass purple" (in Greenwald, 1985, p. 49).

Other consumers framed their comments in less religious and more patriotic terms: Changing Coke was like spitting on the flag or taking Teddy Roosevelt off Mount Rushmore (Morganthau, 1985; Oliver, 1985). The leader of a hastily formed but high-profile protest movement was often quoted in the media, making pronouncements such as "When they took Old Coke off the market, they violated my freedom of choice. . . . We went to war in Japan over that freedom" (in Morganthau, 1985, p. 33).

As one regional bottling company president observed, "What Coca-Cola didn't realize was that the old Coke was the property of the American public. The bottlers thought they owned it. The company thought it owned it. But the consumers knew they owned it. And when someone tampered with it, they got upset" (in Greenwald, 1985, p. 51). Consumers in this case created their own meaning for the new product, that of an impostor, which didn't match up to the "best just got better" message that the company had spent 3 years and US$4 million developing. One disgruntled consumer even turned the new advertising jingle inside out: "For years, Coke *was* it. Now it's gone" (in Morganthau, 1985, p. 33). Or as a restaurant owner said, "They don't make *Coke* anymore" (in Morganthau, 1985, p. 32).

Something had gone wrong, and as the comments make clear, it wasn't so much a matter of taste. Continued blind taste tests still heavily favored the newer, sweeter formulation. The religious and patriotic tenor of the complaints demonstrated the deeper meanings called into question by the reformulation of Coke. New Coke wasn't a different formulation of an old friend, it was a fake trying to pass itself off as the "real thing." What was called into question were the very identities of the product and the company themselves, forming the next moment on the circuit.

Identity

When developing New Coke, company personnel envisioned young consumers as the major target audience. The taste of the product, the packaging, and the advertisements were geared toward a teenager or early twenty-something who wanted to be on the leading edge, part of what was happening, what was "it." What Pepsi had identified as the "Pepsi Generation," Coca-Cola identified as the "New Wave." As part of this strategy, the company tried to gain credibility by identifying itself as a bold risk taker at the forefront of development. But as outlined earlier, a key lesson of the circuit is that competing and conflicting meanings are always being generated. If a campaign doesn't establish a common identity around the product or issue and the target audience, conflicting identities arise and campaign objectives are lost.

In the case of New Coke, the problems began with the identity of the company and its flagship product. For almost 100 years, the only product of the Coca-Cola Company was Coke itself, and the identities of the two had become conflated over time. During those years, the company had spent millions of dollars developing an image steeped in nostalgia and small-town America, which they splashed on calendars, billboards, magazine ads, and myriad other promotional items.

Although the company established an internal identity as a progressive innovator when CEO Goizueta came on board, an identity the media also promoted with talk of bold and aggressive marketing, consumers held on to the old identity. The company, as embodied in its flagship brand, was an American institution built on old-fashioned American values, as noted in the patriotic theme of consumer responses: "People felt Coca-Cola represented Americana, and they don't want Americana to change on them" (in Hollie, 1985b, p. D15); "Baseball, hamburgers, Coke—they're all the fabric of America" (in Morganthau, 1985, p. 32).

What became evident was that consumers didn't drink a particular brand for how it tasted; even confirmed Pepsi drinkers often preferred the taste of New Coke in the taste tests. They drank a brand for what it stood for and what it said about them—for the identification it fostered between the product and their own lives. As one Coke drinker said, Pepsi "is too preppy, too yup. The New Generation—it sounds like Nazi breeding." A Pepsi drinker responded with "I think Pepsi is a little more rebellious, and I have a little bit of rebellion in me" (Morris, 1987, p. 1). Both responses demonstrate that Pepsi had captured the youth market, which identified with its message of hip rebellion; Coke was for those who wanted to celebrate traditional American values as romantically reconstructed—an idyllic, nostalgic past that never really existed but lived on in the identity of Coke as constructed in the minds of loyal consumers. With the introduction of New Coke, consumers felt betrayed, and they felt empowered to act, as explained by meanings produced in the moment of regulation.

Regulation

After the reintroduction of original Coke, a company official flatly stated that the company had betrayed the trust of the American public. What consumers had valued as a personal relationship suddenly had been revealed as an economic one. In essence, the company declared its consumers' values invalid. Consumers tend to reject anything that challenges their shared norms. As a psychiatrist observed, "People felt outraged and ripped off because there was an implicit and explicit contract between the Coke drinker and the company" (in Greenwald, 1985, p. 49).

If shared norms are challenged strongly enough, the group holding them often feels empowered to act, even in the face of corporate power and clout. In this case, consumers exercised several options. They complained directly to the company (one consumer sent a letter to CEO Goizueta addressed to, "Chief Dodo, the Coca-Cola Company") and indirectly through the media. They demonstrated and wrote protest songs, attracting national media attention. The diehard Coke drinkers with greater resources imported original Coke from some of the 153 countries where it was still sold, most notably Brazil. And they boycotted, switching to water or, worse yet, to Pepsi.

When the company caved in to consumer pressure and announced that it would bring original Coke back as Coke Classic, its stock price rose by US$2.37 a share, and 31,600 calls were logged on its hotline in the next two days. Media found the announcement so newsworthy that it was featured on every evening network news show and on the front page of almost every major daily. ABC even interrupted its broadcast of a popular soap opera to share the news with its viewers.

Although consumers rejoiced in the news, one person protested by ending his contract with Coca-Cola. Bill Cosby, who had starred in commercials praising the new formulation, said his credibility had been damaged, and he would no longer work with the company. The strong sense of betrayal felt by consumers and by Cosby empowered them to act. By violating social norms, the company had weakened its relative power and lost the ability to define events. Such a fall from power by a major U.S. corporation was unusual enough to command media attention and force a disruption of accepted media norms.

Completing the Circuit

This brief overview of the circuit has introduced the five moments, but by doing so separately it has not fully conveyed the synergistic, interactive, and discursive aspects of the model. For example, the company's decision to produce a new product line was integral to its new identity. But the identity of consumers was tied to the company's earlier representations, and the betrayal of trust experienced by consumers empowered them to produce oppositional meanings and ultimately to force the company to recreate an identity consistent with consumers' images.

For practitioners, some clear lessons emerge. First is the need to value qualitative data for their ability to provide a picture of how consumers will use products or confront issues in their everyday lives. Second is the need to be up front with consumers. In this case, participants in the taste tests weren't told that original Coke would be replaced, only that a new flavor was being tested. Because the company had not been fully forthcoming, consumers felt empowered to act, ultimately forcing the company to undertake an expensive retooling of their product line and a new marketing campaign.

Third, and perhaps key to this case, is the role of identity in all facets. Consumers had constructed an identity for themselves in relation to the company's old identity and brand. The campaign failed not because of actual product preference (the taste of New Coke was preferred) but because the cultural intermediaries hired by the company failed to create an identification between the new product and consumers. Ultimately, a company's identity, or that of its products or issues, is determined by the publics who consume it, not by the company itself.

Fourth, the interaction of the five moments creates variable and contingent outcomes. As this case demonstrates, science and material resources don't guarantee results. Because of the discursive nature of meaning and how it informs perspectives and subsequent behaviors, the course of a campaign is never absolute or determined. A communication campaign is always a work in progress, not a linear task with a concrete beginning or end. The failure of New Coke doesn't signify an end point on the circuit but a continuing process of redefining meanings.

The implications of the New Coke case form an integral part of cultural understanding today. Contemporary marketing experts say the company made a colossal blunder, even though at the time it was heralded as a bold and aggressive marketing move. The company itself recasts the narrative on its Web site in terms of "the power of taking intelligent risks" and the responsiveness of the company. In the words of CEO Goizueta, the most significant result of the product reformulation "was that it sent an incredibly powerful signal . . . a signal that we really were ready to do whatever was necessary to build value for the owners of our business" ("The Real Story," n.d., ¶ 6), thus emphasizing company responsiveness to shareholders, not consumers.

The continuing implications of the case also have a distinctly international angle. In 1985, New Coke was introduced in the United States and Canada. Many fewer consumer complaints were received from Canada, in part because the original formulation sold in the country was a sweeter product to begin with, so the changes weren't as apparent. But more important, the change did not challenge Canadian cultural norms.

In today's more globalized world, however, issues of national identity loom large. Consumers remarked that anywhere they went in the world, they could be surrounded with unfamiliar signs and symbols, but the Coke symbol would always be there, looking like a piece of home. This identification of Coke with the United States has spread around the world, but in myriad ways. In some areas of the world, Coke has been embraced as embodying the American Dream: opportunity and consumerism. When the authors were in Shanghai during the celebration of the start of the Year of the Rooster, the Coke symbol was prominent throughout the colorful New Year decorations. Yet at the same time, Coke has come to symbolize U.S. imperialism and neo-colonialism, often within the same countries, indicative of the multiple and conflicting identities that often form, as discussed in chapter 2 in terms of the company's operations in India.

This brief overview of the circuit of culture and the case of New Coke illustrates the basic principles of the circuit and suggests how it can inform public relations practice. The next five chapters discuss each moment in more detail to provide an in-depth and more nuanced understanding of how the circuit can inform international practice. To illustrate the circuit in practice, we outline an in-depth case study—the World Health Organization's smallpox eradication campaign—at the end of each of the next five chapters.

CHAPTER SUMMARY

- Culture constitutes meaning; language, culture, and meaning are inextricably intertwined.

- The circuit of culture, which comprises five moments, demonstrates how any cultural product is imbued with meanings.
  - Regulation encompasses the formal and informal controls on culture.
  - Producers encode dominant meanings into their cultural products.
  - Representation is the form cultural products take, including the meanings encoded into them.
  - Consumers actively create meanings by using cultural products in their everyday lives.
  - Public relations practitioners serve as cultural intermediaries, working to create common identities between products or issues and consumers, as in the case of New Coke.

- Articulations are the particular situations that arise from relationships and relative power within the five moments of the circuit.

- Dominant discourses are the "truths" that emerge within articulations based on relative power and difference.

❖ ENDNOTE

1. New Coke, Diet Coke, Cherry Coke, and Coke are trademarks of the Coca-Cola Company. Information for this case study was compiled from the company's Web site (http://www2.Coca-Cola.com) and news reports from the *New York Times, Time* magazine, and *Newsweek*.

4

The Regulatory
Environments of Global
Public Relations Practice

❖   ❖   ❖

Public relations is an important player on the international stage of
regulation, which inextricably links economics, politics, and communication. According to British theorist Stuart Hall (1997b), issues of
culture and power are at the forefront of this stage; how they interrelate
is fundamental to international public relations. The key question we
consider in this chapter is, How does international public relations perpetuate or influence regulation, and to what ends? We discuss forms of
regulation, followed by a discussion of international public relations
campaigns that either regulate or seek to regulate and of the ways in
which culture and power function in those campaigns. The chapter
ends with a case study of the World Health Organization (WHO) smallpox eradication effort and the role of regulation in that effort.

❖   NOTIONS OF REGULATION

Regulation *is essentially a type of control often associated with government
as government regulation carried out through law,* but it is much broader

than that. On a more abstract level, regulation is about an ongoing power struggle between various entities attempting to define the social, moral, and cultural norms of society. Forms include environmental regulation, cultural regulation, and self-regulation. Censorship is a form of regulation, as is the use of stereotypes, which attempt to normalize what users deem not normal by casting uncritical judgment.

The primary area for regulation is at an institutional level. Governments regulate to prevent anarchy in their societies by promulgating laws for certain modes of conduct. They might institute policies to protect their economy, environment, and culture. Cultures also project their own set of rules, and when the boundaries of those rules are crossed, issues of regulation inevitably emerge. Social movements and activist groups might form in an attempt to regulate or influence conduct.

Every country and the worldwide community have regulatory organizations. In your country, consider what organization regulates what you see on television. What conduct is permissible and not permissible? What about nudity, sexuality, violence, and language? Who determines what channels are on your television, what language they are in, and where they come from? In a democracy, the easy answer is that the market decides, but that doesn't account for the presence of local laws, international laws such as those established by the European Union, or the existence of national regulatory bodies such as the Independent Television Commission in Britain. These entities are among the forces that regulate the market, along with multinational media conglomerates in the nongovernment sphere. Here, issues of censorship, power, nationality, imperialism, freedom of speech, and multiculturalism are the currency of discussion.

In the circuit of culture, no single entity or individual owns regulation or any other moment. The moments are concurrently unstable, constantly in flux, interminably creating and recreating meaning. As Hall (1997a) reminds us, meaning is never fixed. The inability to recognize the fluidity of meaning is why many public relations efforts fail. The lesson for practitioners is the need to recognize the shifting meanings attached to changing circumstances and cultural tides, all while simultaneously negotiating regulation. On a fundamental level, complacency portends doom for many public relations efforts. Under this assumption, the process becomes critical to generating ideological and discursive patterns; Hall reminds us that the process is defined by "infinite points" and that culture and power are constantly interrelating. Russia is only one country where we can extend this discussion into the more tangible by relating issues of culture and power to notions of public relations.

❖ SHIFTING POLITICS, EVOLVING PUBLIC RELATIONS

Most studies of Russian public relations agree that the country is rapidly changing in public relations practice. The public relations industry in Russia is growing at a rate of 30% to 40% per year (Sveshnikoff, 2005). Natalia Mandrova, head of a Russian communication counseling firm, estimated the corporate public relations market in Russia at somewhere between US$400 and US$600 million in 2003 (RBC, 2003).

These numbers and facts illustrate that the formalized practice of public relations in Russia is growing, but as we have previously discussed, this doesn't mean that public relations is necessarily a recent phenomenon in Russia. If we take at face value the growth of public relations in Russia through the number of Russian public relations agencies and income figures, then we are projecting Western-based notions of public relations practice. What if public relations was indeed being practiced when Russia became its own country in 1991, only without the formal benchmarks that the West uses to determine the presence of public relations? There's no evidence that public relations agencies were operating in Russia in 1991 or that public relations was recognized as a legitimate profession. Devoid of this formal recognition, most scholars suggest that the evolution of public relations in Russia has occurred in less than 15 years (Sveshnikoff, 2005; Tsetsura & Kruckeberg, 2004).

Before Russia became an independent nation-state, it was part of the Union of Soviet Socialist Republics (USSR). For nearly eight decades, the Soviet Union operated under communist rule, which forbade private ownership and emphasized collectivism in a society without classes. The Soviet government controlled all forms of communication, making the media the mouthpiece for the government and its policies.

Accordingly, many Western perceptions of Russia exist:

When one hears about the Russian Federation, or simply Russia, he or she evokes his or her own set of social and cultural images of this country. Some think about an economically struggling post-communist country, while others see quite developed and prosperous cities such as Moscow. Some imagine everlasting winters and miserable countryside roads of peripheral Russia, the poverty and continuous struggle of Russian citizens, while others talk about the successful transformation of the communist regime into a democracy, in which a free market economy developed giving rise to a large middle class. (Tsetsura, 2003, p. 301)

Each of us brings to bear our own notions of a country before a discussion begins, unless we are hearing about it for the first time. We don't simply create and recreate images of Russia in every discussion; we bring ideas to our discussions, sometimes through stereotypes, which are a form of regulation.

Stereotypes is another elusive term to define. For simplicity, let's assume that **stereotypes** *are unsubstantiated ways of thinking and talking about something, often through oversimplifications and prejudices.* So although stereotypes are generally seen in Western society as negative, they do offer one beneficial aspect: They help us make sense of the world around us, even if that view is inaccurate or skewed. Stereotypes abound in any society. Pick almost any ethnic group and think of ways in which its members are commonly described: lazy, smart, rude, overachieving, arrogant, exotic, self-centered, and so on. Stereotypes can be helpful forms of communication. *Montezuma's revenge,* a common term to describe gastronomic distress contracted in Mexico or Central America, is one such stereotype that isn't inherently offensive and yet is descriptive enough to usually preempt additional elaboration. In these ways, stereotypes don't permit a boundless way of viewing a culture or society. Instead, they form parameters by limiting our understanding of them. Stereotypes, then, regulate our thoughts about other societies or cultures, sometimes positively and sometimes negatively.

It isn't a stereotype to say the USSR operated under socioeconomic, political, and cultural circumstances very different from those of a democratic society. These differences meant that public relations, at least in Western terms, wasn't widely known or understood. Communication in the Soviet era was characterized by **propaganda,** *a type of communication that straddles the line between persuasion and coercion.* The many definitions of propaganda generally cast ethics as the key variable that separates public relations from propaganda. Accurate, honest communication is public relations, whereas propaganda might include inaccurate information, flawed viewpoints, or critical omissions.

The ethical thread separating communication types is extremely narrow, according to Edward Bernays (1923, p. 212): "The only difference between 'propaganda' and 'education,' really, is in the point of view. The advocacy of what we believe in is education. The advocacy of what we don't believe in is propaganda." The effective application of social science principles could generate public support for a cause or initiative, a process Bernays called the *engineering of consent*. According to Bernays, communication is the centerpiece of effective leadership. Only leaders who were able to engineer consent by marshaling public opinion to support ideas and programs would succeed, he argued.

Bernays's work is a reminder that both propaganda and public relations are forms of communication. Decades have passed since the bulk of Bernays's seminal work on propaganda, yet the term is still associated with one-sided communication, such as that from centralized governments, and is still prevalent in many societies. The continued visibility of propaganda and its continued practice in some parts of the world place it in some proximity to public relations.

Scholarly research suggests propaganda is indeed the same as public relations, or at least distinctly related to it. Propaganda shouldn't be ignored in public relations practice or research because of its prominence in some cultures. Rejecting propaganda ignores its contemporary visibility and its role in effective communication in different societies. Certainly arguments can be made that propaganda is harmful, dangerous, and in some cases evil. But regardless of how propaganda is conceptualized, it's almost universally viewed in pejorative terms, and public relations has yet to fully sever ties to propaganda.

In the case of the Soviet Union, propaganda was an instrument of regulation for political ends. The absence of a marketplace of ideas, where pluralism and media could emerge freely, meant that most Soviet government communication was propaganda. The Soviet Union used facets of public relations in its sustained efforts to inculcate communist ideology in its citizens and those of its satellite nations. Its communication apparatus included posters, literature, cinema, political rallies, and print media. Perpetuating communist ideology was only one function of propaganda; maintaining and protecting communism were also signified through regulation by extinguishing all competing influences.

There is some evidence that modern public relations in Russia is evolving from the cultural, political, and economic realm created by the former USSR. A survey of 500 Muscovites conducted by a Russian research agency asked respondents, "What is public relations?" Half had no idea of what it meant, 33% answered correctly, and "a proportion thought it was a synonym for propaganda" (Williams, 2001, ¶ 1).

The nebulous tension between public relations and propaganda in Russia is exacerbated by the polarizing labels that have defined both terms. Two terms evolved in Russia in the early 1990s, according to Tsetsura (2003): *black PR*, affiliated with manipulation and propaganda, and *white PR,* associated with ethical Western designations of public relations practice. Russian communication appears to be dominated by a hybrid public relations–propaganda model in which ethics and transparency distinguish the two, with black PR as the domain of political public relations in Russia.

How is regulation functioning in the evolving democracy of Russia? That there is such an entrenched legacy of propaganda indicates that it is still part of the dominant discourse, despite some attempts by the burgeoning industry to regulate communications in Russia as public relations. Regulation was overt in the Soviet era, where censorship reigned and business and press were government controlled. The presence of regulation has been harder to detect since the country opened up to democratic reform in 1991, but we need to avoid the dichotomy of "state = regulation and market = freedom" (Hall, 1997a, p. 229). Even in free markets, some regulating force prevents anarchy. Hall suggests that markets regulate themselves through policies, procedures, and norms that provide structure and form. Even in freedom, then, regulation is at work. It has switched from overt government authoritarianism to a more subtle, nuanced form Hall places in a different mode of regulation, a reminder that regulation and freedom can coexist, and the presence of one warrants closer inspection for the other.

❖   THE AGENTS OF BLURRING BOUNDARIES

The type of control the Soviet empire sought to exert over its citizens and other countries would be much more difficult to maintain today. Technology has irrevocably changed communication and blurred national boundaries. It is far more difficult for any nation to institute laws and policies that insulate its citizens. Increasing technological sophistication has also affected society in more profound ways. Culture is far from monolithic; it is constantly interacting with other cultures at micro and macro levels and is morphing in unpredictable ways. The rapidity with which technology is proliferating and the unparalleled access by the worldwide community have so deeply changed culture that some theorists believe the global community is engaged in culture wars.

Politics

Regulation is a weapon on the battlefield of the culture wars because it seeks to generate a particular form of discourse or behavior that constitutes culture. For this reason, many governments are fearful of their citizens having unregulated exposure to other cultures. To these governments, exposure can dilute and modify a "true" culture, turning it into an illegitimate version of the government portrayal of the "real" thing. Iran banned satellite dishes in 1995, when the conservative majority in its government saw Western media as a threat to Islam. Evidence indicates the ban has backfired because of a thriving market in bootleg Western media, including DVDs and CDs. Also, Iranians are using their satellite dishes surreptitiously, disguising them as giant air conditioners and hiding them behind rows of dirty laundry (Lancaster, 1998; Taghi Beigi, 2002).

From the collapse of the USSR to pirated DVDs to satellite dishes disguised as air conditioners, one of the lessons from the moment of regulation is that government attempts to legislate behavior often fail. This point centralizes the role of the regulator as much as what is being regulated:

> All our conduct and actions are shaped, influenced and thus regulated normatively by social meanings. Since in this sense culture regulates social practice and conduct, then it matters profoundly *who regulates culture*. The regulation *of* culture and regulation *by* culture are thus intimately and profoundly interrelated. (Hall, 1997a, p. 233)

Any government attempt to regulate a behavior becomes an exercise in legitimizing power and exerting it, a process that both alienates and provides structure. Regulation in this sense isn't only about power but is about how the affected culture responds to, is influenced by, and participates in the discourse of regulation. This overlaying of cultural variables makes regulation a tricky endeavor for any government. It perpetuates power and attempts to place boundaries around culture, which is much too dynamic and amorphous to respond to unilateral attempts at regulation. This isn't to say that all government attempts to regulate behavior will fail. After all, laws are regulations, and laws give society structure. Instead, it's a reminder that government, by its very existence, is in a position of power, and with that comes not only tremendous responsibility but also recognition of how that power fits into complex cultural patterns and technological advancements.

Technology

More than ever before, those patterns are moderated by technological modalities such as the World Wide Web. On the Web, one person can make a difference by setting up shop in a global marketplace.

Dissolving boundaries, space, language, time, and traditional modes of communication, the Web has linked people and information together more rapidly than ever before. People can coalesce around issues on the Web, creating power bases that deeply affect cultural mores. This global regression toward mutual interests in cyberspace has created new communities that revolve around issues and topics. In cyberspace, cultures are temporarily reified by the innumerable worldviews that are present and thriving on the Web. Any Web site is global because its audience is global. Blogs (Web logs), or online diaries, have emerged as the mouthpieces for groups and individuals that can, to a small degree, regulate culture by commenting on and critiquing it for a vast worldwide audience.

Consider Salam Pax, the "Baghdad Blogger," whose wartime blog during the U.S.–Iraqi conflict drew millions. Pax was the pseudonym for an Iraqi architect whose candid and engaging accounts of the war on his blog were quoted in the *New York Times* and the *Guardian* and on the BBC. Pax became something of a cult figure, eventually landing book and movie deals. He's proof that one person with a blog can influence culture by giving voice to a situation or issue. His voice was effective enough to reach millions of individuals and some of the largest news sources in the world. He transcended culture but at the same time spoke for it and shaped it. In this way, he wasn't a cultural bystander; he was an active participant in the worldwide dialogue about the conflict in Iraq.

As we've discussed, technology has blurred boundaries between nations, bringing more cultures into contact with each other than ever before. How cultures are responding to these outside influences is an issue sociologists and anthropologists will continue to discuss and debate. Considering public relations as an international phenomenon, it's crucial to recognize the regional inequities that still exist and modify its practice. In a Western sense, it's easy to consider technology through a range of words and systems; we might think of digitization, satellites, high-speed Internet, computers, cell phones, the World Wide Web, and so on. However, keep in mind that this technology isn't equally distributed across the world. Much of the world still hasn't seen or used a computer, and a majority of the world's people (80%) have never heard a telephone ring. Less than 1% of South Asia's population is online, even though it is home to one fifth of the world's population. Africa, with 739 million people, has only 14 million phone lines, fewer than in Manhattan or Tokyo (Black, 1999).

Technology can be tangible or intangible; it can be a material or thing, or it can be a new idea. Technology is tightly tangled with economics. In the developed world, which has access to computers and cell phones, technology might mean something quite different than it would to a rural dweller in Cambodia. Cultural discourses can shape our understanding of technology, but those same discourses can also trap us into Western notions of technology and public relations practices that depend on that technology. Designing and writing content for Web sites, writing press releases, and holding press conferences are of little consequence for a public relations practitioner working in many parts of the world.

Economy

Underneath technology is the layer of economy, which greatly affects public relations practice. Strong economies aren't associated only with developed countries but also with parts of countries. Despite its size and its ultramodern cities such as Beijing and Shanghai, China is still a largely rural country. The availability of technology influences public relations campaign structure to the extent of the target public's level of development (e.g., loudspeakers mounted on cars have provided information to the citizens of newly independent East Timor). The Chinese government, working with a host of nongovernment organizations (NGOs), has made HIV and AIDS education and prevention the topic of a nationwide public information campaign. In urban areas, advertisements, Web sites, and press releases are ubiquitous (Photo 4.1). In rural areas, education and prevention programs have used radio broadcasts, dialogues, storytelling, posters, advertisements, caricatures, and photos (UNESCO, 2003). A play called *Student Zhao Ping* transmits messages on HIV prevention through a love story. Attendees also receive educational materials about HIV and AIDS (Global Business Coalition on HIV/AIDS, 2005). The BBC World Service Trust (2002) launched a successful public health education campaign in Ghana to combat trachoma, the world's leading cause of preventable blindness, by using street theater, posters, community events, and radio broadcasts.

This section has discussed issues of politics, technology, and economy in regulation. These three factors can influence and shape culture, much as culture can affect each one in turn. This complex interaction is regulated in different ways. The complexity of these relationships is less important than the recognition that there's no complete freedom in any area or interaction. There's always some form of regulation to moderate and shape economic and political systems. From democratic countries with open markets to authoritarian governments with

Photo 4.1   A Typical Billboard Used in China's HIV and AIDS Education
Campaign

SOURCE: Image part of the IISH Stefan R. Landsberger Collection (see http://www
.nsg.nl/~landsberger).

government-controlled systems, regulation is intrinsic in the world
system. The next section furthers the discussion of culture in this
system and ways in which it affects international public relations.

❖ CULTURAL NORMS: THE HIDDEN REGULATORS

By its very nature, culture is constituted at a molecular level, which we
might consider as an unending stream of interactions between people.
The moment of regulation occurs when the public and private spheres
collide, and for this reason it's of particular importance to international
public relations practice. Here, cultural classification systems, social
assumptions, and mores reside. The moment of regulation, then, is crucial in helping form the representations and identities created by both
producers and consumers. Practitioners consequently must evaluate
both their own and their publics' regulatory systems. Consider a well-
worn tale: The Chevy Nova foundered in Latin American countries
because Spanish speakers constructed a meaning of "no go" (*no va*)
from its name. Although the story probably is false, it has endured and
offers a teaching moment in that regulatory systems must be monitored and re-monitored for changes in meaning.

The cultural indices developed by Edward Hall and Geert Hofstede can inform these regulatory aspects of international practice. Cultural indices provide generic, and therefore admittedly stereotypic, descriptions of cultural norms and values, key regulatory considerations. Hall (1977) focuses on language, and his best-known contribution is his categorization of communication as high or low context. In **high-context cultures,** *such as those of the Middle East, much is left implicit and unstated, and relational prestige is more important than logical arguments.* In **low-context cultures,** *such as that of the United States, communication is explicit and information flows freely.* A distinguishing generalization is that high-context cultures tend to value group harmony more than individual desires; conversely, low-context cultures favor individualism.

The degree of context also dictates preferred message forms, with different cultures having different preferences for whether a message comes as words, numbers, or pictures. This might partially explain why storytelling is considered a valuable and effective public relations tool in high-context countries such as China and Ghana. Interpersonal communication is a prominent cultural feature of these countries. High-context countries value interpersonal relationships, and the communication that binds relationships often is in the form of behavioral cues, including gestures, body language, silence, proximity, and symbolic behavior (Würtz, 2005). A caveat for Western practitioners in such countries is that relying on mediated forms of communication might not be enough to transgress regulatory systems as effective forms of outreach.

Another helpful construct is that of monochronic versus polychronic time (Hall & Hall, 1995). In **monochronic cultures,** as in much of the United States, deadlines and schedules are considered firm, privacy is respected, and promptness is expected and rewarded. In **polychronic cultures,** as in much of Latin America, plans are changed easily and often, schedules and budgets are guidelines but not strictures, and furthering relations is more important than property rights or privacy. These cultural differences alone might make public relations different in the United States and Latin America. When other political, economic, and social factors are considered, it becomes easier to understand how public relations has developed along different models in other countries.

Hofstede (2001) proposed five major cultural constructs:

- Power distance
- Uncertainly avoidance

- Individualism
- Masculinity
- Long-term orientation

Power distance is defined as "the extent to which the less powerful members of institutions and organizations within a country expect and accept that power is distributed unequally" (Hofstede, 2001, p. 98). In high–power distance cultures, practitioners can use more coercive strategies, whereas in low–power distance cultures, rewards or premiums bring better results. **Uncertainly avoidance** measures how well a culture copes with ambiguity or difference. A culture that is high in uncertainty avoidance resists anything seen as an "outside effort," and practitioners are wise to hire a local firm and acquire a local sponsor for a campaign.

According to Hofstede's analysis, Latin America's largest country, Brazil, is high in uncertainty avoidance, meaning there is a cultural tendency to avoid ambiguity at all costs. Hofstede (n.d., ¶ 2) writes,

> In an effort to minimize or reduce this level of uncertainty, strict rules, laws, policies, and regulations are adopted and implemented. The ultimate goal of this population is to control everything in order to eliminate or avoid the unexpected. As a result of this high Uncertainty Avoidance characteristic, the society doesn't readily accept change and is very risk adverse [*sic*].

Montenegro (2004, p. 117) offers a different perspective on Brazil from her survey of professional international public relations agencies in Latin America: "Latin Americans, in general, are highly tolerant of uncertainty, particularly because law is respected yet not necessarily enforced, and time is viewed as infinite and abundant." The difference of cultural uncertainty is dramatic between Hofstede and Montenegro. What should an international public relations practitioner make of this difference? One is that Latin America is a large continent, and speaking in general terms isn't good enough for a savvy and culturally sensitive public relations counselor. Second is that although Brazil shares many characteristics with its neighbors, it has a different culture, history, and language. Third is that Brazil is large enough that there are distinct regional differences. Hofstede notes that the perception of Brazilians being lax with time might apply in social situations, but in Rio de Janeiro and São Paulo, business meetings generally start on time.

This thumbnail analysis of Brazil uses only two of Hofstede's cultural constructs; the other three are **individualism,** which *measures the* *degree to which individuals integrate into a group;* **masculinity,** *which refers to the distribution of gender roles in a culture;* and **long-term orientation,** *which measures values such as virtue, thrift, and perseverance.* Collectively, Hofstede's cultural constructs have been used in a wide range of social sciences and to explain areas as diverse as level of economic development and cultural difference.

Critics charge that the indices are inaccurate, the data for developing them are obsolete, and five constructs aren't enough to summarize a culture. These criticisms aside, Hofstede's indices are unquestionably influential, constituting a dominant discourse in cross-cultural communication. The lesson for practitioners using them is to proceed with caution. As cultures change and globalization exacerbates this pace, no one index has sufficient explanatory power to account for culture.

Cultural indices can provide cultural roadmaps, and studies such as Montenegro's can amplify the characteristics of those maps. Ultimately, however, the circuit of culture presents additional considerations through its moments. The implication is that a worldview can be constructed through consideration of all the moments of the circuit, not just cultural regulation, as we have done here. It also points to the need for local public relations advisors who are familiar with the hidden regulators that govern culture and can take into account regional differences. A closer look at one such regulator helps demonstrate this point.

The prevailing sentiment in scholarly circles is that despite its size and regional differences, Asia is a largely collectivist culture, meaning that it values community and family. These cultures prioritize group goals and hold that the community takes care of the individual in exchange for loyalty to the community. As a result of this emphasis on collectivism, we would expect its converse, individualism, to not score highly on Hofstede's scale for Asian countries. The United States scored 91 on Hofstede's individualism scale, prioritizing the individual over the community. Looking at Table 4.1, we see that China's score in the same category was 20, Japan 46, South Korea 18, and Singapore 20.

The sweeping generalization of Asian collectivism in scholarly literature is supported by Hofstede's individualism index. The concealed cultural regulation in these cultures involves the intricate relationship between individuals and groups such as communities and families. A generalization isn't very different from a stereotype until it has some empirical backing to support it. In this case, the evidence is that, in general, collectivism is one of the myriad webs within the sophisticated cultures of Asia. Of equal import is the need to consider these collectivist tendencies as a cultural regulation, which is part of the circuit of

Table 4.1   Hofstede's Indices for Selected Countries

Country	Power Distance	Individualism	Masculinity	Uncertainty Avoidance	Long-Term Orientation
China	80	20	66	30	118
Japan	54	46	95	92	80
Singapore	74	20	48	8	48
South Korea	60	18	39	85	75
United States	40	91	62	46	29

SOURCE: Data from http://www.geert-hofstede.com/hofstede_dimensions.php.

culture and is generic. Asia comprises 49 countries, each with its own cultural and regional nuances.

A classic example is the difference between the United States, a highly individualistic culture, and Japan, which is guided by social norms. Those social norms were questioned when Sony launched its revolutionary Walkman in 1979. The Walkman was produced in Japan so that a consumer could listen to music without disturbing others, promoting social harmony. In the United States, consumers often used it to block out external noise, which gave rise to the criticism that it was creating antisocial behavior. Criticism in the United States also centered on the device as promoting meaningless entertainment, yet many people used it for personal enrichment, such as listening to books on tape while exercising.

Du Gay et al. (1997) use the Walkman as an extended example of how the circuit of culture is realized. For the moment of regulation, it illustrates how social norms can regulate behavior and influence market economies. This is how regulation can function invisibly and latently, presenting a hurdle and an opportunity for public relations practitioners. Ironically, the Walkman is becoming obsolete as cassette tapes dwindle on international markets. Yet the offspring of the Walkman, such as portable MP3 players and the iPod, indicate the widespread cultural acceptance of portable music as a norm. In this way, the Walkman opened a global door by clashing with regulatory cultural forces and nullifying barriers until it became accepted. The moment of consumption comes into focus here, demonstrating how consumers are active and can change dominant meanings over time.

❖ REGULATING GLOBAL PUBLIC RELATIONS PRACTICE

This chapter has presented regulation as one moment in the circuit of culture, demonstrating how it can take a variety of forms. It can be overt, as in censorship, or less visible, as in a cultural regulation based on norms and classifications. Both examples entail an enforcement mechanism; this is where governments are more apt to struggle, however. The lack of enforcement is one reason many codes of ethics provide little regulation to public relations, making its practice largely unregulated internationally. The circuit warns us that regulation is only one moment; ignoring its other parts *and* instituting unenforceable regulations can completely undermine a government program. This is a lesson for government public relations, national awareness campaigns, and public affairs. Cultural regulation is more difficult to decipher. It is more deterministic and pliable, creating hidden regulations based on complex cultural codes. Those codes are embedded in and affected by a confluence of factors that include economy, politics, and technology.

International public relations seems to have some bearing on certain types of regulation, notably cultural regulation. In this area, international public relations can institute communication programs that might engage with cultures in meaningful ways. This is an area of great risk, however; focusing on one part of the circuit of the culture at the expense of the others or failing to adapt to nuance could make any public relations campaign an exercise in futility. Although the challenges in regulation are many, they can be overcome and incorporated into truly effective global public relations campaigns. The next section is a case study of the World Health Organization's smallpox eradication effort, which illustrates the circuit of culture at work, with an emphasis on regulation.

CHAPTER SUMMARY

- Regulation is a type of control in which various entities compete for power to maintain the social, moral, and cultural norms of society.

- Even in democratic societies, forms of regulation exist that influence public relations practice.

- Politics, technology, economy, and culture can all regulate public relations practice.

- Local public relations advisors are needed in international public relations efforts to help unveil hidden regulators.

Smallpox Eradication Campaign

On May 8, 1980, the World Health Organization (WHO) held a news conference at its Geneva, Switzerland, headquarters to announce that for the first time a life-threatening disease had been purposefully eliminated from nature. The news marked the end of a disease that had been in existence for more than 3,000 years, killed hundreds of millions of people, and changed the course of history on every continent except Antarctica.[1] Widely hailed as a public health triumph, the 21-year, more than US$300-million and 80-nation effort to eradicate smallpox is considered the organization's greatest international relations achievement as well. We examine this latter angle of the campaign, particularly in terms of how discourses were framed through formal, and more often informal, public relations strategies and tactics at global to local levels. Adopting the perspective of the circuit of culture, we begin the analysis with the moment of regulation.

INTERNATIONAL POWER AND POLITICS

One aspect of regulation is the role of organizational structure and relations in creating meaning and guiding subsequent action. The WHO is one of 16 specialized agencies of the United Nations created by international treaty in 1948. Its authority stems from its member nations, which meet annually to decide the organization's agenda and budget. At the 1959 meeting, members passed a resolution to eradicate smallpox worldwide, even though they lacked power to enforce a global effort because not all nations of the world were members, including one of the most populous nations, the People's Republic of China. Enforcement was also problematic in countries emerging from colonial rule. For example, in 1965 Rhodesia (now Zimbabwe) declared its independence from the United Kingdom, changing its status from that of a member state to that of a nonmember state.

Even member countries lacked enforcement power. Most delegates to the World Health Assembly did not hold cabinet-level positions in their respective governments and couldn't leverage political support. In many nations, ministers of health didn't want to dedicate a large portion of their scarce resources to eradicating a disease they saw as just one of many health threats facing their peoples. Yet the smallpox eradication unit, as part of WHO, was required by treaty to work with existing health services in each nation, necessitating government cooperation and support. Given these restrictions, the actual power of WHO's smallpox unit to conduct a worldwide eradication campaign was so severely constrained that failure was a very real possibility.

Case Study

Although the delegates voted for the eradication resolution in 1959, they allocated scant resources over the next 6 years to what many believed was an impossible task. So why did members vote for the resolution in the first place? Perhaps because the Soviet delegate proposed the measure, and the Soviet Union had just returned to WHO membership after a Cold War absence. Members may have passed the resolution as a conciliatory gesture to the Soviets; in turn, the Soviets may have been looking for a cause they could own that would boost their status as a supporter of developing countries (Tucker, 2001).

Also contributing to members' lack of enthusiasm was institutional history. WHO initiated a malaria eradication campaign in 1955 that eventually failed because increasing insecticide resistance made elimination of the mosquito carriers of the disease impossible. It was hard for WHO officials to generate enthusiasm for another eradication campaign, even though smallpox was a much better candidate for eradication. Although endemic in 59 countries and claiming at least 16,800 lives annually, smallpox was easily preventable by vaccination (Photo 4.2). Although the Soviet Union contributed vaccines and other logistical support to the cause, overall the program received only minimal support until 1965, when the superpowers' political interests coincided with WHO's goals.

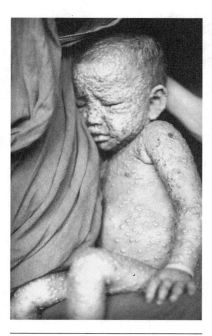

Photo 4.2   A Bangladeshi Child Suffering From a Severe, Probably Fatal, Case of Smallpox

SOURCE: Photo courtesy of the CDC, WHO, and Dr. Stanley O. Foster, M.D., M.P.H.

Cold War Politics

WHO leaders made smallpox the focus of the 1965 annual meeting because medical and technological advances made smallpox eradication more feasible. U.S. officials had been generally unenthusiastic about this Soviet initiative, but at this time U.S. views changed because officials realized the smallpox effort could be used to support political aims. As part of that year's U.N. "International Cooperation Year," U.S. president Lyndon Johnson highlighted the Centers for Disease Control (CDC) measles vaccination campaign in western Africa to demonstrate support for developing nations and compete with the Soviets for influence.

Case Study

The next year, U.S. Public Health Service officials convinced Johnson to pledge support to smallpox eradication in the region as well, although Congress refused aid to Ghana and Nigeria because of their political situations. In turn, Guinea refused U.S. aid because of fears of imperialism (Hopkins, 1989). Both the United States and Guinea eventually gave in to pressure from WHO, which wanted to ensure that all 18 contiguous countries in the region would achieve eradication, leaving no pockets of infection behind (Photo 4.3).

Photo 4.3   Cameroonian Children Show Off the Vaccination Certificates They Received for Participating in the U.S.-Led Smallpox and Measles Vaccination Campaign in Western Africa

SOURCE: Photo courtesy of the CDC.

Another problem developed when the U.S. government refused to cover local costs, such as gas and vehicle repair, because it believed local governments should support themselves. WHO officials, fearing local governments couldn't bear the costs, pledged to cover them from organizational funds, although it forced the global and supposedly nonpartisan organization into the uncomfortable position of subsidizing U.S. Cold War initiatives in the region.

WHO officials credit Cold War tensions for ensuring the success of the program because neither of the superpowers was going to be outshone in its efforts to aid the developing world. This combination of the struggle for ideological domination in the postcolonial era and scientific advances in medicine provided the necessary impetus to boost resource commitment. In 1966, with smallpox still endemic in 33 countries, WHO's member nations agreed to allocate more resources to an intensified effort to eradicate smallpox within 10 years.

Negotiating Boundaries

Although armed with greater logistical support, WHO campaign personnel still struggled to work within the varying structures of the numerous independent national programs, each of which had its own organizational culture. Not only was every national program different, but WHO was asking, in effect, that sovereign nations allow foreign intervention in their internal affairs, a strong breach of the right to self-determination and rule.

In former British colonies of Africa, for example, authority was decentralized, and local medical officers often resented the national eradication program encroaching on their turf. In Ethiopia's feudal system operating within a monarchy, WHO officials worked through 655 separate officials: the leaders of 14 provinces, divided into 102 *awrajas,* subdivided into 539 *woredas.* Pakistan at the time was divided into four autonomous regions, necessitating the establishment of four separate eradication programs, which bickered throughout the campaign. Turnover also slowed campaign efforts; for example, in a 5-year period Brazil had three ministers of health and five smallpox eradication program directors.

In Africa, colonial powers had carved out nations without regard for tribal boundaries. Tribal loyalties often were stronger than national ones, and the hundreds of migrating tribes in western and central Africa paid no attention to national boundaries. Unstable governments in the former French colonies of Dahomey and Togo provided little national leadership, but strong tribal allegiances crossed geopolitical lines. WHO personnel often had to operate under formal, national regulations while simultaneously negotiating the informal constraints of tribal loyalty.

Although WHO had envisioned host countries running their own programs with the organization's aid, in some countries the national health structure was either insufficient to support the program or subject to a regional health authority. For example, in Uganda, campaign leaders were just thankful that "the spread of smallpox was even less efficient than the performance of the staff" (Fenner, Henderson, Arita, Ježek, & Ladnyi, 1988, p. 965). Because Liberia lacked resources to run a program, WHO aided and supplied a religious NGO, which took charge instead. In India, where smallpox was rampant and eradication often seemed impossible, WHO enlisted support from corporate and NGO sources, such as Tata Industries, the Swedish International Development Agency, the Lions and Rotary Clubs, and Oxfam.

Case Study

Coordinating these groups added a layer of complexity to the campaign, but eradication efforts in India certainly would have failed without them. In Brazil, the last stronghold of smallpox in the Americas, the Pan American Health Organization, which wanted no outside interference from the developed world, ran the campaign independently of WHO. WHO had to adapt to each political situation, alternately exercising or restraining power, to gain the cooperation of governments and NGOs. Without such a fluid exercise of power, the campaign probably would have failed.

Applying Moral Suasion

Because officials had no legislative power to compel countries to support eradication, they relied on "the power of moral suasion" to achieve their goals (Fenner et al., 1988, p. 422). To leverage this power, the smallpox eradication unit began releasing incidence numbers by country in WHO's widely distributed *Weekly Epidemiological Record* and in regular information releases to global media. Many health officials didn't want the figures published because they didn't want the high number of actual cases made known. But over time, as many governments saw that other nations, particularly less developed nations such as Afghanistan and those of western Africa, were achieving eradication, they became ashamed and increased their own efforts.

At the 1973 annual meeting, for example, a delegate from a developing country that had eradicated smallpox expressed dismay over the large number of reported cases in India and embarrassed the Indian health minister by asking him whether the country had taken full advantage of WHO aid. Around the same time, Dr. Lawrence Altman, a public health official with the campaign and a *New York Times* medical reporter, wrote a series of articles blaming India's lack of success on neglect and bureaucratic incompetence. Indian officials responded to the resulting excoriation by finally cooperating and providing the necessary support for the program. As global eradication neared, governments of the few remaining endemic areas got behind eradication efforts to avoid the stigma of being last.

But using shame to leverage support proved problematic. If cases were a source of shame, then local officials could avoid the shame and the fear of government reprisal by not reporting cases. In northern India, the director of health services threatened to repost district officers who reported cases to isolated and unpleasant areas (Basu, Ježek, & Ward, 1979), and the secretary of health in Bangladesh threatened to fire local officials if they reported cases (Joarder, Tarantola, & Tulloch, 1980). Indonesia's last outbreak occurred because a regional official did not report the initial case for fear of punishment for incompetence.

Economic and political concerns also led to suppression. In Brazil, the health officer didn't report cases in the Rio de Janeiro area for fear of decreasing tourism. Officials in Iran suppressed notification of an outbreak because the upcoming 2,500th anniversary of the founding of the Persian empire was expected to bring a large influx of tourists. In many areas, such as Togo, local chiefs hid cases from authorities because of suspicion of the unstable national government. One area director in Togo tried imprisoning chiefs when hidden cases were found, which only increased mistrust and exacerbated the situation. In Somalia, where smallpox had been eradicated, officials openly and loudly criticized Ethiopia's program. When smallpox reestablished itself there, Somalian officials, including the WHO advisor, initially hid the cases rather than confront the inevitable loss of face and stigma of being the last.

As nations achieved eradication, governments publicized their success as an overt demonstration of how they were providing necessary social services to their citizens. Ambassadors also became vocal supporters when good media coverage resulted from campaign success in their respective countries. Although WHO employed only two full-time public information officers for the entire agency at this time, they devoted what resources they could to media relations efforts to help the smallpox eradication unit leverage this support.

Overall, the eradication unit had to insert itself into the affairs of many developing nations, but it often lacked any real power to do so. Besides these strictures, the unit also had to function within the bureaucratic structure of an international agency.

BUCKING THE BUREAUCRACY

WHO's director general had not believed eradication possible, and he didn't expect the members to support an intensified effort. Suddenly needing to name a director for the new unit, which until 1966 had comprised one public health physician and one secretary, he recruited Dr. D. A. Henderson, an American working with the CDC, and gave him relative autonomy within WHO. He hoped to make Henderson a scapegoat and blame the United States if eradication efforts failed (Reed, 2002; Tucker, 2001). Henderson agreed to take the position for 18 months only, in part because he was concerned the Soviets would pull their support if an American was in charge. In fact, Henderson successfully cultivated the Soviets, staying in the post for 11 years, leaving just before the last recorded case of smallpox in 1977.

Henderson and a few other members of the team came from the CDC, which had a much more freewheeling organizational culture than did WHO, which was known for its conservative, highly bureaucratic,

Case Study

and almost stultifying approach. For example, WHO required all units to develop standard operation manuals outlining specific objectives, strategies, and schedules. Yet the smallpox eradication unit's operational manual never got past draft form because Henderson believed it was impossible to codify every situation that might be encountered and that pragmatic flexibility was key to success. The operation manual for Zaire was typical in its lack of specificity: "Long-term objectives are to maintain eradication by appropriate surveillance methods as will emerge from experience and evaluation" (in Fenner et al., 1988, p. 916). Henderson also required all campaign leaders to routinely go into the field and encourage innovation at the field level, establishing a more vertical communication flow and institutionalizing flexibility.

In fact, many of the campaign's most successful techniques were the result of bottom-up field innovations rather than top-down bureaucratic decrees. Henderson never second-guessed his field teams, and he encouraged and empowered them to take initiative. For example, a worker in Indonesia renowned for his laziness somehow always submitted more accurate and complete case reports than did his colleagues. On questioning, he revealed that he went to schools first and showed the children a picture of an infected child from one of his WHO training brochures and asked them whether they knew of anyone who looked like that. The children turned out to be keen observers and reliable information sources. Going to schools to gather information soon became standard operating procedure, and laminated smallpox recognition cards featuring pictures of infected children became standard issue to all field workers (Photo 4.4).

The smallpox eradication unit also bypassed WHO's normal budgetary system, which required a paper trail of budget requests, purchase orders, and receipts. Arguing that funding delays contributed to the spread of smallpox, Henderson sent workers into the field with large amounts of discretionary cash, causing a bureaucratic nightmare at WHO headquarters (Brilliant, 1985). When one program advisor found that having travel requests approved could take 6 months or more, he began requesting permission but noting that if he hadn't heard anything within 2 to 3 weeks, he'd travel as planned. He usually came back to find that permission had been denied.

The unit also ignored or usurped government authority as necessary. Although WHO workers were allowed to dispense vaccine only to member governments, when guerrilla fighters in the Sudan requested smallpox vaccine for their area, the vaccine was handed over and marked as lost from inventory on accounting sheets. When a severe outbreak occurred in northern India, the WHO official in charge quarantined the city and established checkpoints along all thoroughfares, despite having absolutely no authority to do so.

The unit's relative autonomy and freewheeling style gave rise to the perception among leaders of other units at WHO that the smallpox eradication unit received special treatment and could violate rules and regulations with impunity. The resulting resentment caused some within the organization to seek to have the program's funding decreased or even removed and the program disbanded (Hopkins, 1989; Tucker, 2001). Yet many credit Henderson's disregard for bureaucracy as key to the campaign's success (Reed, 2002), particularly given the need for flexibility at the local level.

ADAPTING TO LOCAL NORMS AND CULTURES

Differing cultural beliefs had a profound effect on relative campaign progress. In many areas of Asia, for example, it was customary to visit the sick, which increased the spread of smallpox; but in much of Africa, it was customary to isolate victims, which helped halt disease spread and contributed to the quick success rate there.

Photo 4.4   WHO Epidemiologist Dr. Ali Mourad Shows the Smallpox Recognition Card to Schoolchildren in Bangladesh

SOURCE: Photo courtesy of the CDC, WHO, and Dr. Stanley O. Foster, M.D., M.P.H.

Case Study

For the campaign workers from more than 30 different nations in India, the country presented a microcosm of what the campaign faced on an international scale: "The multiplicity of ethnic groups, languages, customs, and associated health beliefs in India is unmatched in any other country. The staggering number of relatively autonomous health and medical organizations at national, state, and municipal levels also compounded difficulties" (Brilliant, 1985, p. 79). English provided an unofficial common language in a country with 15 official languages, more than 350 dialects, and a literacy rate of less than 40% for men and 20% for women. The proliferation of microcultures within India meant that even native Indians had to learn the differing traditional views of smallpox they encountered in the country. Additionally, the caste system, officially outlawed in 1950, remained entrenched in social custom. WHO personnel originally trained only high-caste people as vaccinators because many people would allow only someone of the same caste or higher to vaccinate them. But these vaccinators often were demeaning and abusive to lower-caste people, causing vaccination rates to decline. Eventually, workers had to train people of all castes (Hopkins, 1989).

In many countries, religion proved a cultural challenge, bringing the realm of public health in conflict with the private sphere of personal beliefs. In the Christian nation of Soviet Georgia, believers formed the cult of St. Barbara, patron saint of smallpox, and refused vaccination, believing prevention was a matter of faith (Hopkins, 2002). People in southern India, even devout Christians and Muslims, worshipped Shitala Mata, who could cure, prevent, or inflict the disease. Many Shitala worshippers refused vaccination because they feared it would anger her (Mather & John, 1973). The Yoruba tribe of western Africa worshipped the earth god Sapona, who could inflict smallpox when angered. As part of worship, priests performed variolation, a centuries-old immunizing technique in which live smallpox virus from a victim's scabs was scratched into the skin of a healthy person. WHO workers discouraged the practice because although it often provided immunity to the treated person, it also spread live virus and caused disease among those who had not been treated.

In heavily Muslim areas of Mali, people believed sorcerers inflicted the disease and refused vaccination, seeking a spiritual cure instead (Imperato & Traoré, 1968). For many Sunni Muslims, religious strictures did not block vaccination acceptance, but WHO workers had to train women as vaccinators to avoid compromising cultural norms concerning women. More difficult was containing the spread of smallpox that resulted throughout the Muslim world from pilgrimages to Mecca and Medina.

In 1968, WHO recommended that countries enact supportive legislation to encourage compliance with the program, such as requiring case reporting and vaccination and outlawing variolation. But legal discourse was rarely effective when it contradicted private norms. In India, requiring the public to report cases caused them to hide cases instead so as not to compromise their beliefs. Banning variolation in Afghanistan only stopped the public from reporting variolators; people weren't willing to submit their village elders to a law enacted at the behest of an outside authority. Throughout the campaign, WHO personnel encountered an ever-shifting array of regulatory issues that brought the public and private realms into conflict. No one standardized approach would have worked in all situations; field workers had to be empowered to use discretion.

IMPLICATIONS FOR INTERNATIONAL PRACTICE

Although few formal public relations resources were available to campaign leaders, the case may be more informative precisely for that reason. Whereas standard Western public relations wisdom would have proscribed a management by objective approach, with measurable objectives and detailed strategies and tactics, the more flexible approach taken here allowed the campaign to adapt to the variety of situational particulars encountered in this lengthy international campaign. The case suggests that vertical communication flow, field-level empowerment, and streamlined organizational structures are critical to success. The typical hierarchical structure of many organizations may need to be significantly restructured to achieve cross-cultural goals. To paraphrase one of the public health doctors, who was speaking specifically of health campaigns, "tactics in [public relations] must always be dynamic, not static, changing to meet the ever-changing political, economic, managerial, and [communicative] situation" (Brilliant, 1985, p. 157).

Ultimately, smallpox eradication aid became a tool of neocolonialism, fostering dependence on international aid, interference in national affairs, and increasing Cold War polarization. The campaign succeeded in part because of WHO's fluid management of relative power. They leveraged support from empowered players as necessary; conversely, when they were in an empowered position, they didn't always exercise that power, creating smoother relations that helped lead to campaign success. A notable exception occurred when they asked governments to legislate compliance with the campaign, which blurred the boundary between public and private spheres and led to greater resistance. It was a mistake they didn't repeat.

The issue of relative power is central to international practice. Although WHO's political status limited its relative power, many multinational corporations operating today wield great clout through economic power. As the deputy chairman of Edelman Public Relations recently observed about relationships between global organizations and stakeholders, "some imbalance is natural" (Morley, 2004, p. 17), and any campaign must take such imbalance into account. The issue highlights an important one for international public relations: the North–South divide between the developed world and the developing world and the conflicts inherent in foreign aid packages, trade agreements, and globalization with the right to self-determination. These inherently asymmetric relations result in unequal access to dominant discursive strategies, an issue examined in more depth in the next four chapters.

Case Study

ENDNOTE

1.   Materials from a wide variety of fields (e.g., organizational communication and behavior, management, international relations, anthropology, sociology, epidemiology, and public health) and sources (e.g., technical reports, memoirs, news releases and publicity materials, news coverage, popular media, scholarly articles and books, and trade press materials) were used to gather data for this case study. Unless otherwise indicated, information is from WHO's 1,473-page exhaustive history of the campaign, written by the campaign's major architects (Fenner et al., 1988).

5

The Face and Shape of Global Public Relations Campaign Materials

❖ ❖ ❖

A strong argument can be made that all public relations is a type of *representation,* which is the subject of this chapter. Most, if not all, public relations is about representing a cause, campaign, corporation, nation, or some other entity. An overarching theme in the chapter is that cultural meaning is encoded in the format and content of public relations campaigns and materials. That cultural meaning is constrained by the moment of regulation, discussed in chapter 4, and concomitantly affected by the other moments of the circuit: production, consumption, and identity.

We examine the role of representation through case studies: Russia's trade show efforts to lure high-technology corporations, the marketing of Kentucky Fried Chicken (KFC) in Asia, and the promotion of ecotourism in the Galápagos Islands. Each example reflects the role of representation and its interplay with issues of culture, identity, and power in generating meaning.

❖ REPRESENTING REPRESENTATION

Representation *is the discursive process by which cultural meaning is generated and given shape*: "We give things meaning by how we *represent* them" (Hall, 1997b, p. 3). Therefore, meaning isn't static or inherent in representations but is socially constructed through symbolic systems or discourse. Representation is predicated on power because it propagates the same inequalities inherent in any social system. It also implies that public relations practitioners have great power in their work. Representation is intrinsic in any material they prepare, any document they write, and any activity they undertake; each of these tasks is encoded with cultural meaning and informs a particular discourse.

Some have argued that public relations and advertising have too much power in shaping this discourse. Mickey (1997, p. 271) writes,

> Public relations practitioners can manipulate the image because they know the importance people place on signs and symbols in the culture. But, since media technology today gives us the facts as presented simply because they are presented and have little or no reference to truth, one could pose the serious question of whether the field of modern public relations practice must today and in the future be held to even greater accountability and tighter scrutiny.

Meaning depends largely on how signs and symbols operate in relation to each other. Accordingly, meaning doesn't exist per se; it's created, dependent on situational factors, culture, and the arrangements of its many parts. In simple terms, this means a brochure written by a public relations practitioner has no meaning. Instead, target audiences create their own meanings when they consume it. The codependency of many intervening circumstances, or moments such as consumption, is one reason the circuit of culture is a powerful tool for public relations. The circuit doesn't ascribe total power to consumers at the cost of other actors, such as producers; it locates consumers within a framework that includes production, again giving public relations practitioners great communication sway in how they use the tools of their trade to generate meaning.

The idea that symbols and signs can be arranged to generate a particular meaning is central to hyperreality. According to Baudrillard (1981/1994), **hyperreality** *is a version of the truth, but not the actual truth. The truth is obscured by a conflicting array of symbols, signs, images, and* *representations.* The ubiquity of messages, often from the media, and the technology that delivers those messages obfuscate truth by constructing and reconstructing it. Hall (1997b, p. 11) turns our attention away from the quest for truth and back to the process of representation:

> We should perhaps learn to think of meaning less in terms of "accuracy" and "truth" and more in terms of effective exchange— a process of *translation,* which facilitates cultural communication while always recognizing the persistence of difference and power between different "speakers" within the same cultural circuit.

Both Hall and Baudrillard focus on the process-oriented nature of how meaning is created and how that created meaning relates to truth. The toolbox of the public relations practitioner holds a limitless supply of symbols and text. How these tools are organized and presented becomes the parlance of practical public relations. Practitioners essentially translate organizational policy in their use of this toolbox. To borrow Hall's idea, the structure and presentation of public relations tools are commensurate with his notions of power and difference; and "to what ends" translates to Baudrillard's contested notion of hyperreality and the truth. The two terms are interrelated because truth often is a construct dependent on factors such as point of view.

To illustrate, consider an ancient tale, versions of which appear in China, India, and Africa. Seven blind men happen upon an elephant. One man touches the leg and thinks the elephant is a tree. Another touches the tail and thinks it is a rope. A third touches the tusk and thinks the elephant is a spear. The story continues, with each blind man convinced he has found the true essence of the elephant. This didactic example shows how multiple truths can exist simultaneously. In public relations, the challenge becomes one of operating ethically with multiple truths, a formidable challenge for a discipline that seeks to divorce itself from pejorative terms such as *propaganda* and *deceit.* Public relations has the power to create a particular type of reality, and that power comes with tremendous ethical responsibilities, discussed further in chapter 11.

To provide an example of how a reality might be created, consider the textual analysis of sub-Saharan Africa government Web sites conducted by Fürsich and Robins (2002). In their study, the researchers noted that the national government Web sites of any country are part of their global communication efforts. They concluded that the African governments in the sample created a "reflected" identity that mirrored Western interests. In other words, those nations were constructing a particular type of representation for a particular end. In this case, the authors argued it was to promote tourism and generate investment. They also suggested that the Web sites were reconstructions of the nations themselves:

> Images, texts and hyperlinks are used to reaffirm the nation in its borders, to construct an identity of its people, and to manage its collective memory. . . . The discourse oscillates between motifs of modernity coded as capitalist progress . . . and as tradition. (p. 196)

This example shows how a public relations tool, such as a government Web site, is a text encoded with multiple meanings. A Web site becomes a tapestry of competing—and sometimes complementing—symbols, words, pictures, and phrases. A West African country with a Web site, such as Burundi, ceases to exist as an actual country and instead becomes a creation in cyberspace. Like many western African nations, Burundi is a small country struggling for international recognition and legitimacy. Its Web site presents its point of view, unfettered by intermediaries such as media, and gives the country a storefront in the global marketplace of the World Wide Web. It has power to construct and reconstruct its country, it can position itself as different from or the same as, and it can engage or disengage with its target audiences, creating, in Baudrillard's terms, its own hyperreality.

Whether a Web site is created and maintained as a public relations function depends on the organization or nation creating the site and how it views the public relations function. As a tool, however, there's little debate that a Web site is a public relations vehicle and is one location where public relations practitioners can serve as cultural intermediaries. The circuit of culture posits that the meaning intended by Web architects isn't wholly theirs; it's held up to public scrutiny and inspection. The intended message might differ greatly from the actual consumed message, suggesting that understanding and misunderstanding are narrowly separated. The thin line between the two is enhanced by the circuit, which holds that new understandings are possible.

Web sites are just one example of public relations material embedded with meaning. Many others can serve as contact locations for issues of culture, identity, and power. This chapter only scratches the surface of the content and types of global public relations materials, beginning with Russia's.

❖ NEW DISCOURSES THROUGH
TECHNOLOGY AND TRADE SHOWS

Since the dissolution of the Soviet Union, Russia's emergence into the world economy has been unsteady. Among the challenges facing the developing country are international perceptions that it is still ruled by oligarchs, organized crime is omnipresent, and the economy hasn't opened up fast enough to capitalism: "Say Russia and one thinks of the ballet, of vodka, and of space scientists. Software? Not really. But a lot of action is taking place on the IT front there" (Nair, 2002, ¶ 1).

Elsewhere in the article, Nair discusses the lingering perception grounded in Russia's communist legacy: "One of the predominant issues that Russia faces today is its image from the past: the same KGB, mafia and all that. And then, the industry lacks marketing skills to sell in the global arena" (2002, ¶ 11). Recognition of that questionable image isn't ignored by the Russian press. A reporter for the Russian *St. Petersburg Times* wrote, "When it comes to luring direct investment from the locomotive of the global economy, Russia has a PR problem" (McGregor, 2003, ¶ 1).

One way the Russian government has combated the image problem is by marketing itself as a technology-driven economy with much to offer potential investors. The government has made trade shows and expositions a focal point of those promotional efforts. President Vladimir Putin has said that one of Russia's challenges is reprioritizing its economic sector and modernizing Russia's economy with high technology. The strategic decision to position Russia as a technology-driven, modern economy provides an excellent example of representation at work. As part of a public relations campaign to promote technology, trade shows offer Russia a number of benefits.

A trade show is an ongoing dance between consumer and producer, an exercise in finding middle ground for productive exchange. It's also a meeting place where cultures and business practices collide, creating a composite driven by personal interactions. In many developed countries, public relations, similar to mass media, has become so dependent on technology-mediated communication that personal contact is increasingly uncommon. Trade shows offer the direct contact public relations practitioners often aim to achieve with target audiences. One reason Russia invests so heavily in trade shows is that they are the antithesis of the insular perception of Russia during the communist era. Trade shows also allow the private sector and government to work in partnership, recreating Russia as a technologically advanced country.

Participants in a joint Russia–U.S. business symposium featuring technology toured a costume exhibit featuring this outfit made for Maria Ilinichna, the wife of Tsar Alexei Mikhailovich, for a masquerade ball held in 1903.

Photo 5.1　　Costume Exhibit

SOURCE: Photo courtesy of the State Hermitage Museum, St. Petersburg.

Russia isn't abandoning its heritage in this creation, however. In some trade shows, it has simultaneously represented itself as a country with a rich cultural legacy. At a Pennsylvania–Russia Business Opportunities Symposium in 1998, participants could tour the "Nicholas and Alexandra" exhibition, the last imperial family of tzarist Russia and the largest collection of imperial treasures ever to leave Russia (Photo 5.1). The exhibit brings an aspect of Russian culture to life by giving it form and substance. That culture is uniquely Russian and is on display with Russian technology, creating a cultural space where old and new collide. This space permits a new understanding of Russia to take place, one where meaning isn't related solely to technology but also to culture.

Meanings Encoded in Trade Shows

Hall (1997b) argues there's a politics of exhibiting that makes the invisible visible and therefore subjects the visible to power. Exhibiting technology through a trade show encodes meaning into that decision. At a very basic level it encodes technology into Russia or as a part of Russia. We might assume that the amalgamation of images, symbols, and texts at the trade show would support this rather simple connection of technology and Russia. Remember, however, that Russia is creating this linkage by contextualizing it at a trade show, giving Russia an opportunity to represent its technological prowess. This is a move that both limits and strengthens Russia's power of representing itself.

A cursory examination of Russia's trade show strategy reveals two competing, and arguably conflicting, strategies. On one side, Russia is leveraging trade shows to promote its technology capabilities, many of which were developed under the cloak of the old USSR. It's about recreating Russia from a centralized dinosaur and monocultural economy into an economic juggernaut spurred by technology. This inside-out strategy promotes the country as a technological leader in the global economy. A second strategy is also about promotion but in a different way. Russia is billing itself as a country that is open to multinational corporations (MNCs), technological exchange, and economic partnerships. This strategy doesn't center on the tangible products of technology but rather on the idea that Russia is a progressive place where foreign technology interests can thrive and is a country ripe for foreign investment. In tandem, the two strategies represent Russia as a country associated with high technology.

The Russian investment in technology trade shows has been evident in the past 3 years. The Russian government allocated US$1.97 million for participation in foreign exhibition and fairs in 2003 (UNEXWorld, 2003). A trade show that year, "Partnerships for Prosperity: Building U.S.–Russian Partnerships in Science and Technology," drew more than 250 Russian scientists and engineers to Philadelphia.

Identifying a Discourse of Russian Technology in Trade Shows

By making trade shows part of a public relations campaign to promote technology and improve its image, Russia is trying to recreate a dominant discourse about itself. Public relations through trade shows is an attempt to moderate the dominant discourse by encoding it with a competing discourse, one that's managed by Russia's commitment to technology. Trade shows provide a forum that gives Russia a power to shape its image without mediated sources. Russia is setting its own agenda without relying on the media alone to do it. The new Russian discourses include its cultural heritage and technological advancement, which are bound by engagement, dialogue, and interaction, all of which are far removed from the mechanistic tendencies of communism. This is where difference becomes important; by offering a discourse different from the dominant discourse, Russia gains some relative power because it's actively engaged in an unmediated public relations activity, participating in trade shows. We examine a different kind of power in the next section, which examines KFC's entry into the Asian market in the late 1980s.

❖   THE REPRESENTATION OF A
FAST FOOD SUPERPOWER IN ASIA

Kentucky Fried Chicken is the unquestioned champion of the fast food industry in Asia's largest market, China. It opened its first restaurant in the shadow of Chairman Mao Zedong near Tiananmen Square in 1987. Since that time, KFC, as it's known in China, has opened more than 1,000 stores and is more recognizable as a brand in China than Coca-Cola or McDonald's (Photo 5.2). It's building two KFCs a day in China and opening at least 250 per year, making its growth nothing short of phenomenal by any benchmark (Tutor, 2002). How has a U.S. company built such a dominant market position in China in less than 20 years? The answer lies largely in how it has encoded its brand with symbols, signs, and images that resonate with the Chinese.

KFC has set a record for fast food chain development in China since opening its first store in Beijing, China, in 1987. According to an ACNielsen survey, KFC is now the most recognized global brand among urban consumers in China.

Photo 5.2   Kentucky Fried Chicken in China

The U.S. image of KFC conjures up visions of the bespectacled, avuncular Colonel Sanders with his white goatee; the franchise's red and white color scheme; and its "secret recipe" of "11 herbs and spices." Inevitably, however, we decode these images and words to represent something else: chicken. In other markets around the world such as China, KFC has to create and continually recreate its brand. Kentucky Fried Chicken already has an existing perception in the United States from its 53-year history. Creating that perception and negotiating the cultural tides of Asia to construct KFC has taken an adaptive and reflexive strategy.

The Colonel in China, Malaysia, India, and the rest of Asia looks the same as the Colonel in the United States. That image alone is encoded with a meaning that might include America, Western values, or, more topically, modernity: the idea that a modern superstructure is arriving in Asia. In some of China's rural areas, that cachet of modernity has raised great interest. When a KFC opened in Qiandaohu, a small fishing village, eight security guards were needed to manage the swarm of customers on opening day (Adler, 2003). KFC's emergence in that country was so different from that of any other fast food chain that some people held wedding parties in their stores. In sum, KFC was decoded as a signifier of modernity and advancement. Indeed, the president of KFC's parent company in China remarked, "In many parts of China, the local municipal governments view the arrival of a KFC as a sign of the city coming of age" (Schreiner, 2005, ¶ 6).

KFC has embedded itself in cultures different from the one in which it originated by localizing its products. In China, its chicken burgers use only dark meat, which the Chinese prefer over white meat. American KFC dishes such as coleslaw and mashed potatoes aren't familiar to Chinese, so they were replaced with foods consonant with the Chinese palate, including a shredded carrot, fungus, and bamboo shoot salad; rice porridge; and a soup made of spinach, egg, and tomato. These product changes have created a particular representation of KFC as adaptive to Chinese tastes. KFC isn't decoded solely as a U.S. company imposing its product or image on China; it's viewed as a company that works in concert with Chinese culture by recreating itself for a Chinese audience.

One result is the development of a new understanding of what KFC is in markets such as China. A simple understanding is that KFC is a fast food chain that sells chicken. Even here, however, discursive struggles embody the contestation of meaning. "Fast food" as it's known in the United States isn't a representation that might be consistent with Chinese cultural norms. KFC ceases to be only about food, then; it becomes a site for cultural clashes that, not surprisingly, relegate power to elevated status. The president of KFC's parent company in China, Samuel Su, said after KFC opened its first drive-through store in 2002, "KFC is capitalizing on China's increased mobility, fast-paced lifestyle, greater consumer spending power and desire for luxury items such as automobiles" (KFC, 2002, ¶ 2).

KFC becomes a site where a culture of corporate power competes with traditional Chinese cultures and values. This type of struggle is common in globalization, another contested term with multiple conflicting meanings. In this case, KFC both contributes to the culture of what it means to be Chinese and nullifies it. It becomes a U.S. symbol appropriated for Chinese consumption, making it both propel Chinese culture and change it; some say that change is for better, others for worse. Traditional Chinese culture through food is forever modified by a foreign interloper, the KFC representation of chicken.

An important consideration is that KFC isn't *just* a chicken restaurant; it's part of a much larger sphere with culture, identity, and power as critical determinants. This might be one reason why a KFC in Pakistan was torched by an angry mob after a suicide bomber attacked a Shiite mosque in June 2005.

KFC Negotiates Asian Culture

The creation and recreation of KFC in Asia is apparent in Chicky, a fluffy chicken mascot developed for the company's Asian markets, including China, Singapore, Pakistan, and Malaysia. That you won't find Chicky in a U.S. KFC is an indicator of how KFC is creating symbols that it believes reflect the interests of its target publics in Asia. In this way, KFC is operating in a similar fashion to sub-Saharan African Web sites by mirroring interests based on constructs. The African government Web sites reflect Western interests, according Fürsich and Robins; KFC restaurants reflect what KFC believes to be Asian interests. KFC China president Su believes its success in Asia results partially from its ability to localize its product through "the integration of all aspects of KFC's operations including product development, human resources, supply chain management, logistics, and quality control" (FoodService.com, 2004, ¶ 3). Consider this theory atop a cultural tradition in which chicken has greater appeal than other meats, such as beef.

KFC's entry into Asia hasn't been without bumps. When the company tried to translate its "finger lickin' good" slogan to Chinese, it became "eat your fingers off" (Adler, 2003, ¶ 5). In 2004, an avian influenza shattered Asian interest in chicken, causing nine KFC stores to close in Vietnam alone when their business plummeted (Yanshuo, 2004, ¶ 10). In Tibet, the Dalai Lama joined forces with People for the Ethical Treatment of Animals to discourage KFC from opening up shop in that country, saying that "the mass slaughter of chickens violated Tibet's traditional values" ("Delight Over KFC," 2004, ¶ 3). A food coloring contamination scare caused KFC to pull two products from its menus in China in 2005.

Creating New Understandings of Asia and KFC

Although this section has focused primarily on KFC's booming growth in China, the company is performing well across much of Asia. One inference we can make from KFC's success in Asia is that it's generated meanings that do two things: establish it as a recognizable brand and motivate people to visit its stores and eat chicken. The underlying assumption we might make is that for the most part KFC has successfully negotiated the interplay between culture, identity, and power to formulate a new representation of itself and what it means to be Chinese. Despite concerns about contamination and its other public relations challenges, KFC has created a self-representation that works in Asia. A diner at the KFC in Qiandaohu called the franchise "fashionable," evidence that KFC has inserted itself into a Chinese discourse, irrevocably altering that discourse and its own identity in the process.

KFC has its origins in the United States, but in Asia it has become something else that isn't wholly U.S. or distinctively Asian. It's a hybrid that doesn't belong to any one country or entity per se. Like that of any MNC, the KFC migration into Asia signaled a willingness to divest itself of a central discourse and splinter off into new ones that are, like culture, increasingly complex and dynamic. The company has successfully engaged with new discourses in Asia that are largely dissimilar from those that surround the franchise in the United States, where it's seen as old-fashioned and it has engaged in lengthy media battles with People for the Ethical Treatment of Animals over the treatment of chickens, leading to Web sites such as KentuckyFried Cruelty.com. The emerging discourse in Asia is indeed new. Unlike Coca-Cola, which hasn't been able to completely isolate its public relations woes, KFC has succeeded so far.

The last section of this chapter is a discussion of tourism, one of the world's most profitable industries. More specifically, it examines how Ecuador is promoting the Galápagos Islands under the contested banner of ecotourism. This example is just one of countless others that bring the same issues of representation discussed in this chapter to the forefront of international public relations.

❖ PARADISE FOUND IN THE GALÁPAGOS ISLANDS

Ecuador is one of Latin America's smallest countries, with a population of slightly more than 13 million. Straddling the equator and blessed with the richest biodiversity of any area in the world, Ecuador also includes parts of the Amazon rainforest and Andes Mountains.

Despite its abundant natural wealth, the country has struggled with an economy largely dependent on bananas and oil, which account for more than half of the country's export revenue. As those markets fluctuate, so does the Ecuadorian economy. To offset unpredictable economic cycles and the overdependence on only two products, Ecuador has made an effort to increase tourism, notably to the Galápagos Islands.

This archipelago was made famous by Charles Darwin, whose theory of evolution was inspired by the abundant wildlife, including pink flamingos, penguins, sea lions, marine iguanas, and giant tortoises. The publication of Darwin's *Origin of Species* in 1859 transformed the Galápagos Islands from relative obscurity into a land with international cultural meaning. In the late 1990s, the government of Ecuador began heavily investing in the Galápagos by promoting tourism based on the islands' natural beauty and wildlife (Photo 5.3). That promotion has come with a price, however; as tourism increased, so did international pressure to preserve the islands.

Furthermore, the small year-round population of 17,000 on the Galápagos relies heavily on fishing to earn a living. To maintain good standing with the international community and preservationist organizations, the government enacted regulations to limit fishing, resulting in unrest and protests by a small but spirited group of fishers. To curry favor with international groups such as the United Nations Educational, Scientific and Cultural Organization, the government also instituted tourism regulations that required a naturalist to accompany every tour group and prohibited bringing food, pets, and plants to the islands.

The Politics of Ecotourism

The Galápagos Islands fit neatly into the U.N.'s resolution to make 2002 the International Year of Ecotourism. To capitalize on the international interest in ecotourism, Ecuador poured millions into its tourism

Ecuador has taken advantage of ecotourism by promoting the natural beauty and diverse wildlife of the Galápagos Islands.

Photo 5.3   Galápagos Islands

SOURCE: Photo courtesy of Michael Lejeune.

industry, hiring an American public relations firm, exhibiting at trade shows, and educating island police officers in tourism etiquette (InternationalReports.net, 2001). These efforts positioned Ecuador squarely within the international discourse of ecotourism, including its pros and cons, benefits, and hazards. Ecotourism has since become the Galápagos Islands; the relationship is symbiotic, reflecting the need to balance tourism and economic growth with the preservation of millions of species of wildlife. In a very real sense, the Galápagos Islands are a site of contestation between competing forces with certain perspectives. Those motivations include economic development, preservation of wildlife and culture, and the self-sufficiency of islanders.

Ecotourism gained popularity in the 1980s as a way for developing nations to boost their economy by promoting their natural resources through tourism. An original definition of **ecotourism** comes from Hector Ceballos-Lascurain, a Mexican architect and environmentalist who is generally credited with inventing the term in 1983:

Environmentally responsible travel and visitation to relatively undisturbed natural areas, in order to enjoy and appreciate nature (and any accompanying cultural features both past and present) that promotes conservation, has low visitor impact, and provides for beneficially active socio-economic involvement of local populations. (in Kerschner, 2004, ¶ 4)

Since Ceballos-Lascurain's original definition, the term has spawned multiple definitions from multiple organizations. The offspring of definitions has created the discourse around and within ecotourism. This is one of the perils of creation; any new idea, such as a word, ceases to have original meaning when it's subjected to power in the production process and the accompanying move into the public sphere. Further analysis of this phenomenon might be made in the meanings various audiences have affixed to ecotourism. To a government such as Ecuador, it's revenue. To critics, it's a label—similar to "green friendly"—that permits economic gain along with environmentally irresponsible behavior. To the fishers of the Galápagos Islands, it threatens their livelihood by increasing commercial interest in the area. Ecuador therefore relinquishes its ownership of the Galápagos Islands from the many conflicting positions toward the islands and how they should be handled vis-à-vis tourism and ecology. Similarly, ecotourism as a term is affected by myriad meanings that exert economic and cultural pressures on it, making its definition as contested as the Galápagos Islands themselves.

Trouble in Paradise

Beneath the utopian visions of the Galápagos Islands is a stream of discord from the competing forces attempting to appropriate them for their own ends, whether it's development or conservation. Each cause brings its own discourse to bear, turning the Galápagos Islands into a battlefield pitting discourse against discourse. On yet another level, it's a struggle between global discourses of conservation, nature, and ecotourism and local discourses of survival and right of use. The battles are both discursive and literal.

In recent years, fishers have held tortoises captive, rioted, and vandalized national park offices until fishing quotas were overturned. In 2004, fishers blockaded the entrance to the Charles Darwin Research Station to protest a law protecting the waters of the Galápagos Islands from overfishing. In 2005, 40 turtles were found dead on the island of Isabela, presumably killed by locals for food. One local fisher told a CNN reporter, "An animal is worth a lot more than a human being.

Here, one tortoise, one bird, one sea lion, has more value than a human baby" (in Tyler, 2002, ¶ 19).

Most of the small year-round population of the Galápagos Islands live in Puerto Ayora, a sleepy fishing village without television and with only sporadic electricity until the late 1990s. Now it has Internet access, automatic teller machines, and a Federal Express office. The city's population has tripled in the past 10 years. Building is booming in Puerto Ayora to accommodate those escaping mainland Ecuador for a better life. The downside is in the two ships that have capsized off the coast of the Galápagos, spilling more than 200,000 gallons of fuel—earmarked for the local economy and tourist boats—into the sea. A Galápagos tour operator and the driving force behind the formation of the International Galapagos Tour Operators Association (IGTOA) says the preeminent debate about ecotourism is whether it interferes with wildlife.

IGTOA has lobbied for tighter conservation measures in the Galápagos. In a 2005 "Action Alert" on its Web site, it criticized a government proposal to allow longline fishing, in which hundreds or thousands of bait hooks are attached to a single line. IGTOA said it was "completely against longlining in any form in the protected waters of the Galapagos Islands. To us, is [sic] inconceivable that this form of fishing is even being discussed" (IGTOA, 2005a, ¶ 2).

Its Web site provides the names and contact information for members of the media, Ecuadorian government officials, ambassadors, and international organizations to contact to protest longline fishing. IGTOA paints a bleak picture of conservation in the Galápagos, suggesting that the fight to preserve its wildlife is being lost to mismanagement, political struggles, and marauding commercial interests:

> Chaos reigns in the Galapagos National Park. Eight park directors have come and gone in the last two years. A strike by park staff over political meddling and mismanagement has left park functions in shambles. . . . What has happened? A shift in power. . . . There is big money, not reason, behind all this. Those involved do not consider the interests of the country as a whole, or even the interests of most people living in the Galapagos, whose numbers continue to swell. (IGTOA, 2005b, ¶ 4)

Cultural Encoding of the Galápagos Islands

The emergence of independent voices such as IGTOA signals a shift in power in Ecuador, where the footprints of corruption and authoritarian rule run deep. Tilson (2004, p. 63) described the government of Ecuador as "rooted in a political tradition of corruption, ruled by physical force and manipulation, [that] views communication as an end in itself and will employ deceptive public relations strategies, and violence if necessary, to advance its own interests."

Against this perception, the Galápagos Islands are a commodity capable of being metaphorically bought, sold, and promoted. This **commodification**—*turning an object or idea into something that can be bought or sold and has economic value*—is encoded not only in the government's ecotourism campaign but in how competing discourses have set agendas. The U.N.'s designation of 2000 as the international year of ecotourism politicized the struggle even further, making the Galápagos part of a much larger international dialogue about tourism, ecology, and ecotourism.

The cracks in the tranquil façade of the Galápagos are largely concealed by Ecuador's ecotourism public relations, which the Ecuador Ministry of Tourism Web site says is based on "a promotion strategy which includes the direct participation of the best exponents of our multiethnic culture on international markets." Similar to Russia, Ecuador has invested in trade shows such as the ITB Tourism trade show in Berlin, Germany. At the 2005 fair, Ecuador sent a native shaman to "cure" Berlin, hosted a happy hour for German journalists, held a folklore ballet, and placed a straw hat weaver at a fair reception. An Ecuadorian dance and music group performed at the fair, and Ecuador participated in a handshake ceremony with representatives from Taiwan, Peru, and the World Trade Organization.

At ITB, Ecuador reappropriated cultural symbols to construct its national image. That image becomes encoded with authenticity through culture, meaning that the "real" Ecuador is accessible to fair participants. The symbols of Ecuador include the shaman in traditional garb, promotional materials splashed with vibrant colors, straw hats, and handmade traditional Ecuadorian blankets. The cumulative effect of this public relations strategy is to position the Galápagos Islands and Ecuador as a distinctive "other," different from other countries and tourist destinations. Ecuador is selling an exotic image that is based on its difference from any other place in the world, and it can do so literally because the Galápagos Islands are different from any other tourist destination in the world.

Ecuador has chosen to translate its culture into segments that it thinks will be meaningful to a worldwide audience. This translation isn't real in the sense that it is wholly representative of the Galápagos Islands. Like most communication campaigns, it is a selective representation that ignores strife, tensions with fishers, and the trappings of modernity. These omissions make Ecuador's version of the Galápagos Islands through ecotourism a strategic construction. In this process of representation, Ecuador is walking a tightrope as international conservationist groups watch closely. If the country doesn't appease those groups, it can lose their endorsement and consequently an integral component of how it represents itself. The constructed version of the Galápagos Islands creates one discourse that's simultaneously affected by the other organizations, notably tourism operators, who are creating their own discourses.

❖ OF REPRESENTATION AND NEW UNDERSTANDINGS

The examples of public relations campaigns from around the globe in this chapter demonstrate that public relations doesn't work in a vacuum; it's constantly shaped by exigent forces that often go unrecognized by public relations practitioners. One lesson from this realization is that learning another culture is only the start of an international public relations campaign. Identifying and decoding some of the alternative discourses that surround the topical aspects of a public relations campaign are also important. Public relations practitioners need to decode the discourse surrounding their work, much as consumers decode public relations materials to make meaning. Learning other languages also becomes important in this light; Burns (2001) says that language is the key to culture and understanding and that all public relations practitioners should be multilingual in the future. The circuit of culture instructs us that language is only one key to one lock on the door to international public relations. Myriad other locks must be opened for truly effective global public relations work.

The idea that language is only one such key is consistent with Banks's belief that public relations must be situationally redefined. Banks argues that practitioners must be able to adopt a particular flexible worldview predicated on openness: "The nature, means, and methods of communication must be emergent, allowing specific communication outcomes to flow organically from interaction based on the few basic principles of genuine dialogue" (2000, p. 113). The result is the need for a public relations practitioner who is both a translator—facilitating and managing discourse—and also what we might call a **strategic decoder,** *one who decodes discourses and then appropriates selected parts to in turn encode public relations materials.* The first step in this process is recognized by many Western-based formulas of public relations that begin with research.

The public relations examples in this chapter reveal that a certain type of research is needed for public relations practitioners. That research approaches culture with the same scrutiny as identity and power. It entails the ability to step outside one's point of view to try on other perspectives. It also entails the ability not only to recognize alternative discourses but also to see them on other terms. This is a challenging move that temporarily disempowers public relations as a process but can ultimately empower it by generating new understandings. Those understandings might be dramatically different from what the public relations practitioner originally envisioned but no less effective in addressing a public relations challenge.

This shift to a certain type of research and thinking relates to Freitag's notion that we "may soon see a time where the term *international public relations* becomes unnecessary. Indeed, one can make the argument that *national public relations* does not exist" (2002, p. 225). All public relations materials are encoded with meaning, and that meaning isn't consistent across international borders, nor is it wholly consistent within national borders. The evolution of technology gives international wings to any public relations campaign, making the local global and vice versa.

Thinking internationally becomes a type of thinking in which culture is omnipresent, along with power and identity. To put it another way, it means that culture doesn't relate only to international public relations but to all forms of public relations. This challenging shift doesn't make all public relations relative or situational. Fortunately, there are guidelines for practicing public relations and producing public relations materials. We'll discuss the moment of production in the next chapter as a direct link to practicing public relations in a global environment. But first, we demonstrate how the moment of representation manifested in the smallpox eradication campaign.

CHAPTER SUMMARY

- Cultural meaning is encoded in the format and content of public relations materials.
- Learning another language and culture is only a starting point for launching an international public relations campaign.
- Practitioners must be able to try on different points of view in their work to reach new understandings.
- Issues of culture, power, and difference affect the production and content of all public relations materials.
- Public relations practitioners must serve as strategic decoders who are able to decode discourses and then reappropriate selected parts to encode public relations materials.

Smallpox Eradication Campaign

Although the goal was straightforward and easily measurable—eliminate smallpox—campaign leaders had to carefully choose and tailor campaign materials' content and format to make eradication salient to a wide variety of peoples to gain compliance and support. This section of the case study explores some of the dominant representations WHO developed in four areas of practice: government relations, employee relations, external relations with affected publics, and media relations.

GOVERNMENT RELATIONS

Because WHO is an international organization existing only by treaty, government relations are inherent in all its undertakings. The smallpox eradication campaign was no exception. In any international campaign, government relations often figures prominently because of the regulatory issues involved in cross-national work. Today, dedicated government relations specialists take charge of these crucial aspects to ensure that the organization may operate in any given country. For most of this campaign, however, leaders did not have any dedicated public relations personnel, much less a government relations specialist.

They also lacked professional fundraising experience. The campaign desperately needed support from the wealthier developed nations in which smallpox had already been eradicated and therefore was not a pressing health issue. Lack of funding was a continuous problem for the unit: The final tally at campaign's end demonstrated that during the peak years of the campaign (1967 to 1979) only 12% of funding came from WHO's regular budget. Another 14% came from special voluntary funding within WHO (WHO, 1980). Campaign leaders had to raise almost three fourths of all funds by convincing member nations and other groups to give cash, supplies, and other gifts in kind.

Framing the Funding Case to Developed Nations

WHO traditionally had not sought supplementary funding from governments, giving leaders no precedent to follow. The campaign thus faced two challenges: making the issue of smallpox eradication salient to leaders of developed countries and getting them to adopt a new behavior of making additional, specialized funding contributions to the campaign. Although the public health doctors leading the campaign lacked fundraising experience, they had one distinct advantage. Many of them had worked for government agencies in developed countries, and they understood how these governments and their budgets functioned; they could speak the language of progress and economics.

They used this language in the 1964 report on the program, stressing both the possibility of reinfection in developed countries and the feasibility of the program thanks to scientific progress: "Eradication of smallpox in endemic areas is well within the compass of modern preventative medicine" (WHO, 1964, p. 4). Noting that the current lack of success was attributable to a dearth of resources, the report suggested that "given energetic action and practical help from countries free from the disease the endemic countries could rapidly bring it under control and ultimately eliminate it" (p. 4). To reinforce the point, the conclusion of the report reminded readers that "the success of the smallpox eradication programme within a reasonable period of time is directly linked . . . with the amount of practical assistance in the form of technical advice and the supply of vaccine and other essentials, which the smallpox-free countries are prepared to give to the endemic countries" (p. 30).

Having established eradication as feasible given modern medicine and support, campaign leaders needed to demonstrate to political leaders of the developed nations, which had the most to give but seemingly the least to lose, that smallpox was a losing proposition for them as well. Campaign chair Dr. D. A. Henderson and other key campaign figures had previously worked for the U.S. government's Centers for Disease Control (CDC), and they knew that funding was almost never forthcoming without demonstration of a favorable cost–benefit ratio. For the first time, WHO workers constructed reports and charts demonstrating the savings these governments could garner by supporting eradication: The estimated cost for the entire eradication program was US\$300 million, compared with developed world costs of US\$1 billion per year for vaccinations and quarantine (Auerbach, 1977). For the United States, the total cost of the program was estimated to be only twice its annual expenditure to prevent reinfection (Hopkins, 1989).

As with most cost–benefit analyses, the "facts and figures" presented were, in actuality, best guess estimates. For example, the services of a volunteer worker were valued at US\$750 a month, a figure pulled from the accounting sheets of one donor nation and applied to all. What mattered wasn't whether these figures represented the eventual reality but that they were presented with the authority of science behind them, making them true for discussion purposes. By presenting their case as one based on scientific progress and hard facts, the campaign leaders narrowed the possible courses of action to one: A fiscally responsible government would, of necessity, support eradication.

By framing the issue in scientific and economic terms, leaders wrote out of consideration the moral argument that eradicating smallpox would rid the world of a scourge that killed tens of thousands of people annually, many of them children. They realized that this argument would hold little force with governments. Many serious health problems plagued much of the developing world and devastated vast populations, often affecting children. Framing the argument in these terms made smallpox one problem among many, and eradication wouldn't solve the larger health issues. A doctor with the campaign later reported for the *New York Times* that

> smallpox eradication was undertaken as much for economic as for altruistic reasons. In this era of cost–benefit analysis, justification for wiping out smallpox comes from the saving of $1 billion that will be realized each year. . . . Without such savings, the governments of the world probably would not have overcome complacency to undertake the venture. (Altman, 1979, p. C3)

Officials personally presented their case of cost-effective self-interest to influential opinion leaders because they learned that "personal, often repeated, appeals by individual members of the smallpox programme eradication staff had to be made in order to obtain each contribution" (Fenner et al., 1988, p. 467). The approach worked—from 1967 to 1969, the United States, Sweden, and the USSR contributed more than three fourths of all funds and gifts in kind to the voluntary fund account—but funding remained an ongoing battle. In 1976, with eradication in sight, Henderson had to turn down an urgent field request for additional personnel, saying, "Frankly, at this time, we simply don't have the money. . . . One would have expected all sorts of support at this time but we are simply not getting it" (in Fenner et al., 1988, p. 460).

Smallpox as a Numbers Game in Developing Nations

Estimated costs were much higher for the developing countries in which smallpox was endemic, in large part because the severity of the illness caused a drop in work productivity among those it affected. However, officials realized that cost–benefit analyses would be ineffective here, where many health issues were even more costly and resources to combat them were lacking. The campaign team was also in a precarious diplomatic position. It was one thing for a delegate to the World Health Assembly to vote for global eradication as a nice concept. It was quite another to have an international agency within your sovereign bounds telling you how to run your country's health program. Campaign leaders faced three major challenges:

- To convince national health administrators that eradication was feasible
- To have it singled out from other health programs and given priority
- To do the first two diplomatically so as to garner cooperation rather than engender greater resistance

Case Study

In many areas, smallpox had existed for almost as long as recorded history, becoming an inevitable fact of life. Even WHO's regional health director for Southeast Asia thought eradication impossible, a belief underscored for many by the failure of the malaria eradication campaign. Compounding the issue was the number of competing health issues on the agenda.

A WHO smallpox administrator in Geneva looking at India in 1973 saw a single country that accounted for 57.7 percent of the reported global incidence of smallpox (and by the following year it would account for 86.1 percent). But to the planner in the Indian Ministry of Health or to the Health Cell in the Ministry of Planning, smallpox was not the major health problem in the country. (Brilliant, 1985, p. 29)

Consequently, smallpox workers commonly were reassigned to other areas; in India, for example, the health ministry often diverted staff to the family planning unit. Perhaps not wanting to see others succeed where he was failing, the U.S. malaria program advisor in Ethiopia convinced the minister of health to not even meet with WHO officials to discuss the campaign. Malaria program staff refused any cooperation, even hiding extra unused vehicles in a remote desert area when the smallpox program asked to borrow them. Only when members of the malaria team began to contract smallpox did the hostilities cease.

To convey the feasibility of eradication without simply trying to force a program on unwilling nations, leaders adopted the low-key, behind-the-scenes approach mentioned in chapter 4 of simply publishing weekly incidence figures in their own widely distributed publication, the *Weekly Epidemiological Report,* and in information releases to the media (Table 5.1). Additionally, the unit produced local publications, such as *The Eradicator* in Sierra Leone and *Boletim* in Brazil, which they circulated widely in their countries of origin. Besides local statistics, these publications contained praise for officials and workers when evidence of success mounted.

This indirect approach took time, but it was generally effective and contributed to better government relations. In countries where health ministries supported smallpox eradication programs, such as Indonesia and countries in western Africa, eradication was achieved in just 3.5 years rather than the projected 5 years or more. If eradication could be achieved in these stubbornly endemic areas and under extremely difficult conditions, then it was feasible anywhere. And eradicating smallpox meant one less issue on overcrowded health agendas. WHO gave these facts and figures maximum publicity and let them speak for themselves.

As the campaign progressed, international discourse made smallpox eradication a source of pride and continuing infection a source of shame, as noted in the last chapter. Indira Gandhi, India's prime minister, voiced a

Table 5.1   Monthly Smallpox Incidence Figures Published for
Indonesia in 1971

The breakdown by province showed which health officials were doing a better job of containing outbreaks and contributed to intracountry and intercountry rivalry.

Province	January	February	March	April	May	June	July
Java							
West Java	9	24	17	12	0	0	0
Jakarta	4	0	0	0	0	0	0
Central Java	0	0	0	0	0	0	0
East Java	0	0	0	0	0	0	0
Sulawesi							
North Sulawesi	0	0	0	0	0	0	0
Central Sulawesi	0	0	0	0	0	0	0
Southeast Sulawesi	0	0	0	0	0	0	0
South Sulawesi	149	155	403	220	130	98	142
Sumatra							
Aceh	0	0	0	0	0	0	0
North Sumatra	40	90	20	30	1	56	34
West Sumatra	0	0	0	0	0	0	0
Riau	12	10	0	0	0	0	0
Jambi	62	35	44	5	1	0	0
South Sumatra	0	0	0	0	0	0	0
Bengkulu	0	0	0	0	0	0	0
Lampung	0	0	0	0	0	0	0
Total	276	314	484	67	32	54	76

Case Study

SOURCE: Data from Fenner et al. (1988, p. 653).

growing sentiment when she called smallpox "a disease of economic backwardness" (in Brilliant, 1985, p. 87). Most governments got the message and hopped on the eradication bandwagon. For the few holdouts, WHO officials found ways to bypass recalcitrant health ministers. In Botswana, for example, WHO officials met with the director of the Botswana Red Cross, who just happened to be the wife of the president. Not long afterward, the president signed a bill authorizing the program. In Ethiopia, Henderson waited until the minister was out of the country to meet with Emperor Haile Selassie's personal physician and plead the cause. Soon after, the emperor ordered his health minister to support the program, making Ethiopia the last country to officially authorize a program.

Officials used these backdoor approaches as a last resort because they were bound to breed resentment and damage overall government relations. More often, they let the facts speak for themselves, giving them a global stage from which to do so. Campaign leaders presented smallpox as a numbers game, one that many developing countries wanted to win.

EMPLOYEE RELATIONS: CREATING A GLOBAL ARMY

Most international workers didn't need to be convinced that eradication was a worthy goal, but their work was physically and mentally arduous, endangering morale. However, the majority of workers were poorly compensated temporary government employees, which didn't engender job loyalty. Lacking employee relations staff, campaign leaders had to find a way to unify these disparate groups and maintain enthusiasm and morale. The answer was to characterize the campaign using a war metaphor. The public health doctors, educators, clerks, mechanics, vaccinators, and others from 73 nations operating in 50 countries became soldiers united in the global war on a common enemy: smallpox.

Early training manuals outlined three stages to this "veritable military operation"—preparation, attack, and control—codifying the imagery (WHO, 1968, p. 10). Henderson (1980, p. 4) made "a global war" on smallpox one of his key messages and talking points, referring to needles and vaccine as "the guns and bullets of the campaign." A 1980 special edition of *World Health* magazine commemorating the campaign demonstrates how thoroughly campaign workers adopted the imagery. One from Sierra Leone described the inauguration of the campaign there in martial imagery: "The vaccination team members wore their field uniforms and displayed their jet injector guns for the public to see" (Davies, 1980, p. 8). An interview with the national officer for India outlines that country's "war plan," which included the decision "that instead of expending our resources against the entire enemy forces simultaneously, we would concentrate on their strongholds" (in Tuli, 1980, p. 13). The article opens with an extended war metaphor:

The relentless war against an enemy that knew no mercy had not been going on too well. If anything, it had become a general's nightmare. There was no dearth of "troops" or "ammunition," the problem was to get them to the right place at the right time. Naturally, the casualties were heavy—over 16,000 reported dead and more than five times this number maimed and disabled.

Mobile search teams were "reconnaissance troops"; vaccinators were "commando units that would strike at 'enemy' strongholds at short notice" (p. 12).

The campaign "generals," headquartered in Geneva, spent up to 70% of their time in the field, signaling their personal involvement in the battle (Nelson, 1985). They concluded at the end of the campaign that one of the lessons learned was that these frequent field visits were invaluable. They facilitated problem resolution and efficient redistribution of services and, as important, raised morale. Field workers reported that they found headquarters very responsive and encouraging in large measure because of this personal contact (Hopkins, 1989).

At the end of the campaign, Henderson believed his staff deserved more recognition for their work than they received. At his own expense, he created the mock "Order of the Bifurcated Needle," referring to the instrument used for smallpox vaccinations. Participants received a certificate and a needle shaped into a zero to represent the campaign's goal of no more smallpox (MacKenzie, 2004; Tucker, 2001), giving the campaign war "medals" to round out the imagery.

MOBILIZING PUBLIC SUPPORT FOR ERADICATION

Locating every case was critical to prevent outbreaks, but the public often hid cases for myriad cultural, religious, and economic reasons. To motivate the public to report cases, campaign leaders took the controversial step of offering monetary rewards to citizens who reported cases. Leaders presented the reward program to the news media as recognizing the "importance of public participation" (Altman, 1979, p. C3) and "dependence on an informed public" (Brilliant, 1985, p. 54), but internal critics complained they were paying people to do what they should be doing anyway.

Health educators working in advance of vaccination teams presented four key messages to local opinion leaders:

- Smallpox should be reported.
- Smallpox should be reported to a health worker.
- There is a reward for reporting.
- When an outbreak occurs, people should be vaccinated to prevent illness and loss of income (Brilliant, 1985).

Case Study

Besides these interpersonal channels, the messages were conveyed using mass media in urban areas, including public service announcements, news releases, advertisements, posters, fliers, bus and truck placards, public address systems mounted on cars, slides in cinemas and theaters, and puppet shows in local markets (Photo 5.4). In remote areas, leaflets were dropped from planes, and in one area of India, workers painted a notice on the side of an elephant and rode it through the streets. WHO created posters with ample white space to allow the addition of messages in local languages. In areas of Asia and Africa, notice was stenciled on every 10th house.

Photo 5.4   Two Smallpox Eradication Workers Spread Word of the Reward for Reporting Cases From a Rickshaw With a Megaphone Mounted on Top

SOURCE: Photo courtesy of CDC, WHO, and Stanley O. Foster, M.D., M.P.H.

A *New York Times* article observed that "areas considered a high risk for smallpox are saturated with publicity about the reward" ("India and W.H.O.," 1975, p. 16), and in several countries local officials asked the teams to desist because of the profusion of posters and stenciled notices on buildings (WHO, 1980). The publicity blitz worked: A nationwide survey in India found that 61% of the population knew about the reward and the amount; in Somalia, 77% of the settled population and 70% of nomads were aware.

The reward campaign was successful, with almost two thirds of new cases in Somalia discovered as a result of the program. In Indonesia, the offer of a transistor radio resulted in the discovery of 160 previously unknown cases. In Bangladesh, authorities paid out 220,000 *takas* (US$27,280) of reward money, "a modest sum for the improvement in reporting" (Fenner et al., 1988, p. 509; Photo 5.5). The last recorded case of smallpox outside a laboratory was discovered when a coworker turned in the victim to collect the reward (Tucker, 2001).

A problem arose when local health workers, who were often poorly paid government employees, started concealing reports of cases so they could claim the reward themselves. Campaign officials solved the problem by offering two rewards: one for the member of the public and one for the health worker passing on the report. As suc-

Photo 5.5   WHO Hired Sign Painters in Bangladesh to Paint Notice of the Reward for Reporting Cases on the Backs of Buses

SOURCE: Photo courtesy of CDC, WHO, and Stanley O. Foster, M.D., M.P.H.

cess loomed, the reward amount was increased. In late 1975, a 1,000-rupee (US$125) reward was offered in India, a sum equivalent to about 4 months' salary for many and high enough to invite fraud. On one occasion, people smuggled in a patient from Bangladesh and tried to claim the reward, but health workers uncovered the ruse. Interestingly, in Ghana the reward system was not used because officials there believed it would be viewed as corruption (Hopkins, 1989).

In late 1978, when eradication appeared achieved but not yet certain, WHO's director-general, acting in accordance with a World Health Assembly resolution, increased the award to US$1,000 (Photo 5.6). Despite the high sum, there were no takers: Smallpox had been eradicated (WHO, 1980).

Case Study

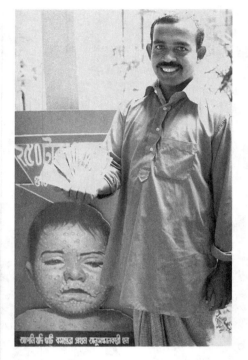

Photo 5.6   A Bangladeshi Ministry Official Holds Reward Money Over a Copy of a Poster Announcing the Reward for Reporting a Confirmed Smallpox Case.

SOURCE: Photo courtesy of CDC, WHO, and Stanley O. Foster, M.D., M.P.H.

MEDIA RELATIONS

Although the medical profession historically has been renowned for its deep-seated distrust of the media and lack of media relations training and skills, the smallpox eradication unit actively cultivated the media. Henderson was remarkably media savvy, although many of his staff weren't. He held numerous news conferences to appeal to potential donors and gave progress reports. The unit was headquartered in Geneva, which wasn't a major media hub, and the little public relations support there came from WHO's general public information office. Joan Bush and Peter Ozorio, public information officers (PIOs) in WHO's office at United Nations headquarters in New York City, provided some additional support, such as setting up transatlantic telephone news conferences. Local media relations were handled by operations officers.

Not until 1977 was the unit authorized to hire James Magee, a full-time PIO, and at that point his job was simply to publicize the campaign's success. The main work of the campaign was already accomplished. The flurry of media coverage that appeared thereafter, and the proliferation of commemorative stamps, medals, and other keepsakes, lends credence to the campaign leaders' observation that "more rapid progress might have been possible if from the beginning, there had been a special staff to handle two other activities—public information and soliciting contributions from donors" (Fenner et al., 1988, p. 1356).

The message sent to the media was the familiar one of eradication as a military operation. Dr. Lawrence Altman was not only a public health doctor with the campaign but also a *New York Times* medical reporter, giving the campaign literally a "journalist in residence." Altman and Henderson had worked together at the CDC, where in 1963 Henderson informed Altman that he thought smallpox eradication was feasible (Altman, 1979). Altman's stories were frequent and informed and served as agenda setters for other news outlets.

Altman (1975, pp. 1, 26) helped convey the military message in articles such as a front-page story that recounted the "global war on smallpox" fought by "battalions of health forces" and an "air force . . . [of] helicopters" so "the troops [can] track down the potential victims by telegraphing or broadcasting to allied forces elsewhere." Other newspaper reporters followed the lead, and headlines such as the "Battle Goes On to Free World From Smallpox" (Borders, 1976, p. A17) and "Total Victory in Two-Century Effort Is Proclaimed by Smallpox Warriors" (Cohn, 1979, p. A2) appeared.

As in all campaigns, events occasionally drove coverage. One notable example occurred in 1974, when reporters from around the globe gathered for India's first atomic bomb test. In an extraordinary collision of circumstances,

- A major outbreak occurred at the same time, with 11,000 cases of smallpox recorded in just one week.
- Railroad and airline employees went on strike, halting vaccine shipment.
- Medical workers in one region went on strike.

Journalists didn't miss the irony of a country joining the nuclear arms race while services were in shambles and smallpox was proceeding seemingly unchecked. They rushed to cover the story. Dr. Lawrence Brilliant, the official in charge, was ill prepared to handle the media, but Henderson and another associate flew in and gave him a crash course in media relations.

A competing representation arose when campaign leaders' determination to receive maximum publicity for the last case led to a virtual media circus surrounding what became a comedy of errors. In October 1975, WHO officials held a news conference to announce that smallpox had not been found in Bangladesh for more than 2 months, only to have a case reported 4 days later. In October 1976, television crews flew to Somalia for WHO's announcement that smallpox hadn't been found anywhere in the world for 10 weeks, only to have smallpox found in Mogadishu, Somalia's capital, on the eve of the announcement. Altman (1976, p. A30) reported a month later that WHO officials had "virtually eliminated smallpox," then 3 months later that officials noted a "setback" but "expressed optimism." He quoted Henderson forecasting that "the last case of smallpox in the world will occur this month" (Altman, 1977, p. A25). Henderson was mistaken.

Soon the story became not the war on smallpox but the seeming impossibility of the task. Even within campaign ranks "it was nearly part of the legend of smallpox that the last case might only be found on the eve of eradication celebrations" (Brilliant, 1985, p. 69). Altman continued to voice Henderson's optimism that eradication was near, but other news reports weren't as optimistic and departed from WHO's script, noting the "many false cries of success in the past two years" (Auerbach, 1977, p. A20). By the time the final case occurred in 1977 in Somalia, however, the unit had its full-time PIO on board, and the media were well represented. Both the U.S. Public Broadcasting System and Japan's NHK produced documentaries, and reporters for many major newspapers and wire services were on hand. *National Geographic, Reader's Digest, Scientific American,* and other publications ran lengthy articles. Most coverage conveyed the dominant theme: The battle was won, the enemy was dead.

Throughout the campaign, the combination of Henderson's media relations prowess, the presence of a journalist in residence, the unit's frequent information releases to the media despite limited public relations support, and the inherent newsworthiness of the endeavor helped the unit build the media agenda and shape media coverage of the campaign along their main talking points.

IMPLICATIONS FOR INTERNATIONAL PRACTICE

Campaign leaders understood the need to develop different representations of the problem for different groups, tailoring them to local conditions, to raise issue salience and garner support. Some of their successful tactics have become common public relations practice and advice:

- They spoke the language of the target audience.
- During a crisis they responded quickly and personally from top levels of management.
- They kept key messages simple.
- They relied heavily on interpersonal communication channels to reach opinion leaders.

A few aspects of the case have particular application to international practice. Campaign leaders realized they had to take a long-term approach, slowly building relationships and taking time to allow target governments to embrace the campaign's perspective, an approach recommended by top international practitioners today (e.g., Crawford, 2004). Current industry leaders have taken many Western-based MNCs to task for trying to move too quickly and not building a solid relational foundation in a country first. The leaders of the eradication campaign also realized the value of face-to-face communication with their employees, no matter how distant, to resolve problems and raise employee morale.

Even with today's technology, face time remains a valuable component of international campaigns. The senior vice president for corporate communications of Unisys states,

> If you're the communications leader, you have to meet people, listen, observe, and show your global and local teams you care by being there in person. You can't run a global organization from headquarters. Face-to-face meetings will never be eliminated. The leader of a company or a communications organization has to travel. (Badler, 2004, p. 20)

The decision to offer rewards for case reports presented a moral issue for the audience as well as an economic one, which created new meanings around how cases were to be understood. In doing so, the campaign disempowered the victims, who were already suffering, and the food, lodging, and clothing given to them amounted to much less than what other people were paid to report them. For victims, the reward system offered the final indignity.

Simultaneously, it made unethical behavior on the part of employees and social disruption within communities inevitable. The reward amount offered was large enough to be coercive, particularly in areas with extremely high levels of unemployment and poverty.

The reward system and dominant war imagery had strong repercussions for the campaign, which we discuss in the moments of consumption and identity. But first, chapter 6 examines how representations come into existence through the moment of production.

Case Study

6

Practicing Public
Relations in a
Global Environment

❖   ❖   ❖

This chapter explores the moment of production, which is given by far the most weight in public relations textbooks and classes. Discussions about the production of public relations commonly center on its tactics, from writing a news release to a public relations plan or a speech, for example. Production of these tools is considered central to the practice of public relations. Much as tactics are generally part of a larger public relations plan, production is part of a larger issue in the circuit of culture. In the circuit, production is another moment that's manifest in all aspects of public relations, introducing and reintroducing power dynamics from creation to implementation. All too often these power dynamics are overshadowed by time constraints and budgetary concerns in practice and by the need to teach basic public relations skills in educational settings.

This chapter builds on those concerns by framing production as part of doing public relations in a global environment, in which power affects both the production of public relations materials and their communication to external audiences. The chapter also frames common public relations production processes, such as targeting publics, around sensitivity to culture. We examine typical patterns of public relations agency growth around the globe and the relationship of that expansion to contested notions of globalization and glocalization. We see how production often is gendered and racialized, creating a product that's inescapably predicated on power. Finally, we consider how the regulatory environments and production constraints of various cultures have led to privileging of different voices in the production process. The global–local nexus is the conceptual thread that connects these topics by recognizing that local and global are constantly clashing and grappling with each other in complex, often unpredictable ways.

❖ GLOBAL DIMENSIONS OF PUBLIC RELATIONS

Look at the Web site of any of the largest public relations firms, and chances are that you'll see either a world map of their office locations or links to their offices around the world. A composite of these Web sites would tout the company's global reach and presence and point out that they're an "international public relations agency." A closer look reveals offices invariably clustered in Europe and North America, with a few dots in Latin America and Asia and fewer still in Africa. If there is a presence in Africa, it tends to be in northern Africa or South Africa and clumped in with regions such as the Middle East. Invariably, the large international public relations agency model consists of dozens of offices in the United States and Europe and either wholly owned offices or partnerships in densely populated areas of other developed countries. What do these observations tell us about international public relations?

One observation is that most international public relations agencies in the United States and the West are selectively international rather than global. They're driven by business and economics, not by the richness of culture or by communication altruism. In other words, power is perpetuated by countries and regions in a position to offer certain strategic benefits or financial gain to large public relations agencies. The same thing occurs when professional athletes in U.S. sports leagues call themselves "world champions," yet their only competition has been domestic.

A second observation is that the concentration of public relations agency office locations in Europe and North America gives most international public relations agencies a decidedly Western orientation rather than a wholly international one. This point is important in production because it reflects the power advantage the West has in projecting a particular discourse of international public relations. This discourse originates in the West. Consequently, global production patterns are tightly controlled by Western interests and capitalist tendencies.

This might explain why international public relations often is associated with a Western public relations agency opening an office in an "othered" country. We might expect a U.S. public relations agency to open up an office in Nigeria or Ukraine, but when was the last time a Nigerian or Ukrainian public relations agency opened in the United States? This doesn't mean these two countries don't have interests associated with public relations in the United States, but a discourse of international public relations is generally one way, from developed to developing, first world to an often nebulous "other" and from large to small.

The president of Uganda, Yoweri Kaguta Museveni, hired the London office of Hill & Knowlton to improve the Ugandan government's image.

Photo 6.1   Yoweri Kaguta Museveni, President of Uganda

SOURCE: Photo courtesy of Wickipedia Commons

The global public relations environment is controlled by actors with power, whether they're wealthy nations, multinational corporations, large public relations agencies, or interests with the necessary resources to go international. This might explain why President Yoweri Museveni hired Hill & Knowlton's London office to "polish the image of the Ugandan government, which is wrestling with civil war, a tarnished human rights record and a wave of criticism from Western media and human rights groups" rather than using a local agency ("Uganda Hires," 2005, ¶ 1; see Photo 6.1).

The primary contemporary model for establishing a global public relations presence is to partner with an indigenous public relations firm or open a regional office. The practice of partnering with local firms began more than five decades ago and has continued unabated, becoming the prevailing way for agencies to pool resources and claim a regional presence. More recently, these partnerships have given way to corporate behemoths such as the Interpublic Group, Omnicom Group, and WPP Group, whose stable of public relations agencies includes Burson-Marsteller, Hill & Knowlton, and Ogilvy. The grouping of agencies under one mammoth corporate umbrella mirrors the centralized media structure that predominates in much of the world.

Implicit in the model is the need for local practitioners who can negotiate the local cultural and business landscape. In this model, many multinational corporations, including large public relations firms, use local talent while being sensitive to local cultural differences. But often inherent in that business philosophy is the notion that the global is dominant and the local dependent, creating a new form of colonization. We often think of colonization as it relates to imperialist countries subjugating others, such as the British colonizing Nigeria or Portugal colonizing Brazil.

From an organizational perspective, however, colonization operates at a micro level with similar core issues. At stake aren't national cultures and identities of traditional colonization but rather the same issues within an organization. Power is the weight that tips the scales toward headquarters, which essentially colonizes its subsidiaries and foreign counterparts by directing activities and using the local office and staff to carry them out. As this example illustrates, the same core–periphery arguments that apply to economic systems and colonialism can also apply to global organizations with local offices.

Gender, Race, Class, and Power

One dialogue surrounding public relations power structures in Western countries involves gender and race imbalances. It's no secret the public relations industry isn't as diverse as the audiences it purports to reach. Minorities are severely underrepresented in public relations in the United States, where women account for two thirds of all public relations practitioners. Nonetheless, men still predominate as top firm executives, demonstrating that the gender distribution at managerial levels is still heavily tilted toward men. This upper management bias toward men has spawned terms such as *glass ceiling* and *velvet ghetto,* signifiers of a corporate power struggle in the United States.

Further embedded in gender discourses are other issues ranging from pay equity between men and women, work–life balance, gender stereotypes, and sexual harassment. The discourses of gender and race imbalance and unequal distribution of managerial status aren't lost in international public relations; they're ideologically transferred when agencies move across borders to establish new ventures.

Power structures can be buttressed in many ways internationally, such as gender inequities at the executive level, the ratio of expatriates to locals in a firm, and the number of minorities employed. Yet another issue is class; it takes some capital to operate a public relations business, and global agencies often have the deep pockets to bring their Western, corporate business models to developing countries. However, the presence of such global agencies can erroneously indicate that public relations is the tool of the economically powerful and can be practiced only according to a Western, corporate model.

On another level, power is institutionalized in how a company defines and carries out its work. One such example is the increasing tendency for U.S. public relations agencies to develop company-specific approaches to public relations. Ogilvy calls its approach to public relations a "360 Degree Brand Stewardship™," Ketchum offers its proprietary "Ketchum Planning Process (KPP)™," and Edelman has its Edelman BrandCARE™, "a proprietary, multi-phased PR-centric process." Such standardized systems are useful and give some agencies an advantage over national competitors, provided the systems are reflexive enough to account for variation in public relations practice.

Formalizing proprietary knowledge at the global level is a risk, however, because the cultural dimensions of globality introduce variables that resist categorization and structure. Moreover, scant evidence suggests that standardized public relations approaches work across varied socioeconomic, political, and cultural systems. The question of whether uniform standards are applicable in places other than their country of origin is at the crux of one of the most topical conflicts of international public relations, that between ethnocentric and polycentric perspectives.

Worlds Apart: Differing Approaches to an International Agency

Ethnocentric and polycentric are two general orientations to international public relations. The **ethnocentric theory** *holds that public relations is no different in other countries than in its country of origin*—the "one-size-fits-all" approach to public relations (Illman, 1980; Maddox, 1993). Proponents of this approach believe that public relations is built around principles that are immune to exterior factors such as cultural diversity. According to Banks (2000, p. 110), this model "assumes people everywhere are motivated by the same needs and desires and are persuaded by the same arguments, and it uses in all host country settings public relations practices that managers believe are effective at home." The **culturally relative perspective, or polycentric model,** *is the exact opposite; it holds that public relations should be practiced differently in every culture.*

These two approaches are described in great detail in many scholarly treatments of international public relations. Verĉiĉ, Grunig, and Grunig (1996) use a **hybrid approach,** *bridging the two competing theories by suggesting there are some generic public relations principles appropriate to all cultures and societies.* A similar hybrid comes from Brinkerhoff and Ingle (1989), whose "blueprint" model includes generic variables for application to unique cultures.

Our position is that a fruitful approach is to separate tenets of effective communication from public relations practice rather than collapsing the two into a single process. We believe certain tenets of effective communication can form a foundation for public relations practice in any culture. But that culture and the many nuances we discuss in this book are what make public relations practice different from the communications that characterize it.

For instance, it's a given that we think in pictures. If you're asked to think of a frog, for example, you picture a frog in your mind; you don't spell it out. This idea—that pictures are the currency of the mind—is common for all human beings. How much weight to give that idea in public relations practice can be affected by cultural considerations and some of the moments of the circuit, among many other factors. To summarize our position, we suggest that there are ethnocentric communication principles that must be viewed in relation to the difference promoted by polycentric models; therefore, we offer another version of a hybrid approach for consideration.

Burson-Marsteller's Asian Expansion

Every organization with a global presence must decide which path to follow. Consider Harold Burson's (2003a, ¶ 15) account of how Burson-Marsteller (B-M) expanded into Japan: "Anticipating a Tokyo office, we hired two young professionals—one in New York, the other in London—and put them through a training program that would enable them to transfer B-M methodology and culture to Japan." The belief that managers in foreign offices must be sufficiently inculcated with the company's norms and culture is common. It ensures some uniformity in company values and approaches to public relations challenges.

At the same time, however, it extends the inequalities and nuances of the headquarters to the other offices. An important consideration is that maintaining some semblance of a uniform corporate culture is what makes a company a global brand. That uniformity must be weighed carefully against cultural norms and values to determine an adequate degree of uniformity. Too much leads to ethnocentrism; too little leads to a relativistic perspective.

Burson also recounts how B-M Tokyo's first general manager, an expatriate who spoke 10 languages, said learning Japanese was the most difficult challenge he'd ever encountered. As we've discussed, learning a language is only the start of understanding much deeper cultural subtleties that undergird global public relations practice. In Korea, Burson (2003a, ¶ 30) faced a formidable regulatory hurdle before opening his first office:

> The Korean economy surged during the years preceding the Olympics, and I was determined that a legacy of our engagement would be an ongoing Burson-Marsteller office in Seoul. At the time, however, Korean law forbade foreign ownership of advertising agencies. Although the law wasn't explicit, the ban was thought to cover public relations firms as well.

The point here is that learning a language and deciding which business theory to follow are all parts of the same struggle of doing public relations in a global environment. By applying the circuit of culture, we can see the infinite complexities of determining what happens when global meets local. The circuit would identify Korean law banning foreign ownership as a regulatory issue. It would also reflect that, not surprisingly, there are other concerns Burson might face: What is the overall environment for public relations in Korea? If Burson can successfully partner with a Korean agency to sidestep the law, what other effects might result from the ban? How might this information be used to determine how Burson should proceed with its business in Korea? Why might the Korean government have thought such a law was necessary in the first place?

In time, South Korea relaxed its foreign ownership ban, and Burson opened an office in Seoul by acquiring a Korean public relations agency headed by a South Korean woman who "was deeply steeped in the ways of Burson-Marsteller and knew many of our people in U.S., European and Asian offices. In a sense, we were starting a new office with someone we identified with and could call our own" (Burson, 2003a, ¶ 32). Within 10 years, B-M had merged with its

chief competitor in Korea and eventually acquired the competitor out-
right. The firm appointed a chief operating officer from its New York
office whose "principal emphasis [was] on instilling Burson-Marsteller
culture and methodology" in its Korean operation (¶ 33). The steps
Burson made seem to have paid off; he proudly calls B-M the "undis-
puted market leader in Korea" (¶ 33). B-M's expansion into Asia is a
drop in an ocean of companies around the world undergoing overseas
expansions and corporate mergers and acquisitions, resulting in an
ongoing collision of ideologies, cultures, and discourses. This trio of
terms forms the basis of the term *globalization*.

❖ THE GLOBALIZATION OF PUBLIC RELATIONS
AND THE CIRCUIT OF CULTURE

The highly contested nature of globalization makes it one of the most
contentious topics of our time. The term in itself is a polarizing battleground of conflicting ideologies and opinions. When the World Trade
Organization, a symbol of globalization, met in Seattle in 1999, clashes
between police and anti-globalization protesters included the firing of
rubber bullets, violent protest, and tear gas, resulting in a "public relations disaster" ("WTO Tarnished," 1999, ¶ 5). In 2001, anti-globalization
protesters again appeared at WTO meetings in Doha, Qatar. Similar
protests have occurred at the EU Summit Meetings and the Group of 7
(G7) and G8 meetings of leading industrial nations in Genoa, Italy.
More recently, Scotland faced thousands of protesters in Edinburgh,
Stirling, and Auchterarder when it hosted the 2005 G8 summit. Protesters generally favor debt relief to poor nations, more equitable trade
packages, environmental reform, and more aggressive attempts by
developed nations to reduce global poverty.

Critics of globalization charge it doesn't give developing countries
any power in international discussions of trade, human rights, and
culture. Critics also commonly cite capitalism as a global tsunami that
obliterates culture, the environment, and fair business practices. A
central issue is one of unequal global power balances. Proponents of
globalization say it's inevitable in a world that has become a "global
community" because of technological advancement and blurring of
cultural lines.

Protecting cultural and local interests is seen as antithetical to the
marauding interests of capitalism. The targets of many critics are
well-known global brands such as Coca-Cola, MTV, McDonald's, and
Nike. You'll notice that these brands are American, which symbolically

makes the United States the producer of a global discourse. It also positions the United States as a prominent global influence in the currents of culture and production of meaning. Production might come through a U.S. discourse that promotes certain ideals such as the "American dream," attainable for anyone who works hard enough; bigger is better; and more is good.

However, that discourse doesn't always align with the cultural norms and standards of other countries, an antecedent to protests and anti-globalization movements. In fact, Hall (1991) argues that U.S. influence around the globe is so pervasive it's nearly synonymous with globalization. More specifically, he asks whether global mass culture isn't actually predominantly U.S. culture.

Glocalizing Public Relations

The new buzzword from the ashes of globalization is the neologism *glocalization*, describing a hybrid discourse that subsumes the dialectics of the global–local nexus of production. The contact site between global and local under the rubric of glocalization makes it a sphere that is infinitely dynamic, complex, and charged. It also can be transformative, producing new meanings that are neither local nor global; in essence, they become glocal. **Glocalization** *is "the process whereby global corporations tailor products and marketing to particular local circumstances to meet variations in consumer demand"* (Maynard, 2003, in Maynard & Tian, 2004, p. 288).

Another definition of glocalization comes from Word Spy (http://www.wordspy.com), an online compendium of new words and phrases: "The creation of products or services intended for the global market, but customized to suit the local culture." A last definition of glocalization comes from Thomas Friedman (1999, p. 236):

> The ability of a culture, when it encounters other strong cultures, to absorb influences that naturally fit into and can enrich that culture, to resist those things that are truly alien and to compartmentalize those things that, while different, can nevertheless be celebrated as different.

Friedman's definition, although more verbose, does more than identify the global–local dialectic. It accentuates the transformational process in which power is productive *and* constructive. In theory, glocalization sounds like an ideal hybrid. Like globalization, however, it carries charged currents that make it controversial.

This framing of glocalization creates an aperture for viewing power in international public relations on two levels. The first level is internal to the public relations agency itself, in which power is intrinsic in the relationship between headquarters and the host country. On the second level, however, power struggles become an external function, produced by the presence of a global public relations agency in a host country. The duality of power illustrates the many competing interests that not only produce power by their presence alone but must harness it for beneficial ends to the organization. The next section examines the glocalization phenomenon through shopping malls in Chile and the Philippines.

Immaculate Perception in Chile and the Philippines

For an example of glocalization at work, look no further than your local shopping mall, a physical forum of local and global interests competing toward different ends. Salcedo (2003, p. 1087) sums up the argument as follows: "The two views have comprised two opposing narratives, one that claims the mall is a public sphere that facilitates community, the other that it is a space of contrived hyperconsumption and social control." Salcedo's account of the global expansion of malls explores how they neatly symbolize many issues of power and culture. Where they're located, their appearance, their functions, what they include or don't include, and how they're used are all questions he deems important to understanding the production of meaning within and surrounding a mall.

In Chile, for example, a newspaper wrote that malls were springing up like mushrooms. Many Chilean intellectuals and cultural leaders criticized the proliferation of malls, claiming they diminished Chilean national culture. At the same time, U.S. department stores such as JCPenney were trying to capitalize on the growth of malls in Chile. The U.S. stores failed, according to Salcedo, because they misjudged Chilean tastes and consumption patterns.

Malls also glocalize by adapting to the cultures of their locations through the redefinition of formal power structures. The Catholic Church illustrates this point. The Catholic Church is a prominent power structure in Latin America and the Caribbean. It holds great clout over millions of people on this continent; figures show that nearly 75% of the region's population, or 416.4 million people in 2003, is Roman Catholic. The Latino and Caribbean cultures therefore are influenced by the Catholic Church, what it says, what it does, and the ideology it promulgates. This gives the Catholic Church a voice of privilege in those societies, elevating its position in the production of cultural meaning. Societal issues such as homosexuality, birth control, and premarital sex are all profoundly influenced by the church's position. Put another way, if a culture comprises a cacophony of discourses, the Catholic Church's discourse rises above most others in Latin America.

However, evidence shows that the voice of privilege is eroding as the church's numbers have dropped significantly in the past 50 years. A Brazilian theologian, Fernando Altemeyer, attributes the decline in part to the population shift from rural to urban and the changing attitudes from that urban migration: "The urban lifestyle is a consumer lifestyle" (in Prada, 2005, ¶ 12).

What do the Catholic Church's relative power in Latin America and its declining numbers have to do with glocalization and shopping malls? Its central activity, mass, is being conducted in new places and new spaces, such as in Chilean shopping malls (Salcedo, 2003). That model isn't limited to Latin America, however; there's a Catholic Church inside the Alabang Town Center Mall in the Philippines. These malls have glocalized their spaces by translating global structures into local products for local consumption. The global presence of the church is dislocated from its traditional realm—a separate church building— into a glocalized arena where the church is absorbed by a mall. This nontraditional location of the church makes it a space where new discourses can emerge, one of the assets of glocalization.

The Alabang Mall developer called the church its "anchor tenant" and "the most consistent of the center's traffic draws" in its more than 600,000-square-foot space (Kenyon, 1998, ¶ 1, ¶ 8). The developer said the church was originally built into the mall to serve the spiritual needs of the community, but it has turned into the mall's economic engine, bringing more than 800 churchgoers per weekend service or, as the developer says, up to 8,100 potential customers on Sundays alone.

Although the church is a dominant voice in Latin America, it is now bound in the same space as other global, capitalist discourses in a mall. This creates a set of oppositional forces, generating meanings that occasionally overlap and occasionally neutralize each other, raising some interesting questions. What happens when the church occupies the same physical space that recently featured the appearance of a *Queer Eye for the Straight Guy* television star? Or when the church is in the same building as *Women's Secret*, an outlet specializing in women's lingerie? What does it mean for Filipino culture when one of its largest malls, the Alabang, has as its merchants Nike, Vans, the Athlete's Foot,

Burger King, Subway, T.G.I. Friday's, and a church? What is the dominant discourse, if any, that's produced by these dynamics?

These questions defy easy answers, but they illustrate the complexities of globalization and glocalization through the power operating on many different levels in the identifiable environment of a mall. And although international public relations operates in a different arena, the issues it faces aren't very different from those at a mall.

Public relations is caught in a dominant stream of discourse and has a role in shaping that stream. It cannot ignore the fact that its operations are always situated in a dialectic that's related to power. To this point, we've examined the overlap of the global and the local and the resultant power struggles; another equally important imbrication is between the internal and external audiences of public relations.

❖ THE INTERNAL–EXTERNAL PARADOX
   MEETS THE GLOBAL–LOCAL NEXUS

Every public relations campaign is a production comprising predetermined tactics and tools for a specified audience. When those techniques enter the public arena, they aren't only for consumption; they are subject to public scrutiny and inspection. On the path from initial idea to project fruition, a public relations campaign is in itself an exercise in power. Organizational culture dictates how a project unfolds internally before it's presented to a client. Some public relations agencies might have a completely homogeneous client team working on a project intended for an audience that is remarkably different from them—a different race, socioeconomic group, or culture, for example.

On top of the social dynamics that guide the internal evolution of a public relations campaign, other factors, including client deadlines, budget constraints, available communication channels, and technology infrastructure, can greatly influence the direction of a campaign. These internal considerations don't take into account the presentation to a client for approval, adding another layer before actual public scrutiny. Finally, after all the internal actors have agreed on the plan, it's released to target audiences through project implementation.

Before the leap from private to public, then, any public relations tactic has been consumed by internal audiences who have approved it. This can lead to what Gladwell (1998, p. 69) calls an **internal audience problem,** *which occurs when agencies become preoccupied with pleasing powerful internal audiences, not the external audiences who actually consume the product.* Gladwell suggests that this theory explains why so many

Manhattan-based magazines look the same. The producers of those magazines are competing with their competition (other Manhattan-based magazines) and losing sight of their target audience: those who actually consume, or use, their product. This process creates what Gladwell (p. 69) calls a **closed loop,** *in which the internal audiences hold more power than the target external audience.* Cheney and Christensen (1997) have similarly studied this problem in the marketing and public relations industries, where internal interests can unwittingly over-shadow external publics. "In these cases, the communication directed to an external audience has the potential of becoming a medium through which the organization addresses its own visions and self-images" (Christensen, 1997, p. 209).

In this way, production affects consumption, not vice versa. Public relations practitioners typically must identify target publics, or audiences, for their public relations campaigns. Those publics form what Anderson (1991) calls an **imagined community,** *publics perceived to form an audience that shares common values and beliefs.* As an actual community, however, these selected publics are not a real, monolithic audience. Salaman (1997) takes this idea a step further by suggesting that organizations themselves, such as public relations agencies, are imagined communities built around shared values, purposes, and objectives. The International Red Cross doesn't exist per se; it can't be touched or held. As a concept, however, it's a community of individuals who share common motivations. The results of their efforts, and how those efforts are communicated to external audiences, make the International Red Cross real.

Audiences as Communities

A target public is a community constructed by public relations practitioners to serve as shorthand for the myriad individuals they wish to reach. Miscalculating the language, values, culture, and beliefs of a community can doom a public relations initiative. There's also no guarantee that the encoded public relations message will be consumed in the way the producers intended. The rationale a public relations practitioner provides for targeting a certain community becomes important, as is an understanding of the discursive elements that bind that community. It's easy to overlook the nuances of target audiences by relying on cookie-cutter public relations techniques. Need to publicize something? Write and send a news release. Preparing a company launch? Write a brochure. Big announcement? Hold a news conference. Going global? Tweak traditional public relations techniques through glocalization.

Although sometimes successful, these rote methods bury the processes of production that occur long before the finished product is cast into the public arena. This notion makes production both a private and a public process of creation, a powerful antidote to concentrating only on the end product of production and bottom-line thinking. As a process, production must take into account not only meaning and how that meaning is generated but also for whom that meaning is intended, making the identification of audiences not a passive step in public relations planning but a strategic imperative.

A sweeping lesson from this chapter, then, is that how public relations practitioners identify audiences and the rationales they use in that process can have great import in any public relations campaign. This lesson teaches us that public relations cannot afford to become grounded in the system of production—tactics and strategies, for instance—without taking into account the fluidity of the communities, or audiences, that the production system is designed to reach. In other terms, a target audience isn't entrenched; the target shifts as the elements that bind that audience change through cultural patterns. Targeting the scope of public relations and keeping it stable and unmoving can cause a public relations campaign to miss the mark.

When practitioners recognize that their target audiences are imagined communities they construct as part of planning, they leave the safe haven of the predictable, fixed, and stable and enter a new world where audiences function like living organisms. Audiences must be constantly evaluated and analyzed. This monitoring function therefore is part of the production process, not an afterthought lumped in with evaluation. We might ask, How were those target audiences identified and constructed? Did the tactics complement the constructed identities? How did the target audience actions, interests, or beliefs change over time, if at all? To put the idea of the imagined community as a target audience into practice, let's consider an example in the realm of cyberspace and global brands in China.

Glocalizing the Web

In chapter 2, we examined the ways in which Coca-Cola modified its Web site in India to suit an Indian audience. The existence of several Web sites to reach different audiences indicates that Coca-Cola is glocalizing its Web presence, according to Maynard and Tian (2004, p. 286), who studied how "top global brands accommodate to different cultures, i.e., how they 'glocalize' on their Web sites." In their study of the 100 top global brands, the authors found that these top brands localized their Web sites by integrating China's political, economic, and cultural characteristics into branding strategies. As a global strategy was not identified in these Web sites, a glocal approach was validated. The top brands customized their Chinese Web sites to cater to local tastes, while at the same time also providing Web links to the Web pages of their head-quarters or other regional Web sites. This approach positioned the brand as local, but with a global reach. (2004, p. 290)

In Maynard and Tian's study, glocalization emerges as a produc-tive way to ease the tension between global and local. However, that strategy doesn't imply that power ceases to become an issue or can be discarded. To the contrary, power is still at the epicenter of glocaliza-tion as it is with globalization. Where would you guess the most top global brands are from? If you guessed the United States, you're cor-rect; according to the study, the United States had 65 brands, followed by Europe with 28. The power differential is again tilted toward the West. The production of meaning in the study is advanced through a typically Western communication modality, the World Wide Web. This tactical choice privileges those with access to the Web and those who can afford it, making the message carrier—the communication modality—an important consideration in the moment of production.

The privilege of the Web shows that these Web sites might be glo-calized for China but only for a certain type of Chinese: those who are reasonably affluent and urban and use the Web. Of that number, there's always the issue of how many will actually find and use the site—that is, consume it. And we might find that the audience isn't Chinese liv-ing in China but a worldwide population of Chinese who might be liv-ing anywhere from the United States to Uruguay to Kazakhstan. That audience isn't limited to the geographic boundaries of China; it's scat-tered around the globe. That population might be linked through the same language, but culturally, that population is influenced by stan-dards and norms of the countries where it resides. This is why the Web is viewed as a tool that creates, builds, and interacts with communities. It's also a reminder that glocalizing is a move toward the local not nec-essarily in a geographic sense but in a cultural sense.

❖ NEGOTIATING ASYMMETRY

This chapter explored the numerous exigent factors that make the process of production in international public relations an exercise in negotiating various power relationships. Brought into the fray were gender and race issues and other discourses pitting global against local and internal against external. International organizations participate in and shape discourses, such as where they open offices internationally, how they staff those offices, how their management is structured, how their corporate culture evolves, and how they approach affiliations and partnerships.

The cumulative effects of these decisions make production a product of both discourse and ideology. In public relations firms, the latter is transferred, to varying degrees, by agencies that open offices abroad or partner with smaller agencies. To maintain their "global presence," they must transfer some characteristics of their headquarters, symbolically placing their global brand on a continuum with two poles, polycentrism and ethnocentrism discussed in this chapter.

Metaphorically, the poles illustrate the lack of symmetry in practicing public relations internationally and producing public relations materials. The moment of production is the process of negotiating this asymmetry to create an identity for a public and create messages for that public encompassing organizational goals and ideology. Of import, however, is that producers subsequently monitor consumption of those messages because the message constructed and encoded is often not the message consumed. This chapter builds on that idea by suggesting that communities, or target audiences, aren't real but are created in how they're imagined or constructed. As created identities, publics then consume these messages, giving both the message and the community meaning. This process defines the moment of consumption, which is discussed in chapter 7.

CHAPTER SUMMARY

- The process of producing public relations materials is an exercise in power influenced by gender, race, internal–external audiences, and management.

- All public relations is situated in a dialectic related to power.

- Target audiences are imagined communities that are constantly in flux, created by public relations practitioners.

- The moment of production challenges practitioners to negotiate internal, or organizational, concerns with ongoing monitoring and analysis of target audiences.

Smallpox Eradication Campaign

At the height of the campaign, from 1967 to 1980, the six administrators of the smallpox eradication unit headquartered in Geneva oversaw 5 to 10 staff in each regional office, more than 150,000 workers in approximately 50 countries, and US$23 million in average annual expenditures. One commentator compared the campaign's vast scale to a Cecil B. DeMille epic film (Nelson, 1985). When it was over, campaign leaders wrote a 1,473-page book chronicling the campaign. We outline its basic parts in many fewer pages, examining the technologies, campaign strategies, and global workforce that guided campaign production.

TECHNOLOGY AND PRODUCTION

All production takes place within technological constraints, which can be empowering or disempowering. Campaign leaders recognized technology's key role and worked closely with government and private industry to ensure that technology empowered the campaign. Their efforts paid off in the late 1960s when three breakthroughs gave much-needed impetus to the campaign: freeze-dried vaccine, jet injectors, and the bifurcated needle.

Previously, only 10% of liquid vaccine met WHO's potency standards. Heat stability was a major problem; the vaccine had to be kept cold to remain viable. The U.S. Agency for International Development shipped trucks with refrigeration units to western Africa for what was to become the combined measles and smallpox campaign. The trucks were too heavy for the roads and bogged down, however, and the refrigerators worked only at temperatures below 90°F. When workers asked the agency how to make the refrigeration units work in the ambient temperatures of the Sahara Desert, they were told to park the trucks in the shade. Workers surveyed the terrain for anything taller than a bush in vain (Altman, 1979).

Unfortunately, technological problems compounded by bureaucratic inefficiency were not uncommon. A campaign assessment team in Afghanistan found that the director of the national program couldn't authorize a truck to pick up a vaccination shipment, so the shipment sat in a hot shed for 8 days, rendering it unusable. The development of freeze-dried vaccine of reliable potency by a laboratory in London provided a major breakthrough. It remained viable without refrigeration until reconstituted with liquid, facilitating shipping and increasing effective vaccination rates.

A second breakthrough was the refinement of the jet injector to give intradermal vaccines. Smallpox vaccine had been administered by either scratching the skin about 30 times with a needle, which was slow, or using a rotary lancet, a medieval-looking device that was painful and often created a large scar. The jet injector was painless and allowed up to 1,000 people per hour to be vaccinated. In areas such as Brazil and Sierra Leone, the jet injectors worked well and greatly increased vaccination rates (Photo 6.2).

Note the line of people waiting to be vaccinated.

Photo 6.2   A Child in South Cameroon Is Vaccinated With a Jet Injector

SOURCE: Photo courtesy of CDC and Dr. J. D. Millar.

Jet injectors were not without their problems, however. A large number of people had to be assembled in one place at one time in a location with electricity, which wasn't logistically possible or culturally feasible in many areas. The units were also expensive and heavy. When vaccinators on floating islands in Chad depressed the foot pedals to power the injectors, they starting sinking through the soft matted reeds forming the islands.

For areas in which jet injectors weren't practical, Wyeth Laboratories developed a low-cost, portable solution: the bifurcated needle, which held a single dose of vaccine between its two small prongs (Photo 6.3). Unskilled workers could be trained in its use in about 10 to 15 minutes, often using an orange or other piece of fruit for practice. The technology became WHO's vaccination tool of choice in most areas because it was efficient and easy; illiterate workers could master it. In some areas, however, workers refused to adopt the new technology, despite WHO's best efforts to persuade them (Thaung & Ko Ko, 2002).

Generally speaking, research and development facilities were generous with their time and donated the rights to use their products. However, when WHO officials tried to persuade plastic manufacturers in the United States and Switzerland to develop a low-cost, easily sterilized needle holder so that bifurcated needles could be reused in poor countries, they were unsuccessful. With much more personally at stake, local producers in the smallpox endemic areas of Bangladesh, India, and Pakistan quickly devised a high-density polyethylene container that solved the problem. Without these technological advances, campaign progress would have been greatly impeded.

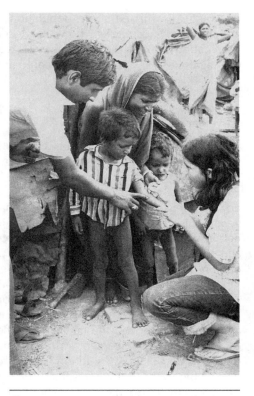

Photo 6.3   WHO Volunteer and U.S. Student Jennifer Alpern Uses a Bifurcated Needle to Administer the Smallpox Vaccine to a Small Boy Living in a Squatter Camp in Bangladesh

SOURCE: Photo courtesy of CDC, WHO, and Stanley O. Foster, M.D., M.P.H.

CAMPAIGN STRATEGIES

To achieve eradication, managers devised a strategy based on what had worked in much of the developed world: mass vaccination. Technology played a key role in guiding planning: Mass vaccination was more feasible with jet injectors. Vaccination quotas, protocols, and records were established to achieve and document the vaccination of virtually 100% of the population.

The strategy proved ineffective over time, however. Despite high rates of vaccination, outbreaks kept occurring. The strategy that had worked well in the developed world wasn't functioning in areas lacking well-developed health services and communication networks. Vaccinators systematically missed some populations, such as agricultural workers and nomads. Vaccinators who were meeting their quotas often did so by vaccinating the easiest population to reach, schoolchildren, over and over again. Mass vaccination appeared impossible, putting the campaign at risk.

Surveillance and Containment

In 1966, in western Nigeria, where 90% of the population had been vaccinated, an outbreak erupted among a religious sect that opposed vaccination. With limited vaccine on hand and shipment of more delayed, Dr. William Foege made best use of what little he had. When new outbreaks occurred, his team vaccinated only the people who were geographically or socially close to the victim, forming a wall of vaccination around each new case. The strategy worked, with eradication achieved in the region in a short time despite less than 100% of the population being vaccinated. A new campaign strategy was born from field innovation, that of surveillance and containment.

Production is guided by organizational culture, and the flattened hierarchical structure of the eradication unit welcomed field innovation and change. Although the new strategy flew in the face of the scientific establishment, management willingly adopted it because it conserved resources and offered a solution to the problem of continuing outbreaks despite high vaccination rates. In 1968, WHO officially advised all countries not only to use mass vaccination to reduce incidence but also to use surveillance and containment to identify outbreaks and eliminate pockets of infection.

However, the program was a hard sell. National governments had invested in the infrastructure of mass vaccination programs, which they thought better demonstrated concrete and quantifiable efforts on behalf of their citizens (Hopkins, 1989). When the Indonesian program director presented a conference paper in 1970 claiming that surveillance and containment was more effective than mass vaccination, most medical personnel attending treated the findings as heresy, and many national health directors refused to adopt the strategy. During an outbreak in India, the director of health services ordered mass vaccination and made it clear that he wanted no new cases found or reported by surveillance teams. In Bangladesh, the secretary of health thought the approach worthless and pulled workers off surveillance and containment operations and assigned them to other jobs, threatening to fire personnel if they reported new smallpox cases. Brazil only grudgingly accepted the new strategy; the French administrators in Gabon never did.

A turning point came when the new strategy proved effective in a region in India. If it could work in this densely populated country with one of the highest rates of infection, other countries were willing to try it as well. WHO's second technical report, released in 1972, emphasized the strategy's success and stressed that "efforts are always made to obtain the maximum participation of the existing health services" (p. 10). Countries began adopting the new strategy, and the last case of smallpox in nature was recorded just 5 years later.

Developing a Proactive Communication Strategy

Surveillance and containment presented a much more proactive approach. Workers had to actively discover cases so they could contain the outbreak, which required rapid and reliable communication methods. Despite the reward offered for reports of confirmed cases, up to two thirds of cases remained unreported in some areas, for reasons discussed more fully in chapter 7. Communications designed to raise public awareness and create a favorable attitude were needed. Public health education materials technically were the responsibility of the ministry of health in each country, but few made significant contributions. Workers learned to develop the materials and techniques they needed as dictated by local conditions, adapting universal principles to local needs.

Initially, news media often provided workers with their first notice of outbreaks, and scanning the papers became standard office procedure. On a more serendipitous note, a sharp-eyed U.S. epidemiologist watching a television news documentary spotted smallpox infections among refugee camp residents. He notified the Centers for Disease Control, which immediately called WHO headquarters, and workers rushed to the scene. In turn, workers used mass media to reach out to the populace. Radio was useful for reaching literate and illiterate populations, and workers enlisted local opinion leaders to tape messages for broadcast. Other media were used as applicable, including handbills, advertising, newspaper articles, posters (Photo 6.4), rickshaw signs, leaflet drops, and letters to medical personnel and local leaders.

Although mass media helped raise awareness, interpersonal channels often were more effective, particularly in low-literacy areas. In Asia and Africa, where local markets formed important social and communication centers, workers stationed themselves by banners and reward notices posted at every entryway, questioning people as they came by and handing out educational materials. More often, workers had to track down populations, and migration and seasonal patterns emerged as large factors in tracing outbreaks. Nomadic tribes and migrant workers often spread infection across wide geographic areas.

Conversely, in areas such as Yemen, the closing of the Suez Canal between 1967 and 1975 helped halt transmission in that country, despite

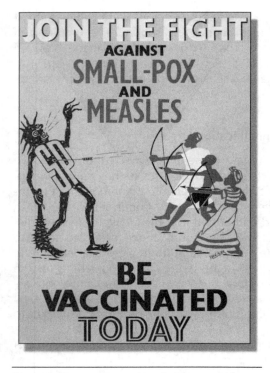

Photo 6.4   A Poster Used to Promote the Combined Measles and Smallpox Vaccination Campaign in Western Africa

SOURCE: Image courtesy of CDC and Stafford Smith.

its low vaccination rate. In the Ogaden Desert of Somalia, workers mapped water holes and used them to trace tribal movements. Nomadic groups traveling between Pakistan and Afghanistan were intercepted by search parties so often that they started claiming harassment. Workers responded by giving them certificates proving that they were vaccinated and free to pass. During extended droughts, populations would migrate, necessitating greater surveillance along migration routes.

Workers went from village to village with the smallpox recognition card, which after its original development in Indonesia had been localized to show victims of different ethnicities and distributed to workers in all areas. In the final push in West Bengal alone, 10,000 small and 3,000 large recognition cards were used. Workers showed the cards to opinion leaders (Photo 6.5), such as local political figures, teachers, watchmen, postmen, health officials, and religious leaders, and to schoolchildren, who were often more uninhibited sources of local information. Workers also showed the cards in shops and areas where people gathered, including tea shops, bazaars, bus stands, betel nut shops, migrant camps, and brick kilns (Basu et al., 1979).

To overcome resistance to case reporting, workers also developed more indirect methods of discovery. In Bangladesh, they visited graveyards in major cities to collect information on recent deaths and track down possible cases. In India, workers often searched railway stations, which served as major transportation hubs, and performed night searches in cities to monitor the often overlooked street-dwelling population, which in Calcutta alone numbered 48,000.

In some areas, particular customs indicated the presence of smallpox. In Sierra Leone, for example, a dead bird hanging outside a village warned of infection (Davies, 1980). In India, smallpox was worshipped as a manifestation of Shitala Mata, and workers would stand outside her temples and follow worshippers home, often locating active cases that way. Workers also searched houses with neem tree branches hanging outside because the branches were thought to offer smallpox victims relief. In Somalia, a worker saw people with fresh pockmarks, but no one would admit to a recent outbreak. As he was leaving the village, he drove the truck into deep mud, knowing that local custom would demand that the villagers assemble to help him. He found four active cases among his rescuers.

Targeting Opinion Leaders With Health Education

Surveys demonstrated that these communication efforts were successful in raising awareness of the campaign, but campaign leaders recog-

Photo 6.5   A Local Volunteer Shows the Smallpox Eradication Card to a Village Elder in Bangladesh

SOURCE: Photo courtesy of CDC, WHO, and Stanley O. Foster, M.D., M.P.H.

Case Study

nized that to change behavior they needed the support of local opinion leaders. To obtain cooperation in a given area, a health educator or team would talk to local leaders in advance of vaccination teams. Workers were briefed about local customs to ensure that they treated leaders with respect, and they tailored the length of lead time, leaders targeted, and messages presented to each area. In Zaire, village chiefs were contacted 1 to 2 days beforehand; in other areas of Africa, teams arrived 1 week beforehand to observe the long formal greetings required to establish working relationships. In all instances, the members lived with the villagers to establish a bond. For extended visits, care was taken to keep the advance team small, just one or two people, so as not to overwhelm local hospitality. When cooperation was difficult to obtain, workers would stay in the area for extended periods to try and wear down resistance.

As in any persuasive venture, the degree of cooperation obtained varied. In some parts of Africa, such as Guinea, securing the advance support of its active and well-organized national political party led to cooperation throughout the country. Other African countries, such as Sierra Leone, were strongly divided along tribal lines, and workers had varying degrees of success with each tribe. One Nigerian chief insisted on personally witnessing all vaccinations to ensure that his people complied. In other areas outbreaks occurred among seminomadic groups with no strong tribal allegiance, which made organizing cooperation difficult.

Village leaders and missionaries provided their support for the campaign in much of eastern Africa, which allowed it to succeed despite poor government administration. In some areas, such as much of India, religious leaders were more easily persuaded and effective than local government leaders. In traditional Muslim areas, religious leaders had the power to assemble large groups of people, facilitating vaccination and spot checks to locate outbreaks (Hopkins, 1989).

Advance teams also recruited local people to work on the campaign, which helped garner compliance. Illiterate locals often were more effective than educated urbanites because they were familiar with local dialects and customs, and the population more willingly accepted vaccinations and house-to-house searches from one of their own. Special efforts were made to enlist villagers who were recognized medical opinion leaders, such as herbalists in parts of Africa. When workers could persuade these figures to serve as vaccinators, their status combined with their zeal as new converts proved a winning combination.

MANAGING A GLOBAL WORKFORCE

Enacting the surveillance and containment strategy required a huge workforce of public health doctors, health educators, search workers, vaccinators, mechanics, pilots, and office staff, among others. In India alone, workers numbered almost 64,000 in 1973, more than 116,000 in 1975, and almost 135,000 in 1976 (Basu et al., 1979). The majority worked for their national governments, which either transferred them to the unit from existing health units or recruited them specifically for the program. Another 687 people from 73 countries served mainly as short-term consultants on foreign assignment (WHO, 1980). In Bangladesh, for example, personnel were brought in from Brazil, the United Kingdom, Czechoslovakia, Egypt, France, the USSR, Sweden, and Switzerland, with new recruits arriving every 2 weeks.

Recruitment and Supervision

Personnel shortage was a perennial problem. In the early 1970s in Ethiopia, the program enlisted workers from a leprosy program, mission groups, a scientific expedition staff, and emergency relief workers. In

Pakistan, 50,000 schoolchildren served as volunteers in a special 2-day search. In Ethiopia, the government combined literacy and smallpox efforts, teaching 60,000 students, then sending them to their home areas as health educators. At times, the program was a victim of its own success. When the number of cases started to drop in the Punjab province of Pakistan, for example, the local health director pulled staff to work on cholera instead. In Kandahar, team members were conscripted for military duty.

When hiring nonnatives, preference was given to those with international experience, such as Peace Corps volunteers (Hopkins, 1989). Director Henderson looked for attitude more than experience in his field staff. He purposefully recruited younger people, believing they would be more open to new ideas and innovation (Tucker, 2001), although the final campaign report also stresses that "youth was an advantage in the more remote areas where travel by vehicle was at best rough and walking often the only possibility" (WHO, 1980, p. 64). Overall, two personality traits were considered key: an ability to deal with other cultures and minorities in their home cultures and a positive attitude. As Dr. William Foege, of surveillance and containment fame, noted, "Don't send a pessimist to India" (in Hopkins, 1989, p. 63).

As the campaign progressed, WHO hired fewer medical staff and more advisors to avoid encroaching on the turf of local health officials. Sensitive to Muslim restrictions that prevented men from vaccinating women, officials recruited more women as health workers over the course of the campaign. New recruits from developed countries often were overwhelmed by culture shock when they arrived, however. They received crash courses on local customs and scenario-based training. The epidemiologists, many of whom had never worked in rural areas, thought it almost inconceivable that hospitals often served as sources of outbreaks. By the end of training, they realized that home rules no longer applied: Conditions in developing country hospitals often were more conducive to the spread of disease than to its eradication.

National workers experienced different problems because they were government employees and not directly employed by WHO. In Pakistan, vaccinator positions were doled out as political favors to people already otherwise employed, giving them little time to devote to their new responsibilities. In Indonesia, the government paid vaccinators the equivalent of US$2 per month, which didn't even cover food expenses. Underpaid workers in Bangladesh created dummy villages because the government paid them by the number of houses searched. In Somalia, some local staff thought their pay was justified only if they located smallpox, so they spread rumors of outbreaks. In Afghanistan, a search team was fired when it turned out that they were filing fictitious reports from the comfort of their office; vaccinators there often went on strike because they hadn't been paid by the government.

Given the scope of the campaign, adequate supervision was difficult or impossible. Campaign leaders did what they could by developing assessment tactics to serve as system safeguards, but the lack of supervision remained problematic.

Life in the Field

Field conditions were physically demanding, with the average worker in India losing 10 to 20 pounds in a 3-month tour of duty (Tucker, 2001). Insect bites, parasites, injuries, lack of safe drinking water, and heat exhaustion were common. Additionally, working in the field in the days before e-mail and cell phones meant little contact with home. Workers often operated in war zones and areas of civil unrest, making field work even more dangerous. In the early years of the campaign, fighting often brought a halt to operations in an area, and refugees spread smallpox into neighboring countries.

But as the campaign progressed, search teams anxious to carry out their missions often worked to receive special dispensation from fighting forces to cross lines and continue vaccination. In 1972, warring Sudanese and Ethiopian forces agreed to allow team members to cross the border area freely to investigate outbreaks. As hostilities increased, however, some helicopter pilots served only a couple of days before asking to be returned home, and all countries except Japan pulled their volunteer workers from the area. In Somalia, guerrilla forces warned WHO personnel beforehand of planned attacks and advised teams to leave, giving them safe passage. When warring forces captured workers, rebel leaders recognized their mission, and the workers usually were well treated and soon released to national authorities.

Transport was often by boat, bike, or pack animal or on foot. In some areas, such as Nepal, chartered helicopters delivered workers to a mountaintop, where they set out on foot along trails, returning a specified number of weeks later to be picked up. In Ethiopia, more than 85% of the population lived more than 30 km (almost 20 miles) from an all-weather road, and many areas of endemic countries were impassable during the rainy season (Photo 6.6). When the last case in Bangladesh occurred on Bhola Island, it took team members 24 hours to get there, traveling by speedboat, steamer, Jeep, and motorcycle and on foot.

Field work was further complicated by communication difficulties. Workers in Ethiopia often needed two or three layers of interpreters to navigate the 70 languages and dialects spoken. In Zaire, a telegraph message took 1 month to travel to a neighboring province, and in Yemen reports had to be hand carried to the capital. Field personnel often used radio transmitters to keep in touch in remote areas, but in Ethiopia they were banned because of civil war.

Many endemic areas were impassable during the rainy season.

Photo 6.6   Team Members Slog Through the Backwaters to Locate
Smallpox Cases

SOURCE: Photo courtesy of CDC, WHO, and Stanley O. Foster, M.D., M.P.H.

The problems spilled over into field offices as well. All requests for supplies in eastern Africa had to go through the regional office in Brazzaville, which then forwarded the requests to Geneva. This communication chain often took 4 to 8 weeks, inhibiting campaign progress. Workers there learned to put their requests in to the regional office and headquarters simultaneously. Geneva gave them a quick response, but protocol had been honored with Brazzaville. An assessment team in Afghanistan in 1969 found that the national program office lacked a phone, secretary, stationery, files, forms, and records; in short, they had no way to run an effective program.

From this overview of working conditions, it becomes clearer why, as outlined in chapter 5, campaign leaders worked hard to keep morale high. Field work was hard work, and the leaders did their best to ensure that the workers knew they were appreciated.

IMPLICATIONS FOR INTERNATIONAL PRACTICE

Given the scope of this epic production, it is indeed a miracle, as proclaimed by many news reports at the time, that eradication was achieved.

One campaign historian suggested that "some of the most critical variables in the campaign proved to be those of problem definition, organization, and management" (Hopkins, 1989, p. 18), and this analysis reinforces that conclusion. Throughout the campaign, the organizational culture was open to change and encouraged innovation, refusing to be limited by current technology or conventional wisdom. Leaders didn't enforce or even endorse a one-size-fits-all approach. Rather than supplying workers with a strategy to be used as a single tool, they provided workers with a wide-ranging box of tools to use as they saw fit.

Dr. D. A. Henderson said smallpox was eradicated only by the narrowest of margins, with "quixotic circumstance" often tipping the scales in the campaign's favor (Henderson, 1998, p. 17). For example, the surveillance and containment technique came about because of the collision of an oppositional religious sect and a vaccine shortage. But sheer chance alone isn't enough to account for the campaign's success; credit must be given to an organizational culture that recognized serendipity as opportunity. To some extent, this approach was driven by the fact that campaign workers didn't have the time to perform much strategic research before it began. They had to adjust as they went along, being open to moments of discovery and changing strategies and tactics as necessary: "The global programme had to evolve within a framework of broad principles and expectations, pragmatically modified by reality, rather than within the confines of a comprehensive master plan having specific and enforceable time-limited goals" (Fenner et al., 1988, p. 422).

Despite the lack of formal public relations staff or training, a hallmark of the campaign was its strong communication focus. Dr. Lawrence Brilliant, sounding more like a public relations practitioner than one of the campaign's doctors, concluded that one of the major lessons of the campaign was that "communication within the organization and between the organization and the outside world needs to be consistent, rapid, and honest" (Brilliant, 1985, p. 158). Mass and interpersonal communication channels were widely used to garner community-level support. Workers took time to cultivate local opinion leaders, selecting them according to local norms. The deputy chair of Edelman Public Relations recently encouraged practitioners to take a similar approach, noting that "all relationships are local and vary by geographic market" (Morley, 2004, p. 14).

Problematic aspects are WHO's use of covert methods to discover cases, which blurred the boundaries of the private and public spheres, and the concomitant empowering of workers, with few checks on their behavior. Both acts had consequences for the campaign evidenced in the moment of consumption, which is the subject of chapter 7.

7

Consumption

Rethinking Publics and Practice

❖ ❖ ❖

The moment of production, covered in chapter 6, tells only part of the story. Meanings encoded during production aren't fully realized until the moment of consumption, when consumers renegotiate the meanings generated during production through use of products and ideas in their everyday lives. Although scholars and practitioners often have considered consumption the antithesis of production, increasingly they're viewing the two as interrelated parts of a process. In public relations terms, target audiences, or publics, are no longer simply the end point of a linear transmission chain, the passive recipients of practitioners' labors. Instead, scholars and practitioners are increasingly viewing publics as active meaning makers who often challenge the dominant discourses surrounding an issue or product. This chapter examines the active role of consumers in constructing meaning for both campaign messages and material goods and how that affects international public relations practice, particularly in light of new technology and globalization.

❖ THE MOMENT OF CONSUMPTION

The moment of **consumption** *encompasses how publics make use of a cultural artifact, such as a campaign issue or product, in their everyday lives and form new meanings around it as a consequence of its use* (du Gay et al., 1997). In China and Singapore, for example, schoolchildren visit McDonald's not so much for fast food or playgrounds but because their living quarters often are small, and the tables at McDonald's provide a place to spread out and do homework (Zukin & Maguire, 2004). This new meaning of McDonald's as a workspace emerged not from corporate campaigns or policy but from consumer use.

The idea of consumers as active participants in constructing meaning is new. Traditionally, theorists have represented the communication process using a **linear transmission model,** *such as Lasswell's (1948) classic "who says what to whom in what channel with what effect" model, which positions consumers or audiences as the passive recipients of communicated meaning.* Although the model has evolved over time to include a feedback loop, it remains a linear process in which the audience either gets the correct message or fails to grasp the intended meaning because of noise, or interference, in the communication chain. This linear notion underlies most Western forms of public relations practice, built on research, action and planning, communication, evaluation (RACE) or research, objectives, programming, evaluation (ROPE) models.

Bourdieu (1979/1984), espousing a more active view of consumers, posited that we consume according to who we are. Consumption is the prime indicator of social class, with the dominant discourse of aesthetics and taste defining and maintaining class distinctions. However, his analysis doesn't take into account context, that is, other factors besides class that could influence consumption. To oversimplify Bourdieu's approach but make the point, it would be like trying to segment publics for a campaign by income level only. It might prove somewhat helpful, but it would leave a lot unaccounted for as well. Postmodernists, such as Baudrillard (1988), have suggested that we become what we consume; meaning resides not in an object but in how that object is used by consumers. Although this approach fully empowers consumers, it goes to the other end of the spectrum by downplaying any role for production in determining the meaning of an issue or product.

The circuit of culture balances these approaches by situating production and consumption as overlapping, intertwined processes in accordance with de Certeau's (1984) notion that consumption always takes place within the bounds proscribed by production. During the moment of production, practitioners encode campaign messages with a possible range of meanings directed at target audiences. Because audience members appropriate and use these messages in the context of their lives and situations, however, meanings other than the dominant encoded ones may emerge. The result is that production and consumption exist not in binary opposition but as equally integral parts of the process of circulation, in which an ongoing tension exists between the bounds set by production and consumer creativity (Acosta-Alzuru & Kreshel, 2002).

Consumers actively decode public relations campaign messages in reference to their own contexts, such as demographics (e.g., ethnicity, religion, age, education), psychographics (e.g., political persuasion, tolerance for risk taking), their own cultural competencies, and perceived saliency of the message to their lives (Moores, 1997). Consumption becomes both appropriation and resistance, taking in what resonates and resisting what doesn't. Edward L. Bernays alluded to this notion when he observed that he didn't think of practitioners as powerful; instead "people go where they want to be led" (in Wilcox, Ault, Agee, & Cameron, 2001, p. 40). Marketing scholars and professionals have operationalized this concept as *consumer value* (Overby, Woodruff, & Gardial, 2004).

The Swedish-based multinational firm IKEA, which manufactures inexpensive, flatpack furniture for home assembly and has stores in more than 30 countries, has successfully dominated discourse by encoding meanings that resonate with consumers. For many consumers, the company has changed the meaning of furniture as a major purchase that becomes a family heirloom to be handed down over generations to that of something transient and disposable. In doing so, it has created a meaning for the company that goes well beyond that of just another furniture store and becomes a major part of people's lives:

> For a broad demographic swathe of Britain, IKEA has defined our lives. . . . [It's] as if it were not a shop at all, really, but something far more emotively substantial: a football team, or the Church of England, or the government. (Burkeman, 2004, ¶ 10)

In contrast, the Pleasant Company has been only partially successful in conveying the meaning encoded in its American Girl Dolls line. In-depth interviews with mothers and daughters who owned the dolls revealed that whereas mothers adopted the manufacturer's meaning of the dolls as educational and empowering for girls and therefore were willing to spend large amounts of money for the dolls, the girls who owned the dolls didn't fully adopt the message of diversity and empowerment the company intended but brought their own meanings to bear instead (Acosta-Alzuru & Kreshel, 2002).

The moment of production, then, is never fully realized until the moment of consumption, when consumers appropriate messages and create new meanings through their use. Consumption feeds new meanings back into campaigns: "Consumption is not the end of a process, but the beginning of another, and thus itself a form of production (and hence we can refer to the 'work' of consumption)" (Mackay, 1997, p. 7). Consumer appropriation has driven production of the Logan, French automaker Renault's low-cost, no-frills car designed for sale in emerging markets such as Poland and Romania. When consumers in developed countries saw the car, they clamored for them, creating a 5-month waiting list at Renault's upscale Champs-Élysées dealership (Edmondson, 2005). What Renault produced and marketed as the chance for first-time car ownership in the developing world became the no-frills, shabby chic ideal of the developed world, forcing Renault to retool its production line and strategy.

❖ PUBLIC RELATIONS PRACTICE AND CONSUMPTION

As we discussed in chapter 3, the role of public relations practitioners within the circuit of culture model is to act as cultural intermediaries. Practitioners mediate between the moments of production and consumption, between the public and private realms. They shape producers' actions and messages, delimiting the range of possible interpretations presented to audiences. Just as important, however, they must monitor audiences' decodings of those actions and messages to determine the new meanings that arise during consumption. Precisely because audience members are active meaning makers, public relations practitioners have the crucial, and often difficult, job of creating meanings with which audiences will identify and of documenting the efficacy of their efforts. Because of the active nature of audiences, the moment of consumption has three important consequences for public relations practice:

- The need for ongoing research
- The need for more ethnographic methods of research
- The need to recognize and account for relative power in relationships

Recasting Research and Issues Management

Delivering a message to audiences is no longer enough when consumption isn't the end of a campaign but the beginning of another production cycle. The circuit of culture demonstrates the need for ongoing research, not research as bookends of a linear timeline, with formative or strategic research marking the start of a campaign and evaluative research the end, as in the RACE and ROPE models. Instead, research must be recast as continuous environmental monitoring, traditionally the domain of issues management.

Issues management emerged in the 1970s as *a strategic, proactive means to counter activist groups and influence public policy* (Gaunt & Ollenburger, 1995). Traditionally, public relations practitioners used **environmental scanning** *to monitor publics and their opinions to identify emerging issues of concern to the organization and formulate ways to defuse the issue* that avoid regulation, confrontation, and trial in the court of public opinion. Heath (1997), using the linear communication model, outlined four issues management steps for practitioners:

- Anticipate and analyze issues.
- Develop organizational positions on the issues.
- Identify key publics whose support is vital to the public policy issues.
- Identify desired behaviors of key publics.

The circuit of culture model suggests that environmental scanning is better understood as a necessary, ongoing process of identifying fluid meanings as they emerge, of continuously monitoring the public opinion environment in which the organization is operating. The goal isn't to defuse issues but to learn how audience members' meanings of those issues are incorporated into their daily lives and relate to organizational meanings. The desired result isn't consensus or accommodation but balancing and absorbing of the competing meanings that unavoidably arise in a way that enriches organizational understanding of the issue and allows public relations to in turn contribute to public opinion formation (Dougall, 2005). Issues aren't obstacles to be resolved. Instead, they become part of an ongoing negotiation between an organization and its audiences, with the realization that some articulations will gain stability and undergo far less change over a given time period.

Leading international public relations firms recognize the value of ongoing environmental monitoring of audience meanings and incorporate the process into their campaigns. Weber Shandwick Scotland, as part of its almost 2-year Save the North Sea environmental campaign, regularly convened focus groups drawn from members of 24 target groups in five different nations to monitor audience reactions and incorporate changes on an ongoing basis (Save the North Sea, 2004). The campaign, designed to reduce pollution, was highly successful, as determined by the ongoing focus group feedback, the observed change in target publics' specific behaviors, the continuation of campaign projects by private groups after the campaign's end, and the awards it received from the International Public Relations Association and the United Nations.

Privileging Ethnographic Methods

Using the circuit of culture as a model for practice not only changes when and why we perform research but also changes how we do it. To determine how audiences consume messages and use them in their daily lives, practitioners need to use ethnographic methods, such as observing behavior through participant observation and determining subjects' meanings through in-depth interviews and focus groups. Measuring awareness or attitudes on pretest and posttest surveys presents a partial picture at best: "The realm of day-to-day life and of household cultures of consumption . . . does not lend itself to being measured because it exists as a dispersed domain of lived experiences and cultural meanings—not as a calculable object" (Moores, 1997, p. 227).

Although the objective of most public relations campaigns is almost always to change behavior, we often measure awareness and attitude change as proxies. Yet attitude changes don't necessarily lead to behavioral ones. To determine behavior and the meanings informing behavior, we need to feed the results of ethnographic studies back into campaign planning to align campaign and consumer meanings in ways that can promote effective understanding.

Ethnography remains an underused tool in public relations, however. It's time-consuming and therefore expensive. It lacks the power of scientific discourse in the Western world. But as demonstrated by the New Coke® case, a greater reliance on ethnographic methods may be less costly in the long run than the mistakes that can result from not using them. In much of the West this will entail a change in dominant corporate culture, in which ethnographic research happens only serendipitously. When IKEA opened its first North American store in Vancouver in 1976, it sold a disproportionately large number of vases. Astute clerks asked consumers why they were buying eight vases at a time and learned that North Americans thought European-sized glasses were too small. They fed the information back up the company chain, and soon larger glasses appeared in IKEA's North American line (Burkeman, 2004).

A few successful multinational companies recognize the value of ethnographic research and have incorporated it, despite its cost and "unscientific" basis. Sony showrooms are constructed as "playrooms" to gather data on how consumers actually use Sony products. Sony used participant observation in toy stores when designing and launching their children's line of products. In May 2005, McDonald's opened a public restaurant as a test site to see how customers use and react to new products, such as menu items, plasma televisions, wireless Internet access, and digital media kiosks offering ring tone downloads, photo printing, and CD burning. One goal is to see whether the meaning of McDonald's can be remade in customers' minds from "fast food" to "hangout" (Carpenter, 2005).

Public relations agencies around the world more often use focus groups and in-depth interviews to inform campaigns. For example, USAID South Africa commissioned GreenCOM, a strategic participatory communication organization, to raise awareness of the impact of global climate change and encourage consumers to adopt behaviors that would reduce greenhouse gas emissions. Through 10 focus groups held in three provinces in South Africa, the firm developed effective key messages for the campaign focusing on health benefits, financial savings, and better overall quality of life that garnered corporate buy-in and informed educational materials (GreenCOM Project, 2005). Likewise, when the Greek Trade Commission hired Shanahan Advertising and Public Relations to regain market share for Greek marble among U.S. architects and designers, the firm chose focus groups over surveys to obtain more insights into the target audiences' attitudes and perceptions, particularly cultural differences. The award-winning campaign is credited with increasing imports of Greek marble to the United States by 400% in a 4-year period (Shanahan & Prabhaker, 2003).

The Role of Relative Power

Another insight from the moment of consumption is that practitioners need to recognize the role of relative power within relationships, particularly those between producers and audiences. Consumers, though active producers of meaning, are seldom empowered producers of meaning (Mackay, 1997). Producers often have the upper hand in relationships with consumers. For example, public relations practitioners are usually employed by those with more relative power, making two-way symmetric communication impossible.

Just looking at one aspect of empowerment, economics, illustrates the point. An old joke says democracies have a free press for anyone who can afford to buy one. In like manner, public relations counsel is available to anyone who can afford it. Three of the 2005 Public Relations Society of America's Silver Anvil Award winners for multicultural campaigns listed campaign budgets ranging from US$600,000 to US$12 million. In the face of such overwhelming producer resources, talk about consumer empowerment may seem a poor joke at best.

Yet as we noted in chapter 3 and the case of New Coke, when consumers believe their norms have been violated, they often feel more empowered to act. These actions may be individual, such as that of the political activist in Indonesia who quietly protested the restrictive Suharto regime by taking his son to eat at a symbol of Western freedom, McDonald's, once a week (Friedman, 1999). At other times, protest actions involve organized civil disobedience, such as the nude protesters in Pamplona, Spain, organized by People for the Ethical Treatment of Animals to highlight issues of animal cruelty (Photo 7.1). When groups lack relative power, they often must resort to civil disobedience to attract media attention to their cause.

When people believe their norms have been violated or organizations have betrayed their expectations, audience empowerment can arise under otherwise unlikely circumstances. In China, for example, increasing privatization and industrialization are starting to dominate traditional rural life. As the government has established factories and industrial parks on traditional farmlands, farmers are protesting the land seizures, resulting pollution, and unresponsiveness of local government to their complaints, as well as the fact that the economic prosperity promised from such development hasn't benefited them. In 2004 alone, more than 70,000 recorded clashes between rural residents and government officials took place (Bodeen, 2005).

In one such incident, residents frustrated by a lack of local government responsiveness built a tent city to barricade an industrial park entrance and manned it with members from the local Elderly Association, believing the government would abide by cultural norms regarding respect for the elderly and not take action against them. Ignoring cultural convention, the police sent to break up the protest beat the elderly protesters to get them to disperse. Even a factory manager from the industrial park, which had been under siege for 4 years, asked the police to stop but was himself beaten. At this point, the crowd fought back. More than 20,000 area residents joined the tent dwellers and attacked police, running them off and destroying their vehicles. As one participant noted, "We saw the other face of the police.

Civil disobedience often is used by activist groups who otherwise might not command media or world attention.

Photo 7.1   PETA Protesters in Pamplona, Spain, Protesting the Running of the Bulls

SOURCE: Photo courtesy of PETA.

At first, the ordinary people had been afraid. But by then, it was the police who were afraid" (in Cody, 2005, ¶ 38).

The lesson from these demonstrations is that relative empowerment in the moment of consumption is highly influenced by the moment of regulation, which encompasses cultural norms and expectations of organizational behavior. It serves as a good reminder that although we're discussing the moments of the circuit separately, they remain bound in every articulation, requiring practitioners to take all of the moments into account during campaigns.

❖ THE CHALLENGES AND AMBIGUITIES OF NEW TECHNOLOGY AND GLOBALIZATION

Relative empowerment in the producer–consumer relationship figures into two aspects of international public relations practice: the use of new technology and globalization. Both bring us into contact with different cultures and customs, an often uncomfortable process as our ideas about ourselves and others are challenged. Critics alternately have hailed new technology and globalization as great democratizing forces, empowering consumers, or as another means for producers to take control. We examine the challenges for international public relations practice in light of these inherent ambiguities.

The Role of New Technology

Common public relations knowledge in the West holds that the Internet is "changing the definition, meaning, understanding and practice of PR" as the "PR audience is becoming more diverse in an increasingly integrated global economy" (Ihator, 2001, p. 15). Most U.S. public relations scholars believe the World Wide Web holds great promise for the field because new technology allows practitioners to create texts that bypass media gatekeepers and directly reach consumers and to track consumers' surfing habits and buying patterns (Hill & White, 2000).

In turn, consumers can use new technology to become producers of texts and transmit, reproduce, and distribute messages at low cost. In the digital world, the roles of producer and consumer collide. Personal blogs, or Web logs, become news sites; the marketplace becomes more competitive as consumers price compare global products; and peoples in widely disparate geographic areas become organized entities. This development of online activism has caused public relations practitioners to perceive new technology as a possible threat and to devise strategies to respond to Web-launched activist attacks (Ragan Communications, 2001).

For example, a consortium of six U.S. environmental groups has launched the http://www.exxposeexxon.com site, designed to generate grassroots support for a boycott of Exxon Mobil. The well-designed site offers easy-to-use tools for both consumers and journalists, including automatic e-mail updates; prewritten letters to send to Exxon and to members of the U.S. Congress; an action center; links to fact sheets, FAQs, and research reports; a dedicated newsroom with a journalist registration area; and even T-shirts for sale. Although the site makes it easy for people with environmental concerns to take action, the fact remains that the Web, by virtue of being computer mediated, does not promote the same feeling of solidarity that may come more readily from face-to-face group membership. To date, successful activist campaigns on the Web have often required a larger, human presence. The Web-based, grassroots activist campaign to ban land mines, for example, may not have been as successful as it was in the 1990s without the high-profile support of Princess Diana.

What these examples demonstrate is that although the Web blurs the lines between producers and consumers, it doesn't necessarily empower either group just by virtue of its use in a particular articulation. Studies show that the most visited Web sites belong to the major players, such as CNN, Disney, Microsoft, and the major search engines, such as Yahoo! and Google. Marginalized voices often are marginalized in e-space as well, with startup costs for a major Web site now running in the millions of U.S. dollars (Croteau & Hoynes, 2002). What the Internet has done is increase the speed of information availability and its reach. Consumers with access can keep in touch with world events as they happen and shop the globe from the comforts of home.

The key, of course, is access. As Thomas Friedman (1999, p. 28), the *New York Times* foreign affairs columnist, notes,

> For millions of people in developing countries, the quest for material improvement still involves walking to a well, plowing a field barefoot behind an ox or gathering wood and carrying it on their heads for five miles. These people still upload for a living, not download.

In fact, figures for 2004 show that only about a tenth of the world's population is connected to the Web, whether from home, work, Internet café, or other public facility (Global Reach, 2004). Of those, less than one third are native English speakers, yet 75% of Web pages are written in English (Hesmondhalgh, 2002). To have a Web presence is by definition to be global, leading the creators of the circuit of culture to conclude that "the language of global consumerism is, of course, English (or, actually, American)" (du Gay et al., 1997, p. 26).

But as the circuit continuously points out, generalizations must be used with care, as illustrated by the Web presence of a Mexican political movement:

> The struggles of the Zapatistas in Chiapas, Mexico has become one of the most successful examples of the use of computer communications by grassroots social movements. That circulation has not only brought support to the Zapatistas from throughout Mexico and the rest of the World, but it has sparked a world wide discussion of the meaning and implications of the Zapatista rebellion for many other confrontations with contemporary capitalist economic and political policies. (Cleaver, 2003, ¶ 1)

New technology, then, can be either empowering or disempowering for both producers and consumers. It can bring like-minded people together from around the world who otherwise would never meet and inspire action and discussion. But most of the world's population remains far from a paved road and even farther from the information superhighway. For those who are connected, American English is performing a hegemonic function, privileging those who command the language. The dominance of the United States in the global marketplace and what this means for international public relations practice are discussed next.

Consuming the Globe

It's through consumption that most people experience cultural diversity, whether it be food, music, travel, or, increasingly, a visit to their local big box discount store. Target, a U.S.-based discount merchandiser with more than 1,300 stores in 47 states, has incorporated a "Global Bazaar" section in its houseware department, which offers, according to the company's Web site, "spicy décor galore . . . discovered in markets around the world. Destination décor for your home." The world is packaged and divided into easily consumable chunks for U.S. consumers: Latin America and Africa are single, undifferentiated entities, despite their diverse ethnicities and colonial backgrounds; Europe is divided between north (Sweden) and south (Tuscany); all of Asia is collapsed into the two leading economies, China and Japan; and Eastern Europe, Russia, Australia, and New Zealand are conspicuous by their absence, conveying that they aren't exotic or design conscious enough to produce "spicy décor galore" in the transnational discourse.

Chandra Muzaffar, president of a Malaysian human rights group, believes this spread of products from developing to developed world demonstrates that globalization isn't another form of colonization and therefore not inherently disempowering (in Friedman, 1999). But many take a more critical view, noting how the developing world becomes the exotic other that is commodified and sold by producers in developed countries, based in part on a romanticized colonial heritage (Lester, 1992).

This same tension is apparent in tourism, which according to the World Tourism Organization is the world's largest export earner and is experiencing the fastest growth in employment, making it the number-one industry in many developing countries. In 2004, global tourism earnings grew by 10.3% to 500 billion euros (US$622 billion), and international tourist arrivals increased 10.7%. Fast-growing tourist destinations include northeast Asia (up 30%), the Middle East (up

22%), and Africa (up 6%), which was the leader the previous three years (WTO, 2005). Travel and tourism are also large parts of the global public relations industry, with active divisions of professional organizations devoted to their development. In some parts of the world, such as the Middle East, public relations and tourism and travel are so linked that the public relations function is almost synonymous with hospitality and receiving delegations (Creedon et al., 1995).

Tourism is an economic locomotive for much of the developing world, as noted earlier in the discussion of ecotourism in the Galápagos Islands. In Cuba, tourism surpassed sugar in dollar revenues for the first time in 1996 and remains the primary source of hard currency there (Foley, 2005). Throughout the Caribbean and South Pacific Islands, tourism accounts for more than 50% of the gross domestic product in many nations, and ecotourism is steadily increasing as a key economic earner throughout Central America and much of Africa (CIA, 2005).

For consumers with disposable income, much of the world is now available as a vacation destination. Tourism increases the consumption not only of global goods but also of ideologies, as evidenced by the spread of Eastern religions in the West. Tourists visiting Kenya can bring back not only 5-foot-tall carved wooden giraffes and pictures of animals taken on safari but also a greater understanding of the problems of tribal migration, the AIDS epidemic, the influence of Roman Catholicism on social programs and politics, and the early trade routes that have created a heavily Arab influence on coastal areas.

On the receiving end, tourism can reinvigorate local cultures as traditions and arts are reappropriated and revived for tourists. But the tension is obvious: For some, the packaging and selling of local culture for tourists marks its death as it becomes commodified; for others it becomes the cultural savior, renewing local customs and pride (Fürsich & Robins, 2004). In her book *The God of Small Things,* for example, Indian author Arundhati Roy devotes an entire chapter to the traditional *kathakali* dance of her native state of Kerala. Through her characters, she examines how the dance has been repackaged for tourists, much like the traditional family cottages of the area have been bought by area resorts and reassembled on their grounds to provide tourists with an "authentic" lodging experience.

In like manner, although tourism is contributing to the economic development of many developing countries, all too often the tourism infrastructure, such as hotels, transportation networks, and restaurants, is owned by foreign interests, and the economic benefits don't reach local populations. In Cambodia, tourist arrivals increased 15% in

2004, drawn largely to Siam Reap, home of Angkor Wat, a UNESCO World Heritage site. Although national regulations state that Cambodians must have at least 50% controlling interest in all hotels built, government corruption has caused many working as guides in the tourist industry there to question just how well the rules are enforced. They see the growth in tourism as simply increasing the gap between rich and poor, developed and developing worlds.

Despite these regulations, lack of infrastructure has led to increasing privatization and foreign investment in tourism throughout Cambodia. The Choeung Ek Killing Fields, located just outside Phnom Penh (Photo 7.2), are a grisly reminder of the genocide inflicted by the Khmer Rouge, serving as a memorial to the victims and a major tourist attraction. Recently, authorities in Phnom Penh proposed leasing the site to the Japanese J. C. Royal Company for 30 years. The company would pay US$15,000 a year, pave the road to the memorial, build a visitors' center, and raise admission prices by 600%, bringing about upgrades and improved facilities that the government cannot afford (De Launey, 2005). But rising controversy in Cambodia has put a halt to the deal for now, with the population protesting the commercialization of a major national memorial by foreign investors, despite the possible economic benefits.

The memorial tower contains the skulls of approximately 14,000 of the victims found there, including women and children.

Photo 7.2   The Choeung Ek Killing Fields

SOURCE: Photo courtesy of Wickipedia Commons.

As these examples demonstrate, global consumption through tourism is a complex phenomenon. It conversely empowers local peoples and changes their cultures, bringing economic development and greater economic disparity.

The lesson of the circuit of culture is that no simple answers exist to questions of globalization. The issues raised remain contested articulations that must be approached carefully on a case-by-case basis, recognizing the competing discourses of economics and the right to self-development they entail.

Globalized Consumption in the Developing World

In many emerging democracies, knowledge of products has preceded the products themselves, with meanings formed before they even become available. The symbolic meaning of Western goods often has been one of modernity, of prosperity and freedom (Clarke, Micken, & Hart, 2002). Nikes may be made in Asia, but they symbolize Western freedom. What is being consumed is the symbol, not the manufacturing reality. Consumption becomes indicative of global belonging, a badge of citizenship in the modern world (Clarke et al., 2002).

For those in the developing world who don't have the resources to travel, going to McDonald's can constitute a trip to the United States. In the late 1990s, the owner of all KFC franchises in Malaysia observed,

> Anything Western, especially American, people here love. They want to eat it and be it. I've got people in small [rural] towns around Malaysia queueing up for Kentucky Fried Chicken—they come from all over to get it. They want to be associated with America. People here like anything that is modern. It makes them feel modern when they eat it. (in Friedman, 1999, p. 235)

Global consumption means that the same texts are interpreted in many different contexts, with different peoples bringing their own cultural references to bear on them. Empirical studies have demonstrated that consumers in different countries create different meanings for the same products, and those meanings cannot be forecast using demographics or cultural indices. They are more idiosyncratic and less subject to segmentation and national cultural constructs.

When entering new global arenas, the public relations practitioner is to "articulate and recontextualize alien meanings [symbols] into local cultural imaginations and consumption patterns" (Ma, 2001, p. 449). Practitioners introducing a new product or idea to global consumers have to culturally interface within specific local articulations to gain acceptance, coping with what scholar Grant McCracken (1988) called the **Diderot effect:** *the destabilization of lifestyles and discourses brought about by new* *acquisitions and knowledge gain.* The term comes from the Enlightenment philosopher Diderot, who upon receipt of a new dressing gown as a gift began to upscale all the furnishings in his study because they began to appear shabby in comparison. As something new or different enters our cultural space, it has a wider ripple effect.

When consumption of new products and ideas becomes institution-alized through media channels and markets, consumers appropriate these products and ideas in localized ways, resulting in glocalization: Consumption becomes "the mechanism that promotes localization" (Miller, 1997, p. 37). Savvy multinational corporations and international public relations firms have realized the need for glocalization, and today much localization is being driven as much by producers as by consumers.

Photo 7.3   Harajuku Girls Performing as Street Musicians

SOURCE: This Wikipedia and Wikimedia Commons image is from the user Chris 73 and is freely available at http://commons.wikimedia.org/wiki/Image:Harajuku_bridge_02 .jpg under the creative commons cc-by-sa 2.5 license.

The result is a consumer culture of appropriation or **bricolage:** *taking pieces of global culture and adapting them to localized meanings and uses to create new subcultures.* In the Harajuku area of Tokyo, for example, in the 1990s, a subculture developed among teens who dressed in a bricolage of fashions, in part a rebellion against the uniformity of Japanese culture (Photo 7.3). In turn, Harajuku has become an iconic symbol of teen, and particularly female, empowerment. Gwen Stefani recorded "Harajuku Girls," launched her Harajuku Lovers concert tour, and began her own Harajuku fashion line, available in the United States at Urban Outfitters (Photo 7.4). The appropriation of Harajuku resistance by Western mainstream culture led to the demise of the original: Japanese teens no longer dress in Harajuku fashion, and the idea has been appropriated into U.S. culture and given new form there.

The Harajuku girls prompted Gwen Stefani's U.S. fashion line of the same name and the demise of the original subculture.

| Photo 7.4 | Harajuku Fashion in the United States |

SOURCE: Photo courtesy of Urban Outfitters.

Ideally, "the whole purpose of glocalization is to be able to assimilate aspects of globalization into your country and culture in a way that adds to your growth and diversity without overwhelming it" (Friedman, 1999, p. 236). As this chapter has demonstrated, however, globalization is not a straightforward process, and it is fraught with issues of relative power that cannot be ignored by international public relations practitioners, a point well demonstrated in the smallpox eradication case.

CHAPTER SUMMARY

- Consumption and production are two aspects of the same process.

- Consumers actively create meanings for products and for issues through their everyday use.

- Campaign research must be an ongoing process throughout all phases of a campaign, using ethnographic methods to capture the meanings consumers are continuously creating.

- Consumption and regulation are closely tied; when organizations violate consumers' norms, activist or protest groups are likely to form.

- New technology can be both empowering and disempowering, but the majority of the world still lacks access.

- Globalization and glocalization result in cultural appropriation and change, which, like new technology, can be both empowering and disempowering.

Smallpox Eradication Campaign

The ultimate measure of campaign efficacy lies in the moment of consumption. If consumers don't adopt meanings consonant with those of producers, then the campaign probably will fail. In this portion of the smallpox eradication case we examine how the main audience for the campaign, residents of endemic countries, made sense of campaign messages and put them to use in their everyday lives. Because consumers negotiate meaning based on their particular cultural contexts, it's not surprising that local customs and norms played a major role in this aspect of the campaign. The moments of production, consumption, and regulation are closely intertwined, and the moment of consumption brings the issues inherent in the overlap of the private and public spheres to the fore.

Salience, *or how personally relevant something is,* is one factor contributing to how audiences understand issues in their lives, and practitioners often must work to construct messages to raise issue salience. For the many people in endemic countries, however, smallpox was already a salient issue. Smallpox regularly killed, blinded, or disfigured a large proportion of every generation and had done so from time immemorial. As one WHO official observed about India, "Over the centuries during which smallpox struck . . . diverse and widespread legends, beliefs, and practices developed, reflecting the varied religious traditions. Smallpox was incorporated into the very fabric of Indian society" (Brilliant, 1985, p. 2).

Although smallpox was a salient issue, eradication wasn't necessarily as relevant. Because smallpox was so prevalent, many people regarded it as an inevitable and recurring fact of life, a fact reflected in local names for the disease. One Chinese dialect called it "inevitable pox," and in Myanmar it was "the disease of the world" (Hopkins, 2002, p. 131; Thaung & Ko Ko, 2002, p. 105). In Ghana, smallpox was *naba,* the chief of all diseases. In Borneo's creation myth, smallpox is the price paid for the creation of the world, suggesting that as long as the world exists, smallpox will as well (Hopkins, 1989). In some regions, the name of the disease was the same as the name of the season in which it usually occurred, making smallpox as inevitable as the changing of the seasons. How smallpox was identified had larger ramifications for how consumers adopted and adapted campaign messages.

SMALLPOX DEIFIED

For many people in endemic countries, smallpox was such a powerful part of everyday life that it was incorporated into religious beliefs. An 11th-century Buddhist nun introduced T'ou-Shen Niang-Niong as the goddess of smallpox in China. By the mid-1800s her worship was widespread among Buddhists, Taoists, and Confucians, indicative of how widely acknowledged the power of the disease was. She particularly enjoyed disfiguring children with pretty faces, making her more feared than loved, which may have contributed to the ability of the Chinese government to eradicate smallpox by the early 1950s without encountering significant religious objections (Hopkins, 2002). In other areas, however, differing religious beliefs often created opposition to the eradication campaign.

Shitala Mata in India

No region of the world was more devastated over the years by smallpox than was India. In the mid-1800s, a survey of Calcutta found that 13% of all recorded deaths and 75% of all recorded cases of blindness were due to smallpox. Smallpox was so prevalent throughout Indian history that by 1500 B.C.E. it had become incorporated into the large Hindu pantheon of gods and goddesses as Shitala Mata. By the late 1800s, Shitala Mata became one of the most worshipped goddesses, with 32 temples dedicated to her in Calcutta alone and numerous homes displaying her image. Smallpox knew no religious bounds, and her worship spread among Christian, Buddhist, and Muslim groups as well. Even *harijans*, the untouchables of the Indian caste system, were allowed to enter her temples for worship, indicative of the stronghold smallpox had on Indian daily life.

Also known as Mariammai in Tamil areas of southern India, she was the oldest of seven sisters who could all cause or cure particular diseases associated with rashes, including measles, mumps, and chicken pox. Her name meant "cooling mother" because she could bring relief to the hot rash associated with smallpox. One sacred text describes her and her abilities as follows:

> In every house your power is established,
> As beautiful as the full autumn moon.
> When the body burns with poisonous eruptions
> You make it cool and take away all pain.

> — (Prabhudas, *Sitala Calisa,*
> in Hopkins, 2002, p. 158)

Getting smallpox meant you had been visited by the goddess. Although Shitala could decide to visit for no particular reason, she was generally considered easy to anger and prone to visit when displeased. Regular worship was greatly pleasing to her during her annual spring festival and could keep her away (Mather & John, 1973). Treatment for victims consisted of cooling them through feeding them a special diet, surrounding them with the branches of neem trees, which were thought to have cooling powers, and making offerings to the goddess at her temple.

Because many worshippers believed trying to prevent smallpox would anger the goddess, they resisted reporting cases and being vaccinated. Vaccination resistance may have been reinforced by the fact that the vaccine came from cows, which are sacred to Hindus. Not all believers were equally fervent in their resistance, however. Interviews conducted between 1965 and 1970 found that not quite 20% of people were strongly opposed to vaccination and that educational level was not a factor (Mather & John, 1973).

At the other end of the spectrum, a small percentage viewed vaccination as an even stronger spiritual force than the goddess and were open to it. WHO workers closely monitored the various responses, creating a strategy of co-opting religious practice when possible. They recast vaccination as a form of worship, coining the slogan "Worship the goddess and take a vaccination too." Vaccination was accompanied by rituals and hymns sung in Shitala's honor (Brilliant, 1985; Morinis, 1978). For those who adopted vaccination as a form of worship, the vaccination pustule became a manifestation of the goddess, a visible symbol of worship. An active case meant Shitala was in residence, however, and most believers refused to report cases and risk angering the goddess.

Sapona in Western Africa

By the late 1600s, Sapona worship was widely established among the Yoruba tribe, found mainly in Nigeria and Benin, and the Fon tribe of Dahomey and Togo. As one of the sons of the creator of the world, Sapona was given control of the earth. As the earth god, he could make crops grow when pleased, but when displeased he could cause seeds or grains to grow on humans, causing smallpox (Photo 7.5). Similar to Shitala worship, Sapona worship crossed traditional religious boundaries, with many Christians and Muslims also worshipping the earth god (Morgan, 1969).

Worshippers believed Sapona empowered his priests, allowing them to cause smallpox as well. This belief may have stemmed from the fact that priests often served as variolators and incorporated the practice into worship, which led to outbreaks. In the early 1900s, the British outlawed Sapona worship in Nigeria to try to stop the practice of variolation and the resulting outbreaks. The ban only drove the practice underground, however, and worship, including variolation, continued outside government oversight (Hopkins, 2002). Some people resisted vaccination because they believed it would actually confer smallpox, perhaps because they equated the practice with that of variolation.

Case Study

Photo 7.5   Sapona, the God of Smallpox in Parts of Western Africa

SOURCE: Photo courtesy of CDC and Global Health Odyssey.

For some worshippers, eradicating smallpox was equivalent to threatening the very existence of the earth that grew their crops and sustained them. Vaccination represented an assault on their god and on their own lives, leading one group to kill a vaccination team in Dahomey in the early 1960s. In a part of western Nigeria, WHO workers, not realizing that Sapona and smallpox were so strongly identified that in the local dialect the two had the same name, put up the usual advance posters to publicize the campaign. When the vaccination team arrived a week later they were met by angry villagers armed with knives. The posters had used the usual military slogan, "Make War on Smallpox," and villagers thought they were being asked to kill their god (Challenor, 1971). In this case, the meaning decoded certainly was not the one intended by the campaign workers.

After interviewing religious and political leaders to learn their perspectives, workers adjusted their strategy. They persuaded local variolators to become vaccinators instead, which associated vaccination with local religious figures and rituals. In some locales, children were traditionally tattooed to ward off smallpox, and workers convinced parents that vaccination scars were an effective substitute (Hopkins, 2002).

Omolu in Brazil

The slave trade brought many members of the Yoruba tribe to Brazil, along with their gods, including Sapona. The Portuguese attempted to ban worship of the Yoruban gods and enforce Catholicism as the dominant religion as part of a strategy to subdue the slaves, but the tribal members simply melded their old gods with the new saints, forming a new set of deities, the orixas. By the time of the smallpox eradication campaign, Sapona had evolved into two brothers: Obalyuye, the King of the Earth, and Omolu, who was responsible for much disease, including smallpox (Photo 7.6). The practice spread to Cuba, where Obalyuye and Omolu once more merged to become Babaluaye in Santeria practice. In these regions, vaccination was not construed as a threat to the god, perhaps in part because of the infusion of Catholicism, and vaccination was readily accepted by most people in these areas.

The straw surrounding him represents the earth and the coarse skin that results from an active smallpox infection.

Photo 7.6   Omolu, the Brazilian Smallpox Deity

SOURCE: Photo courtesy of Dara Curtin.

Christian Sects in Southern Africa

In South Africa and Botswana, some Christian sects, such as the Mazezuru, vehemently opposed any kind of medical treatment, believing it a violation of God's will. They lived in closed communities and refused to report cases, making surveillance difficult. When a Mazezuru child reported a case in one of his schoolmates, workers approached religious leaders to convince them of the necessity of vaccination. Church officials promised workers they would persuade their members to cooperate, but in actuality they preached continued resistance. Unable to find a way to co-opt religious beliefs and practices that opposed medical treatment of any kind, WHO workers eventually asked the president of Botswana to deport the group if they continued to refuse vaccination. The group considered deportation the worse threat and agreed to be vaccinated.

Overall, religious beliefs generated the most widespread resistance to the campaign. Because believers often identified the disease with their deity or as a manifestation of the deity's will, they weren't likely to accept messages that threatened their deity's very existence or power. When campaign leaders had difficulty finding methods and approaches that would resonate with worshippers, workers used interviews and observation to ascertain local meanings. They often managed to create new meanings that religious audiences could adopt. However, it's important to note that not all religious groups took oppositional readings to campaign messages, and even within religious groups a number of dominant meanings emerged. No religion represented a single, unified group of individuals who all created the same use of campaign messages in their everyday lives.

Religion was just one factor contributing to consumption, however. Next we examine other cultural contexts, as well as demographic and psychographic factors, that either helped or hindered eradication efforts by leading audience members to create preferred, negotiated, or oppositional readings of campaign messages.

CULTURAL FACTORS LEADING TO PREFERRED OR NEGOTIATED READINGS

The people who most readily adopted vaccination often were those who lived in areas with established health services, which typically practiced mass vaccination techniques. Accustomed to lining up for vaccinations for measles and other diseases, peoples in these areas accepted lining up as a routine part of the health care system, particularly when vaccinations were given at convenient times and places (Photo 7.7). These patterns of consumption were apparent mainly in Africa and South America. In Zaire, for example, despite low literacy levels and a lack of cooperation from local officials, vaccinators were able to use jet injectors to fairly painlessly vaccinate a large number of people in a short time, and eradication was achieved fairly quickly. The method also worked in Brazil, where people readily assembled at vaccination points. For these people, such behavior was already part and parcel of their everyday lives, and the campaign didn't require them to adopt new beliefs or behaviors.

In other areas, many people also accepted vaccination, but they weren't used to coming to main collection points for it. In much of Asia and countries such as Sudan, vaccinators went house to house with bifurcated needles to gain compliance. Still others accepted vaccination,

In many areas of western Africa, people were used to lining up for health services, making mass vaccination a viable strategy.

Photo 7.7   People in Niger Line Up to Receive Smallpox and Measles Vaccinations

SOURCE: Photo courtesy of CDC and Dr. J. D. Millar.

but the times and places had to be negotiated. Farmers often refused vaccination during harvest time because they didn't want a sore arm to slow them down. For them, vaccination meant an inability to work, which dictated the times of the season at which they would allow it. Nomadic groups in Afghanistan and Pakistan resisted vaccination when they were traveling because it would slow them down. They readily accepted vaccination when in camp; unfortunately for WHO workers, they often settled in fairly inaccessible areas (Photo 7.8).

Still others readily accepted vaccination because it was a demonstration of attention. For groups in remote areas, a visit by a vaccination team represented a rare glimpse of the outside world and an excuse for feasting and conveyed the message that others cared about them. In Afghanistan, some villagers sent in false outbreak reports so a team would respond quickly and pay them a visit. In the southern and eastern parts of Ethiopia, villagers from as far as 50 km (30 miles) away would

The injectors were heavy and often broke down, making their use in remote areas such as this difficult.

Photo 7.8   A Nomadic Tuareg Girl in Mali Is Vaccinated With a Jet Injector

SOURCE: Photo courtesy of CDC.

leave notes on trails requesting visits, often falsely claiming an outbreak. Workers never could determine what meaning some of these people had constructed for vaccination that made many of them line up for it again and again. The problem for workers became not wasting vaccine on people who already had adequate immunity.

People accustomed to variolation, which usually was performed on the wrist, often would accept vaccination, but only if it was also given on the wrist rather than the preferred upper arm location. Some Muslim women would bare only their wrists for male vaccinators and declined for religious reasons to expose their arms.

How cultures treated and cared for their sick also affected how they complied with campaign messages. In many areas of Africa and in Pakistan, those who succumbed to smallpox traditionally were isolated, which helped prevent outbreaks. In Somalia, for example, isolation huts were established far from main living quarters; in Sierra Leone, patients were confined to their houses; and in Pakistan, smallpox survivors who had some natural immunity were sent to care for quarantined victims. In these areas, reporting a case not only meant business as usual, it could also mean obtaining a reward. Case reports often were provided readily in these areas.

CULTURAL FACTORS LEADING TO OPPOSITIONAL READINGS

Other people refused to report cases in part because they traditionally visited the sick, believing it to be a crucial part of encouraging better health, and they didn't want victims to be quarantined. In India and Indonesia, families carried sick children to relatives' homes to be comforted. In Java, with its high population density and year-round occurrence of smallpox, the practice led to a very high incidence of the disease. In Nepal, one group would go to the home of the sick person to provide solace, whereas another granted any wish to a sick child, and often that child asked to visit family and friends. In many Muslim societies, particularly areas of Bangladesh, the ill would travel miles from their jobs in the cities to return to their rural homes to be cared for during illness, which also spread the disease.

Although many people in Somalia practiced isolation, the nomadic tribes there tended to visit the sick, and when they were placed in isolation huts they would simply leave. To develop a culturally acceptable way to gain compliance, workers interviewed members of the group to determine why they left. Finding that most nomads considered the food and shelter inadequate, they constructed lean-tos and latrines surrounded with thorn barriers. Patients were paid to stay inside, and if they left at the proper time they were given a new set of clothes, making them stand out and become walking advertisements for the program as well. The new arrangement met with much greater success.

A host of meanings led to passive resistance. Some groups in Afghanistan, Pakistan, and Ethiopia preferred variolation because it was their traditional means of gaining immunity and had been used for a long time. Additionally, because WHO recommended that vaccinations be updated in cases of severe outbreaks, suggesting that the immunity granted by vaccination was temporary only, these groups viewed vaccination as inferior to variolation. Again, training variolators as vaccinators helped overcome resistance by transferring their authority to the new technique.

Others simply deemed vaccination ineffective. In Hindi, for example, the same word is used for chicken pox and smallpox. When people still succumbed to chicken pox after being vaccinated, they assumed the vaccine was worthless (Brilliant, 1985). Health educators learned to distinguish the two diseases carefully. In parts of India, where the rotary lancet was traditionally used to administer the vaccination, people offered to pay health workers not to vaccinate them because the device was so painful. Introduction of the bifurcated needle helped overcome these objections. In other areas, the only type of smallpox present was variola minor, a less virulent form that seldom led to death and did not disable its victims. In these areas, smallpox simply wasn't considered a serious threat, and vaccination was deemed unimportant. The main answer workers formulated to this problem was the reward system, paying people for reports of confirmed cases.

In other instances, relative power dimensions played a more direct role in fostering the development of oppositional meanings. Some people used vaccination as a bargaining tool, submitting to it only if vaccinators would meet their other needs as well. In areas of Ethiopia and Somalia, for example, village chiefs would agree to let their people be vaccinated if general medical exams and care were provided as well. Starving beggars in India often consented only if they were fed. What was the use of vaccination, many argued, if they were going to die of starvation anyway?

Others simply declined on principle what they saw as another attempt at colonialism. In India, because British colonizers had pushed vaccination, those who accepted it were deemed British sympathizers, an interpretation that lingered over the years, making vaccination synonymous with colonization. In Nigeria, workers found that religious opposition to vaccination often was not nearly as strong as distrust of the government officials who were part of vaccination teams. Traditionally, government officials showed up in villages only when collecting taxes or conscripting men for military service. Resistance in these instances was fostered not by religious beliefs as much as by those who were promoting the alternative.

People engaging in illegal behaviors also weren't eager to come to the notice of authorities for any reason. Surveillance and containment depended on the ability to trace all people who had been in contact with the victim in the previous weeks, but when smuggling or prostitution was involved, victims often refused to name names. One of the last cases in Afghanistan occurred in a nomadic tribe, many of whose members weren't vaccinated. Workers arranged to travel with the group to ensure that the case was isolated. But the group was smuggling cloth and stole off in the night, leaving the workers and victim behind. In southern Malawi, many illegal aliens from Mozambique fled from government vaccination teams rather than face possible detention and deportation, a situation similar to that in the United States today, where many Hispanic immigrants do not avail themselves of health services or aid for fear of deportation.

IMPLICATIONS FOR INTERNATIONAL PRACTICE

Many factors contributed to the ways in which individuals interpreted campaign messages and incorporated them into their daily lives. We've touched on only a few of them here, and only in broad strokes. But as the case makes evident, interpretations were often shifting and sometimes conflicting. Campaign leaders couldn't simply label worshippers of Shitala Mata, for example, a nonpublic and move on. They realized that this one target public comprised individuals with individual meanings for and attitudes toward eradication. Some remained adamantly opposed to vaccination, some welcomed it, and some could be persuaded through constructions of new, negotiated meanings of vaccination.

Additionally, for any individual, religion is only one of many factors that determine how messages are interpreted; age, gender, ethnicity, and a host of other demographic and psychographic factors act simultaneously to shape attitudes and behavior. The public isn't a static target waiting to be hit but a host of individualized factors that change over time. The lesson for international practitioners is that they cannot think of publics in monolithic terms. As one former congressional press secretary recently warned, "There is no 'typical' Arab. In fact, there is no one 'Arab world' as many Westerners have come to imagine it" (Crawford, 2004, p. 31). Practitioners need to step outside the usual static constructions of publics and reformulate how they think of them and approach them in their work.

Certainly it's easier to think in monolithic and static terms. Planning a campaign becomes infinitely more complicated when a more fluid notion of publics is adopted, but such an approach more adequately addresses the complexities of international practice. Because many articulations are stable over time, situations are not always constantly in flux, but practitioners must remain flexible and constantly monitor the environment for change in the public opinion climate. The eradication campaign was successful in part because workers changed strategies and tactics as necessary to accommodate audience meanings as they arose. A continuous assessment system using interviews allowed workers to gather ethnographic data to guide strategy. For example, in May 1975 workers interviewed 4 million people in India, an amount equivalent to talking to every single person in Ireland or New Zealand today. This commitment of time and resources to assessment monitoring was extraordinary and necessary. It also requires that organizations take a long-term view of campaigns rather than simply look at short-term gains.

Dr. D. A. Henderson (1998) said he learned from the failed malaria eradication effort that continuous research to guide ongoing strategy was necessary. The other team leaders expressed this same sentiment: Continuous assessment was necessary to define and redefine the problem, adjust strategy, and create new tactics tailored to local conditions. The goal of public relations campaigns is to create messages that resonate with consumers' lives, and the success of those efforts can be judged only by observing people's lives and learning their perspectives. When practitioners are successful, they create shared identities between producers and consumers. Next, we examine the moment of identity and the central role it plays in public relations campaigns.

Case Study

8

Contested Identities, Shifting Publics in a Globalized World

❖ ❖ ❖

I dentity may be one of the most contentious words of the new millennium. An Internet search produces the following modifiers for *identity: corporate, sexual, digital, public, racial, national, brand,* and even *Christian* (a U.S.-based white supremacist group). The same search finds *identity* used as a modifier for *theft, management,* and *theory.* Is it any wonder we talk about an identity crisis?

Particularly in an age of globalization and the concurrent mixing of peoples and cultures, identities and their attendant meanings and connotations have become contested at levels ranging from individual to international. Yet in this increasingly fractured world of identity formation, public relations practitioners must function as cultural intermediaries to create shared identities between products or issues and publics. For this reason, perhaps no single moment of the circuit of culture so epitomizes the challenges of international practice as the moment of identity.

This chapter examines many levels of identity—individual, group, organizational, cultural, and national—and how they interrelate. What becomes readily apparent from this examination is how the moment of identity is inextricably intertwined with the other four moments of the circuit: You can't discuss identity without discussing how it

- Shapes and is shaped by regulation
- Is formed and maintained in representations
- Is created to achieve strategic goals
- Is consumed in a variety of ways, resulting in a wide variety of new meanings and identities

Of particular import are the consequences of multicultural and global identities on international public relations practice. But first, it's necessary to outline what we mean by identity as a constructed, rather than an essentialist, notion.

❖ CONSTRUCTING IDENTITIES

Some aspects of identity are based in physical reality, such as motherhood. For some women, motherhood is an essential part of who they are; it's a basic biological fact of their existences. But even this simple notion becomes complicated when we consider in vitro fertilization, surrogate mothers, and adoption. What does "being a mother" mean in these cases? The issue becomes more complicated yet when we step beyond essentialist considerations and examine the concept in discursive terms. Supermom, stay-at-home mom, and soccer mom are just a few of the different meanings and behavioral expectations that have grown around the concept of motherhood.

In turn, these identities inform the larger cultural construction of family. We often struggle to categorize blended families, families headed by a lesbian or gay couple, single moms, or couples who choose not to have children. These constructions don't fit the dominant discourse of family in many countries as a heterosexual couple with biologically related children.

Identities, then, are not just essentialist notions, existing as scientific, biological facts. They are also *social constructions emerging from discursive practices, and they form in relationship to something else.* Derrida (1974) proposed that identities are constructed through what they aren't, through difference and exclusion. We know what female is because it's part of a binary opposition; it's not male. In every such binary opposition, one pole has more relative power. In this case, for many societies, it's the male. But without male, female would cease to have meaning because it exists only in relation to the other. Identity "is not the opposite of, but *depends on,* difference" (Woodward, 1997a, p. 29), or in Hall's terms, "identities are constructed through, not outside, difference" (1996, p. 4).

Identities emerge from cultural classification systems. They're marked by similarity, by placing something with a family of things, and by difference, by distinguishing something from the other members of the family. Male and female are both part of gender, but they're constituted within dominant discourse as mutually exclusive. Relational power includes the power to define who is included and who is excluded. **Binary oppositions** *provide the strongest demarcations of difference, which can lead to stereotyping as the oppositions become ultimately reductionist, ignoring the many degrees of relationship that exist between the poles.*

Within certain articulations, differences can have more relative importance, such as racial polarity during apartheid or the Rwandan genocide. Gender polarity is evident in many regulatory environments, such as certain parental leave policies in the United States that do not recognize fathers' rights or by the Japanese legislature's quick approval of Viagra, while approval for birth control pills languished until 1999, when only partial approval was granted.

In these examples difference has a negative connotation, highlighting issues of marginalization and oppression, but difference can be enabling and constructive, celebrated and enriching, as well. From travel along maritime routes, diverse musical traditions collided and created vibrant new forms, such as Brazil's Afro-reggae and New Orleans jazz. Diverse voices can create an enriched climate of discussion and support, as in India's Rural Institute for Developmental Education (RIDE) program. Bringing together village women of differing, and often mutually exclusive, castes and religious backgrounds into self-help groups, the RIDE staff empowers them to work together toward common goals, challenging the gender, caste, and religious identities and inequalities that have been imposed on them.

Subjectivity and Individual Identities

Our identity gives us our place in society; it informs us "of who we are and of how we relate to others in the world in which we live" (Woodward, 1997b, p. 1). Because we interact within a number of social systems, however, our identities are necessarily multifaceted; we assume different roles, in sociological terms. Identities stem from a number of cultural classifications, such as ethnicity, nationality, social class, gender, and sexuality. The result is that the whole is seldom unified but remains fragmented and even conflicted.

Because identities emerge from relationships, they're always contingent, always in flux. No identity is ever fixed for all time, nor is it a process of simple linear unfolding. The identities we assume and that are assigned to us have concrete effects as identities are created and maintained in both the symbolic (i.e., how we make sense of our world) and social (i.e., how we operate in relationship to others) spheres. We choose to invest in certain identities through which we want to represent ourselves. However, such choice always operates within the socially constructed world of identities that are thrust on us. With new technology it's easier to construct new identities in cyberspace that break some of these bounds and to adopt group identities unbounded by geographic restrictions, but these identities often lack discursive power outside e-space.

Active Publics, Fluid Identities

All public relations campaigns begin by assigning an identity to target publics through segmentation. Typically, practitioners divide publics in terms of demographic and psychographic data. Weber Shandwick Scotland, representing a consortium of research, corporate, nonprofit, and government groups in Sweden, the Netherlands, Norway, the United Kingdom, Germany, Belgium, and Denmark, divided publics in its Save the North Sea campaign along demographic lines:

- Commercial fishers
- Other professional mariners
- Educators and students
- Recreational boaters
- Researchers

In this case, publics were picked for their relevance to organizational goals and segmented by occupation or avocation.

SRI International, a U.S.-based nonprofit research organization with an office in Tokyo, specializes in psychographic segmentation. Their Values, Attitudes, and Lifestyles (VALS) survey segments Japanese consumers into 10 psychographic categories, such as Ryoshiki Adapters, who are concerned about both personal advancement and family and social status, and Traditional Innovators, who tend to be socially conservative, holding traditional religious beliefs. Practitioners use these psychographic categories to determine which groups they should target for particular products or issues of concern to their organizations.

But if identity is constructed and fluid, not an essential part of physical being, then how we define publics for any campaign becomes problematic. The usual approach assumes that publics are undifferentiated individuals just waiting for organizations to group them into meaningful units—a target waiting to be hit. It supposes a transmission model of communication, in which an organization imposes identities on publics by segmenting them according to criteria important to the organization. The organization targets messages to the publics deemed of greater importance and assumes that if the targeting is based on research, results will follow. If that were the case, however, New Coke® shouldn't have failed. In the words of two public relations scholars, "This approach to publics has generated little work acknowledging publics as reflecting the will, aspirations, intentions, or relationships of human beings" (Botan & Soto, 1998, p. 25).

Publics actively create identities; they're self-actuated and self-defined. Publics are dynamic, "constructed and reconstructed through the discourses in which they participate" (Leitch & Neilson, 2001, p. 138). Because identities are constantly unfolding, publics are never concretely formed into static units: "There is no point in time at which the public is definitely constituted" (Botan & Soto, 1998, p. 38). We cannot assume that an individual fits into a single category of public, be it based on activity levels, lifestyles, or even demographics.

The consequence for organizations is that the relationships between organizations and publics are better characterized as ongoing processes of trying to find shared zones of meaning (Heath, 1993). Publics are fully vested partners in the creation of meaning, not the end point of message transmission. In practical terms, as practitioners we must be open to a more fluid construction of publics, realizing that individuals may elect to join in multiple relationships with others that form possibly conflicting opinions on an issue. We shouldn't ignore demographics, which provide some basic essentialist aspects of identity, or psychographics, which provide somewhat stereotypic measures, as long as we remember that they represent reductionist and static simplifications of a complex process. But we must also examine the situational particulars, often using qualitative methods of inquiry, such as talking to and observing publics throughout a campaign, to determine how audience members self-identify and the multiple identifications they hold of our organization. Working to ascertain the identities of publics is an ongoing campaign process, not simply a starting point.

❖ ORGANIZATIONAL IDENTITIES

Everything we've outlined concerning individual identities holds for corporate identities as well. Organizations also accumulate different, fluid identities: "Organizations create meaning through every action or inaction, every statement or silence. These multiple meanings constitute identity—not as an object, but as a mutable and dynamic process" (Motion & Leitch, 2002, p. 52). Since the 1980s, the dominant identity of IBM has gone from personal computer leader to no longer even a bit player in the PC market, from "Big Blue," which took almost paternal care of its employees over the course of their careers, to just another employer experiencing downsizing and restructuring.

An organization's identity, like an individual's, varies by context. Every interaction that an organization has with any public, internal or external, contributes to its multiple identities. Different identities for Médecins Sans Frontières (Doctors Without Borders) emerge from patient groups and countries where it operates, from governments and pharmaceutical companies it lobbies to improve access to healthcare, from donors it solicits for support, from employees, and from potential volunteers.

Even single individuals often hold conflicting organizational identities. For example, in a case study of State Farm Insurance, Moffitt (1994) found that depending on whether a person was referring to the company as an area employer, a claim processor, or any number of other roles, the same person could hold both positive and negative identities of the company simultaneously. Because of the importance of context, however, a crisis may crystallize a dominant identity for an organization for a period of time, such as the vilification of Enron following reports of financial wrongdoing and the heroic mold cast for New York City firefighters after the events of September 11.

Fractured Identities, Activist Publics

The identity presented by an organization is less contested and fractured by publics if it's consonant with organizational actions. IKEA has created an identity based on small-town values: practicality and egalitarianism. Company actions reinforce the identity. Headquarters of the 35-nation company remain in the same small town in a rural area of Sweden where it was founded, company executives fly budget airlines and stay in low-cost hotels, and product design is simple and practical and represents value for the money. Little wonder that in 2003 Swedes voted IKEA the second most trusted national institution, behind only universities (Brown, 2003). Conversely, multinational corporations that work to establish a narrative of themselves as social movements, such as the Body Shop, Starbucks, and Apple, often find themselves the target of activist groups that carefully scrutinize their actions to point out any disjunctures with corporate narrative.

Activist publics are themselves organizations with fluid, conflicting identities. Although they may stand in opposition to other organizations, it's simplistic and reductionist to assume that they exist only in bipolar opposition to organizations. Their complex narratives of identity provide multiple meanings, some to gain organizational legitimacy, some to leverage power by adopting the identity of the victim, some as defenders of issues of concern that present a multitude of meanings.

The goal for practitioners becomes not to achieve consensus of meaning by dominating discourse but to manage dissensus and conflict—to realize how to adapt to diversity and difference and turn it into a strength, respecting competing systems of meaning rather than trying to co-opt them. The implications for practice deriving from this notion of relational identity are discussed more fully in chapter 11, which examines the ethical basis of international public relations.

Forging New Organizational Identities

In a world of mergers, acquisitions, partnerships, subsidiaries, sponsorships, and multinational reach, organizational identity is easily fragmented. The almost 300-year history of GlaxoSmithKline pharmaceutical company encompasses at least 17 acquisitions, three mergers, and numerous reorganizations, joint ventures, collaborations, and divestitures. Each of these new formations required internal and external communications to establish a new, unified identity to which stakeholders could relate. Substantial resources often are necessary to present a unified corporate image, as when German-based multinational Adidas corporation recently partnered with the New Zealand All Blacks rugby team. Marketing personnel had to disarticulate the old identity that existed between the All Blacks and their former sponsor and rearticulate a new identity that encompassed the international relationship (Motion, Leitch, & Brodie, 2003). Because people often hold on to old, familiar patterns of thought, creating a new, unified identity that will resonate with publics can be problematic if the old identity is not deconstructed, as demonstrated by the case of New Coke®.

Changing relationships create new articulations, and the complexity of organizational identity may be best visualized as a three-dimensional web (Leitch & Richardson, 2003). Change reverberates along the entire web of relationships, making unified discourse difficult, but it can have a synergistic strength. Weber Shandwick Scotland, for the Save the North Sea campaign, combined the individual research, corporate, nonprofit, and government member identities to leverage the power of scientific discourse with the formal regulatory power of government control and the informal regulatory power of environmental causes. The result was a larger, unified identity with the power to dominate discourse and action. To successfully partner, however, individual organizations have to be willing to cede some of their power to the other groups. Organizational history is full of partnerships that failed because one or both organizations were unwilling to relinquish the power necessary for a new identity to emerge and dominate.

This power dynamic can be particularly problematic for public relations firms or organizations looking to operate internationally. Often companies expand internationally, claiming that they're making use of local talent while being sensitive to local cultural differences. Too often, however, headquarters remains the locus of control, and international training consists of telling the home country majority how to adjust to "the other" (Banks, 2000), disempowering the local office and undermining the ability of the organization to effectively address local issues and markets.

Business analyst Kenichi Ohmae (1989) points to Honda Corporation as a model of the decentered, equidistant organization, which has equally empowered units operating on different continents. Although some critics hold that a truly equal sharing of power is impossible, it's telling that the head of *Adweek's* 2003 Public Relations Agency of the Year believes it's not only possible but necessary. CEO Adehmar Hynes of Text 100 says the company philosophy isn't to buy foreign agencies and "bolt them on to the side" ("2003 PR Agency," 2003, p. 27). The firm's international reach is successful, she says, because they put the local before the global "to ensure that we are not becoming European-centric, Asian-centric, or American-centric" (p. 27). New technology aids the effort, creating a nongeographic space in which team members from around the world meet. Although "no one person or perspective can fully know 'the world' and no company can ever actually be global in anything but a partial way" (du Gay et al., 1997, p. 78), some organizations do a better job of decentering themselves and working to create shared spaces and identities that share power.

❖ DEFINING NATIONAL IDENTITIES

Although organizational identities formed through diverse partnerships and consortia can be a rich source of strength, national identities
often are constructed in one-dimensional terms. Kenneth Boulding
noted in 1959 that national images were "the last great stronghold[s] of
unsophistication" (p. 131), and the insight appears equally apt today.
National identities often spring from a shared, reductionist history,
such as the reconstruction of the takeover of lands from Native
Americans in the developing United States as Manifest Destiny, that is,
territorial expansion as an inevitable right.

Theory demonstrates that tapping into these shared myths can be a
powerful persuasion tool because they resonate with people's deep-
seated emotions and beliefs. National identities develop through the
concept of internationalism, through relationships of one of "us" among
many of "them." In Anderson's (1991) terms, a nation is, in fact, an
imagined community, constructed and maintained by those who claim
membership. The first challenge of a new nation is to gain international
recognition, to demonstrate how it's both similar to and different from
other nations. The national flag becomes symbolic of this difference
(Billig, 1995), as in 1994 when South Africa adopted a new flag after
abolishing apartheid to symbolize its definition as a nation (Figure 8.1).
Conversely, national identities become fractured when the historical
narrative is ruptured, as when British colonizers brought troops from
India into regions of Africa and Indonesia to serve as security forces.

Despite the inherent simplicity of national identity discourse, however, the actuality is far more complex. Yet it's these simplifications that
dominate, reverting to the binary oppositions of identity. All of Africa
becomes "the Dark Continent," a land of white explorers on safari
viewing animals, not a rich mixture of ancient civilizations, diverse
tribal groups, and philosophies and religions. This dominant reductionist discourse is evidenced in remarks by U.S. President George
Bush at a 2001 European news conference when he referred to the
whole continent of Africa as "a nation that suffers from incredible
disease" (in Von Bormann, 2003, ¶ 1). Similarly, during the Cold War,
communism became the basis of identification and polarization.

Now, religion dominates, leading to a Middle East–West split in
which each side constructs the other as a monolithic binary opposite.
For the West, the Middle East has become an exotic world of terrorists,
oil, and Islam as a single, unifying force rather than a complex and rich

(a)

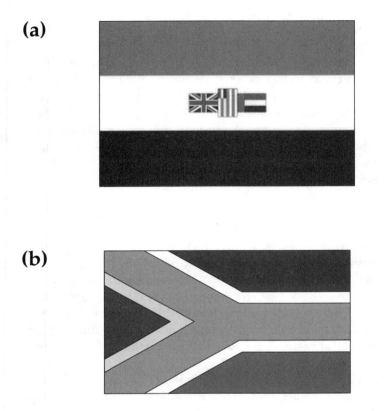

(b)

At top is South Africa's flag from 1927 until 1994. To the Dutch flag were added three small flags, representing the other colonizing and emerging national groups. The flag adopted after the end of apartheid is shown below it. Although officials said at the time the design possessed no symbolism, it's generally understood now that both the Y design and the colors represent unification.

Figure 8.1   South African Flags

religion comprising diverse forms (Said, 1979, 1981). Conversely, the Middle East has constructed the West as amoral and imperialistic. The resulting bipolarity is hauntingly obvious in the September 11 attacks and the war that the U.S. government dubbed Operation Iraqi Freedom.

At other times, the results are more subtle, as in the case of Turkey. In today's discourse, what is of the West cannot, by definition, be Islamic. Turkey, which has historically fallen within European geopolitical boundaries, is now finding its bid for European Union membership blocked. Although it is blocked on ostensibly economic grounds, the underlying discourse revolves around Turkey's Islamic identity. The question becomes, What does it mean to be European? The answer has been, in part, "not Islamic."

Cultural Identity and Authenticity

Similar to individuals and organizations, nations have essentialist characteristics such as geopolitical boundaries, governments, and physical infrastructures. As Salman Rushdie (1991) wryly noted in regard to questions of nationalism, "Does India exist? If it doesn't what's keeping Pakistan and Bangladesh apart?" But national identities are more than their geographic outlines, economies, technologies, and industries, with culture as an additional characteristic. National culture is the site of contested meanings, with the groups who wield more relative power able to define national identities and affect national regulatory bodies, which means national identity becomes closely linked to the notion of cultural identity.

One of the most common ways in which companies and individuals are referred to during everyday discussions is through the discourse of national identity, the idea that people and things from and within specific national borders have very particular, idiosyncratic, national characteristics. When one is attempting to make sense of practices or sounds and images from other places in the world, one of the most common tactics is to attribute an identity in terms of national distinctiveness (du Gay et al., 1997, p. 48).

Hofstede's cultural variables, discussed in chapter 4, are examples of this essentialist form of discourse and its prominence. Hofstede surveyed workers of different nationalities to determine average national values on four scales:

- Power distance
- Uncertainty avoidance
- Individualism
- Masculinity

When the results for members of each nation are compared, a unique cultural identity is declared. Members of Eastern European countries, for example, value hierarchy and formality, but these same power distance values are of almost no consequence to those from Scandinavian countries. But these average values for each nation obtained in surveys don't capture the context or the fluidity of identities, causing Edward Said, among many others, to question this approach: "The notion that there are geographic spaces with indigenous, radically 'different' inhabitants who can be defined on the basis of some religion, culture or racial essence proper to that geographic space is a highly debatable idea" (in Clifford, 1988, p. 274).

From such essentialist approaches to national identities, cultural stereotypes form, including what it means to be an authentic representation of the culture. In terms of the links between national and cultural identity, authenticity often is bound to a mythical past, a constructed heritage viewed nostalgically. In the United States, people of Scottish ancestry, or supposed Scottish ancestry, gather at Scottish festivals, where they dress in tartans assigned to them by tracing their genealogy, real or imagined, to clan membership and celebrate "traditional" arts and sports. The culture exhibited is far more aggressively and nostalgically "Scottish" than anything found in contemporary Scotland itself, but by faithfully recreating and representing the heritage vision, it acquires authenticity; it becomes the essence of Scotland in a way that Scotland itself isn't. In Baudrillard's (1981/1994) terms, it forms a **simulacrum,** *in which the simulation of reality becomes the reality.* Photo 8.1 shows a typical Scottish festival activity—the parade of tartans—in which "clan members" dressed in tartans associated with the clan march in solidarity with their newly constructed families and heritage.

This felt need on the part of some U.S. citizens to reclaim an authentic heritage based elsewhere may arise from the belief often found in Europe that the United States is too young as a nation to possess its own "authentic" culture. As with many postcolonial societies, the search for a cultural identity becomes carried on the back of combined identities such as Irish American, Italian American, Asian American, and African American.

The rooting of these identities in a constructed history and nostalgic past doesn't allow for modern intrusions. One Semester at Sea student was despondent after leaving Kenya because she had received e-mail from a Masai tribesman she had befriended there. In her view, his use of modern technology had removed any chance of his being a "true native"; he obviously couldn't be "authentic." Her experience had lost its luster of legitimacy; she felt cheated. Such encounters have led Chow (1993, p. 27) to sardonically ask, "Where have all the natives gone?"

At the U.S. Grandfather Mountain Highland Games, representatives from each clan in attendance march in the Parade of Tartans. The tartan has become an iconic symbol of Scottish heritage despite the fact that it wasn't a particularly common form of dress until the English outlawed its wearing in 1746 and Scots adopted it as a sign of rebellion.

Photo 8.1   Parade of Tartans

SOURCE: Photo courtesy of Hugh Morton.

Nation Building and Branding

The import of national identity can be evidenced in nation-building efforts and the growing practice of nation branding. Postcolonial nations must create a national identity where often unity doesn't exist along ethnic, religious, or other lines. Kenya, with its seven major tribal groups and division between the predominantly Muslim coastal areas, a relic of Arab colonization, and Christian inland areas, a relic of British colonization, is a good example. Many tribal members were uprooted and "repatriated" during British rule, breaking cultural ties with the land and undermining self-sufficiency and tribal membership. After many years of corrupt political rule, another legacy of the colonial system, the country suffers today from an average life expectancy of less than 48 years because of the growing AIDS epidemic. Additionally, regulatory sanctions taken by the United States and other Western nations have hurt its tourist-dependent economy. The gross domestic product per capita is $1,100, and 50% of the population lives below the poverty line.

In many such countries, the media are at least partially government controlled and often work in conjunction with the government on nation-building efforts. In these countries, the lines between government affairs, media, and public relations often are more blurred because of their shared mission. The Media Institute in Kenya, for example, is a press freedom organization that brings together practicing journalists and professionals in law, human rights, corporate communications, and human development. Although such partnerships seem antithetical in many Western nations, they play a crucial nation-building role in much of the developing world.

Previously, national images were constructed through diplomatic processes in times of peace and military propaganda in times of war. Now, part of the public relations function in many countries is the formation of a unified national brand that can attract foreign investment and tourists (Chong & Valencic, 2001). A government-backed public–private partnership in South Africa, including marketing, public relations, and media companies, funds a national branding campaign to reposition the country on the basis of its peaceful democracy and eco-tourism as "Alive with Possibility" (Von Bormann, 2003). The recent Brand Estonia project resulted in a successful campaign to promote the former Soviet republic as "a Nordic country with a twist" and a "small economic tiger" (in Gardner & Standaert, 2003).

A consortium in Nigeria is working without government support, in large part because the Nigerian brand to date has been one of government corruption (e.g., Transparency International rated the country the most corrupt in Africa for 2005). The thrust of this joint public relations and media effort isn't so much a unified brand as constructing a way for the world to deal directly with Nigerian companies, bypassing the corrupt government structure ("We Can Re-brand," 2004). As a senior research fellow in international relations noted, "Having a bad reputation or none at all is a serious handicap for a state seeking to remain competitive in the international arena. . . . Image and reputation are thus becoming essential parts of the state's strategic equity" (van Ham, 2001, pp. 2–3). National brands are supplanting nationalism, removing some of the inherent bipolarity of nationalism and replacing it with a "unique one among many" view, a trend that arises, in part, from globalization.

National and Cultural Identities in a Hybrid World

In a globalized world, geographic place no longer provides a strong sense of cultural identity, and conflating national and cultural identities becomes particularly problematic. For example, the second largest Spanish-speaking population in the world lives in Los Angeles, California (Katz, 2005). And what does the "Buy American" campaign mean when cars are produced by Japanese-owned companies in the United States from parts manufactured in Latin America? Combined with geographic displacement is the flow of ideas through new communication technologies, forming "a new communications geography" (Morley & Robins, 1995, p. 1), which brings issues of the relationship between culture and identity to the fore. When cultural communication is no longer based on shared history or space, it becomes difficult to define who constitutes the "other" in networked societies (Castells, 1996).

The term *multicultural* has acquired a wide range of meanings. It's become synonymous both with *diversity*, as developed countries are increasingly identified in terms of narrow market niches, and with *identification*, as a single world culture and globalized market segments emerge (Bhabha, 1996). Those who hang on to nostalgic notions of the authentic are appalled by the latter, as found in world music, fusion cuisine, and Masai tribesmen with e-mail accounts; for others, it represents the brave new world of emerging hybrid identities. Either way, the fact remains that lovers of Bob Marley's music form a global culture that is much more tangible in some ways than any national culture (Gilroy, 1997; Morley & Robins, 1995). Marley has become more than a deceased Jamaican reggae singer; he's become the living symbol of pan-African unity.

At the heart of these differing discourses surrounding multiculturalism is the global–local nexus, which we discussed in chapter 6. The global traditionally has been viewed as the more empowered of the bipolar pair, with the local the inevitable loser in any meeting. Following the reductionist logic common to national images, the concept of globalization has been reduced to Westernization, which has been ultimately reduced to Americanization and the fear that a monolithic, culturally bereft, materialistic, fast food nation was overtaking the world in a process of coca-colonization (Morley & Robins, 1995).

These concerns gave rise to the global imperialism thesis, which states that Western, and particularly U.S., media and influence are wiping out local cultures. But the thesis presumes that audiences are inactive, and, as we discussed in the last chapter, audiences are active partners in the production of meaning. Additionally, the rise of Japanese popular culture and its influence first in Asia and then throughout the West has also problematized the notion of Western-only domination.

In place of global imperialism, the circuit of culture suggests that what's happening is a concurrent development of a transglobal identity and resistance to it, which is strengthening localized identities. The rise of a transglobal identity has led companies such as Saatchi and Saatchi to define market segments in global terms: "Globalisation does not mean the end of segments. It means, instead, their expansion to worldwide proportions" (Morley & Robins, 1995, p. 113). Yet, to date, what appear to have worldwide appeal without concomitant localization are the high-end brands that globally convey a sense of belonging to the elite, such as Gucci, Prada, and Mercedes (Ohmae, 1989). For most products and issues, the key to global success is **polysemy:** *Products and issues can generate numerous possible meanings that can be interpreted and used locally.*

McDonald's is a case in point. Although it is a global brand, the experience of going to McDonald's is polysemic and locally interpreted. In the United States, the restaurant often is associated with children: Happy Meals® and playgrounds give parents a chance to eat out in a relaxed atmosphere with their children. In many Asian countries, the restaurant represents the American Dream and is a favorite place to take a date, particularly on Valentine's Day. As we noted earlier, in some Asian countries McDonald's is a place to spread out and get work done. In Europe, where the United States is often associated with a lack of social class, McDonald's often signifies a "there goes the neighborhood" identity with older citizens, which appeals to the rebellious sense of the younger.

As consumers appropriate global culture in local ways, identity is arising not within particular national boundaries but in the relationships between cultures and identities, forming an infinite variety of hybrid identities. Geographic space is no longer the defining element, which raises the question of difference and how we are to define identities without falling back on national boundaries or a constructed organizing dichotomy, such as East versus West.

Also noteworthy in this chapter is that much of the discussion references points made in earlier chapters. It reminds us that the moments are inextricably intertwined, and each informs the others. Examining the moment of identity as found in WHO's smallpox eradication campaign reinforces this point while allowing us to see the interplay of individual, group, organizational, cultural, and national identities.

CHAPTER SUMMARY

- Identities emerge from social constructions of meaning and in relation to what they are not.

- Identities are multiple, fluid, and both assumed and imposed.

- Stereotypes are a shorthand cultural classification system that depends on reductionist binary differences.

- New organizational identities cannot be assumed unless old identities are first disarticulated.

- Organizational identities are less fragmented when organizational actions are consistent with the identity constructed.

- National identities are both gaining in importance as a way to attract foreign investment and losing relevance as globalization brings an increasing mix of cultures across national boundaries.

- Globalization results in the formation of a transglobal identity and the creation of infinite hybrid identities.

Smallpox Eradication Campaign

The last case of smallpox outside the laboratory was reported in Somalia in 1977. For the next 2.5 years, WHO retained an independent commission to certify that smallpox was gone except for laboratory specimens. At the 33rd World Health Assembly in 1980, WHO's director general made the official announcement: Smallpox had been eradicated (Photo 8.2). From the original Soviet proposal at the 11th World Health Assembly in 1958 to the start of the intensified campaign in 1967 to the realization of campaign success, many identities of smallpox, of the campaign workers, and of the victims emerged.

We've touched on some of these identities in previous chapters. In the early years of the campaign, WHO created an identity of smallpox as an expensive nuisance to the developed world, which led these countries

Three former directors of the smallpox eradication program, Dr. J. Donald Millar, Dr. William H. Foege, and Dr. J. Michael Lane, look over the May 1980 issue of WHO's *World Health* magazine, which was devoted to coverage of smallpox eradication.

Photo 8.2   Three Former Directors of the Smallpox Eradication Program

SOURCE: Photo courtesy of CDC.

to contribute resources to the eradication campaign. Within WHO, many officials imposed an identity on the smallpox eradication unit under Dr. D. A. Henderson's direction as a bunch of mavericks who bucked the system. Although this identity led to internal bickering and a lack of cooperation, Henderson's flexible management style also empowered field workers, which was crucial to campaign success. On the consumption side, many peoples of the world worshipped smallpox as a deity, an identity that had large implications for how they responded to campaign messages and actions.

In this section, we further examine the identities that the campaign produced and imposed, and those that emerged and were adopted, over the course of the campaign. Because identities are defined by difference, we outline the major dichotomies that emerged, beginning with the national identity of the smallpox eradication unit.

NEGOTIATING NATIONAL VERSUS INTERNATIONAL IDENTITIES

As we mentioned in the regulatory discussion of the case, the United States, working through the Centers for Disease Control (CDC), took an early lead in eradication efforts in western Africa as part of a Cold War effort to gain influence over developing countries and thwart growing Soviet influence. Around the same time, the World Health Assembly voted to support the intensified effort, at which point WHO's director general placed Dr. D. A. Henderson of the CDC in charge, hoping to blame Henderson and the United States if the effort failed. Henderson was reluctant to take the post, in part because he was afraid his nationality would alienate the Soviets, who were crucial to the effort. The confluence of Henderson's leadership and the U.S. role in western Africa caused many international leaders and some of those in the WHO hierarchy to identify the campaign as a U.S. effort, despite the fact that the initial eradication proposal was a Soviet one and the body that ratified it was an international consortium. This U.S. identity was bolstered by the fact that a number of the high-profile public health doctors involved in the campaign were also from the United States.

Henderson actively fought this identity because he realized it could inhibit international cooperation (Hopkins, 1989). He worked to cultivate the Soviets, stressing the ultimate campaign goal and actively acknowledging their key contributions to the campaign. He surrendered control and gave the Pan American Health Organization autonomy to run the eradication campaign in Brazil because he knew it would not welcome aid linked to the United States. Within the overarching Cold War context, Henderson often had to prove to international leaders that he wasn't a CIA operative, a move that often proved difficult (Hopkins, 1989) given the discursive nature of identity.

Case Study

Case Study

Despite the perceived U.S. identity, the public health doctors who led the campaign came from many nations, including the Soviet Union, Japan, and France, although they shared notions of what constituted the identity of a public health doctor. For example, Dr. Lawrence Brilliant, age 29, had been living and studying in a Hindu temple in India with his Indian wife when the intensified campaign began there. Brilliant's religious instructor told him to leave the temple and use his skills to help the Indian people. When he applied for a position at the WHO office in New Delhi, however, Dr. Nicole Grasset of France repeatedly turned him down because of his youth, long hair, bushy beard, and indigenous clothing. After repeated applications, during which his appearance became increasingly more conservative, his persistence and ability to speak Hindi won out. Grasset hired him as an administrative assistant. Eventually he was able to step into a medical role, and he became one of the most successful members of the leadership team (Tucker, 2001; Photo 8.3).

Photo 8.3   Dr. Lawrence Brilliant Working in India

SOURCE: Photo courtesy of Dr. Lawrence Brilliant.

FIRST WORLD VERSUS THIRD WORLD VALUES

Just as Western notions determined what image was appropriate for a public health doctor, Western notions of science and medicine guided the campaign. For Western scientists, smallpox was a known entity and a scientific fact. WHO publications devoted pages to the exact scientific description of the disease: its specific size in nanometers, genetic structure, etiology, taxonomy (genus *Orthopoxvirus,* subfamily Chordopoxvirinae, family Poxviridae), and two major forms, variola major and variola minor. It was this very identity of smallpox that made an eradication campaign possible in the first place: Although modern medicine could not cure the disease, it had developed a vaccine. Because of this identity, the dominant discourse used throughout the campaign was one of scientific rigor and authority bolstered by technology, such as the development of freeze-dried vaccine and the bifurcated needle. Science was the strategy and technology the weapon in the war on smallpox.

For many consumers of the campaign, however, smallpox was not a scientific fact but a spiritual being. Vaccination wasn't a preventive but an abomination; it defied the deity's will. Faced with this competing discourse, Western scientists dismissed it as ignorant and an impediment to progress. Anthropologists and public health specialists blamed "fear and superstition" (Morgan, 1969, p. 80) for "hav[ing] substantially retarded the progress and success of the . . . smallpox eradication programme" (Mather & John, 1973, p. 195). An official WHO account of the campaign in Bangladesh blames vaccination refusal on "ignorance of its benefits" (Joarder et al., 1980, p. 179). Within the prevailing scientific discourse, the answer to ignorance was education, leading WHO to prepare numerous educational materials for campaign use.

As the campaign progressed, however, many workers found that educational approaches sometimes failed to achieve campaign objectives because they didn't create a shared identity between producers and consumers; the language of Western science didn't address the spiritual issues of audience members. As noted in chapter 7, workers were more successful when they co-opted the religion and put campaign objectives in terms of religious values and language. However, many workers remained dismissive of these measures, seeing them only as means to an end. Some observed rather paternalistically that a spiritual cause demanded a spiritual cure, even if it was an inherently "pre-scientific" and "irrational" approach (Imperato & Traoré, 1968, p. 228; Mather & John, 1973, p. 195). The authors of this book found only one instance in which a Western scientist acknowledged the legitimacy of the people's closely held religious views, suggesting that attributing vaccination resistance to ignorance was incorrect and that a more holistic approach to medicine and spirituality was needed to connect with the attitudes and beliefs of worshippers (Morinis, 1978).

Case Study

Concurrent with the dominant discourse that labeled many potential victims ignorant, an emergent identity was that of smallpox as a disease of the poor. Although smallpox crossed all race, class, and income lines, as mentioned earlier, India's prime minister Indira Gandhi called it a "disease of economic backwardness" (in Brilliant, 1985, p. 87). Early technical reports stressed the possibility of spreading infection through bedding and clothing, making the disease more likely among lower socioeconomic groups, such as chambermaids and laundry workers. These same reports warned that mild ambulatory cases were likely among "tramps and other itinerants" (WHO, 1964, p. 11). In India, workers developed separate strategies to target the lower castes, namely "beggars, hawkers, rickshaw and handcart pullers, daily laborers, cobblers, scrap pickers and domestic servants" (Basu et al., 1979, p. 173). From these representations, smallpox's identity became that of a disease of the poor, despite all evidence to the contrary. Victims became disempowered and disenfranchised because their disease equated them with indigence and ignorance.

In turn, potential victims often rejected foreign intrusion in their personal lives, distrusting vaccinators as colonizers and construing vaccination as a threat (Thaung & Ko Ko, 2002). The situation was similar to that of the 19th-century United States, when many Native Americans declined vaccination because they believed that anything the white invaders were pushing on them must, by definition, constitute another means of subjugation (Hopkins, 2002). Many people distrusted government officials because they were often associated with tax collection, military conscription, or, in the case of India, family planning campaigns. WHO field workers there had to dispel rumors that they were performing vasectomies (Hopkins, 1989). The inherent power difference between government health officials and target publics led to distrust and vaccination resistance, threatening the success of the campaign. WHO workers had to find a way to overcome lingering resistance if the campaign was to be successful.

HOLY WARRIORS VERSUS THE ENEMY

Most WHO workers did not self-identify as colonizers or subjugators, although one Western worker in India candidly reported that "I was a white man in that society, and I could do things that others couldn't do . . . and get away with it" (T. Stephen Jones, in Greenough, 1995, pp. 637–638). However, most workers self-identified as saviors, expressing an almost religious devotion to the cause. They endured the harsh field conditions because they were true believers in the righteousness of their work.

In 1974, for example, Henderson met with a team that had been in the field in India for 4 months straight. Besides being clinically underweight and exhausted, they were variously suffering from severe kidney and fungal infections, shingles, and pneumonia. But they refused to quit, saying, "We've considered the question and have decided that things can't get worse therefore they must get better" (in Fenner et al., 1988, p. 764). Dr. Lawrence Brilliant described this religious fervor toward eradication as becoming caught up in the "infection of zeropox": the belief in the need to achieve eradication at all costs (1985, p. 71).

Although the workers' zeal resulted in a strong esprit de corps remarked on by many campaign observers, when it was combined with the key campaign message of a global war on smallpox, the workers became holy warriors united against a dehumanized enemy. Potential victims in developing countries, disempowered through their identification as poor and ignorant, became collateral damage in the war as workers used force to subdue the enemy. As one worker recalled,

> I was doing good. I was religiously fervid. I was a crusader. . . . There was a clear commitment to working on something that was for the benefit of people. . . . I became so convinced of that, that I did some very excessive things in the name of righteousness. (T. Stephen Jones, in Greenough, 1995, p. 637)

Or as a Peace Corps volunteer with the campaign simply stated, "I just did not take no for an answer when looking for smallpox" (in Andersson, 1996, p. 2).

The use of force to achieve eradication took many forms. Workers withheld food ration cards from the poor in India and relief supplies from east Pakistani refugees unless they agreed to vaccination. They used military escorts, roadblocks, and police cordons throughout Africa to force vaccination acceptance. People in endemic areas were forcibly restrained and vaccinated regardless of age, nutritional status, or medical condition, even though in nonendemic countries WHO (1972) advised that vaccination was contraindicated in cases of compromised immune system and pregnancy. When workers discovered active cases, they isolated the victims, posting four to eight watch guards around the isolation house or hut to prevent the victim's escape. The guards were not paid until the end of the quarantine period, and if one was ever found missing, all were dismissed without pay. The victim became an involuntary prisoner; the watch guards were imprisoned by their conditions of employment.

As the number of endemic countries grew fewer and success seemed imminent, workers used increasing degrees of force. Before the start of the intensified campaign, workers in India avoided force because it was contrary to the basic tenet of Indian society of respect for the individual (Basu et al., 1979). One CDC epidemiologist working in India recalled that when "Operation Zeropox" went into effect, however, it was

Case Study

marked by an almost military style attack on infected villages. . . . In the hit-and-run excitement of such a campaign, women and children were often pulled out from under beds, from behind doors, from within latrines, etc. People were chased and, when caught, vaccinated. . . . We considered the villagers to have an understandable though irrational fear of vaccination. . . . We just couldn't let people get smallpox needlessly. We went from door to door and vaccinated. When they ran, we chased. When they locked their doors, we broke down their doors and vaccinated them. (S. Music, in Greenough, 1995, pp. 635–636)

When an outbreak occurred in the state of Bihar in northern India, Dr. Lawrence Brilliant barricaded all roads surrounding a major city, and no one was allowed to pass without being vaccinated. When an outbreak occurred at a pilgrimage site for the Jain religion, a nonviolent sect who refused smallpox vaccination because of its animal origins, Bihar military police surrounded the village and placed 24-hour watch guards on duty. Pilgrims, who had gathered to mark the anniversary of the death of the religion's founder, could enter the sacred site only if they agreed to be vaccinated. Some agreed, but many didn't, resulting in workers forcefully vaccinating pacifist worshippers on one of their holiest days.

Brilliant recalls that during this outbreak "zealous epidemiologists occasionally made night raids to vaccinate a whole village at a time" (1985, p. 57). In one instance, a district magistrate authorized a late-night raid on a family compound because the residents had refused vaccination for religious reasons. Workers scaled the walls and vaccinated family members after a protracted struggle during which the male head of household bit the doctor. As soon as the struggle was over, the man quietly offered the workers food. He explained that he understood the workers had been conscientiously following their beliefs just as he had been following his, which included offering anyone in his house, no matter the circumstances, the hospitality of food (Brilliant, 1985; Tucker, 2001). He explained his actions this way:

My dharma [moral duty] is to surrender to God's will. Only God can decide who gets sickness and who does not. It is my duty to resist your needles. We must resist your needles. We would die resisting if that is necessary. My family and I have not yielded. We have done our duty. We can be proud of having been firm in our faith. It is not a sin to be overpowered by so many strangers in the middle of the night. Daily you have come to me and told me it is *your* dharma to prevent this disease with your needles. We have sent you away. Tonight you have broken down my door and used force. You say you act in accordance with *your* duty. I have acted according to mine. It is over. God will decide. (Brilliant & Brilliant, 1978, p. 5)

The shamefaced workers retreated. WHO's official campaign record observes that many of the "workers were suffering at one time from human bites" (Fenner et al., 1988, p. 1017).

Not all workers used force. Some decried it, such as Dr. David Greaves (2001), who worked on the campaign in Bangladesh in 1975. He blames the "battlefield mentality" and "jingoistic fervor" generated for spawning colonial attitudes in many workers and a feeling of success at any cost at WHO headquarters (p. 1190). However, campaign leaders retrospectively concluded that coercion, such as withholding food and supplies from war refugees, was effective in some circumstances. By not condemning its use, they implicitly condoned physical violence. For them, the ends of the campaign justified the means, and force became a strategic campaign tactic.

Photo 8.4   Media Gathered to Photograph 3-Year-Old Rahima Banu, the Last Variola Major Case

SOURCE: Photo courtesy of CDC, WHO, and Stanley O. Foster, M.D., M.P.H.

Case Study

CREATING CAMPAIGN ICONS

As campaign success appeared imminent, WHO worked to achieve maximum publicity for the last case in each of the remaining endemic countries. They ferried media to remote areas to record the last case for posterity and made stock photographs available to media who couldn't, or didn't, make the trek. In Bangladesh, 3-year-old Rahima Banu, living on a remote island, was the last case of variola major, the more virulent strain of smallpox (Photo 8.4). In India, 30-year-old Saiban Bibi, an itinerant woman living by begging on a rail station platform, was the last recorded case. WHO workers placed her in isolation in a hospital, sur-rounded by watch guards, and shut down the whole hospital except for emergencies, strictly limiting and controlling staff activity.

The last endemic area encompassed the disputed Ogaden Desert area between Ethiopia and Somalia. Despite ongoing border skirmishes, officials from both countries met to discuss eradication strategy, but each side exaggerated the measures it was taking to appear superior to the other. These meetings became increasingly acrimonious, with each side disparaging the other's program. When WHO finally declared one—Ethiopia—free of the disease, the Somali WHO representative reported large repercussions for international relations:

> Government authorities have resented the fact that Ethiopia has been declared free of smallpox almost at the same time as Somalia was declared as the last known infected focus in the world. This is viewed as some kind of international conspiracy and the influx of WHO smallpox experts as adverse publicity for Somalia. (Fenner et al., 1988, pp. 1046–1047)

The stigma of being the last fell on Somalia when Ali Maalin, a 28-year-old part-time hospital cook, went into the history books as the last recorded case of smallpox outside the laboratory. Maalin, who had been misdiagnosed with chicken pox, was a former temporary vaccinator with WHO, and he was fairly sure he had smallpox. He didn't report himself because he wanted to avoid isolation, but a hospital coworker turned him in for the reward. As a hospital worker he had been in contact with many people, and WHO workers rushed to vaccinate his entire ward, put up a roadblock into town, established checkpoints along footpaths, widely publicized the reward for reports of any new cases, and held their breath.

When no new cases appeared, WHO invited media in to record the event, and Maalin found himself the center of a global media circus (Photo 8.5). Typical of the resulting coverage was a *New York Times* arti-cle that called him "a living, contagious threat to one of the world's great public health accomplishments," as if he were personally responsible for the near demise of "humanity's first successful war of annihilation against an infectious disease" (Schmeck, 1978, p. E9).

In each of the three last cases, ordinary people who otherwise would never be known to the outside world became the center of global media attention. A 3-year-old girl, a beggar, and a part-time cook, living in rel-ative obscurity in developing countries, became involuntary war heroes in a global battle not of their choosing. Their private lives became public fodder. WHO publicity made them iconic figures, and their images became synonymous with the triumph of Western science and technol-ogy over the ignorance of the developing world.

WHO held a ceremony marking the 10-year anniversary of eradication, during which a WHO representative presented Maalin with a bouquet of roses, an event also recorded for posterity (Bazin, 2000). One can only imagine what Maalin thought of the occasion and what he did with the flowers, especially because his little sister died of measles, another disease preventable by vaccination and the focus of earlier U.S. efforts to gain support on the African continent.

IMPLICATIONS FOR INTERNATIONAL PRACTICE

One implication for any "international" public relations campaign is that publics often don't view the campaign as truly international, even when it stems from an international body such as the World Health Assembly. Publics imposed a U.S. identity on the eradication campaign, which proved hard to shake. Almost invariably, publics define groups, organizations, and causes by assigning them to certain geopolitical units: Toyota is Japanese, even when the cars are assembled in the United States; Nikes are American, despite being made in Asia. Although companies such as Honda have actively worked to avoid geocentricism and assume an international identity, consumers in the United States who subscribe to "Buy American" campaigns boycott the company's products based on an identification of the company as Japanese.

Power differentials, which draw attention to the political aspects of identity, are inherent in both assumed and imposed identities. In the case of the eradication campaign, "encounters with government vaccinators

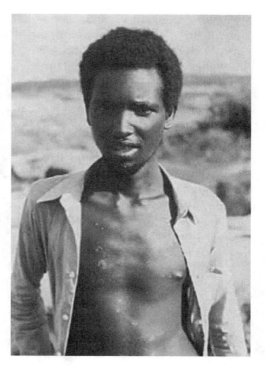

Pockmarks are readily visible on his chest and abdomen.

Photo 8.5   Somalian Hospital Worker Ali Maalin, the Last Documented Case of the Campaign

SOURCE: Photo courtesy of WHO.

Case Study

are never about immunization alone. Public health measures derive their authority from the police powers of the state" (Greenough, 1995, p. 635). Given WHO's organizational mission of "the attainment by all peoples of the highest possible level of health" and the feasibility of ridding the world of a deadly disease, smallpox eradication was an inherently worthy goal. But the political ramifications of the campaign extended well beyond the organization and its mission, and the campaign accumulated new meanings among consumers from national to local levels as new identities formed.

Another lesson of the campaign is that short-term objectives must be weighed against long-term consequences. Although the architects of the campaign believed coercion was effective in some instances, many disagreed. Just a few months after eradication was announced, the eradication program was criticized at a major public health conference as "anachronistic, authoritarian, [and] 'top down'" (Henderson, 1998, p. 17). It's a criticism that continues to haunt WHO today.

When working cross-culturally with populations who have limited and infrequent contact with an organization, memories can be long and missteps continue to resonate many years later. In 1988, WHO launched another eradication campaign, this one against polio (Photo 8.6).

Photo 8.6   Polio Eradication Campaign Workers in Sierra Leone Encouraging People to Have Their Children Vaccinated During National Immunization Day

SOURCE: Photo courtesy of WHO.

In northern Nigeria, however, vaccinators have met with strong resistance from Muslims, who are skeptical of Western motives in sponsoring the campaign. As in India about 40 years previously, rumors are flying that the campaign is really an attempt to render Muslims infertile ("Nigeria Polio Vaccine," 2003, ¶ 4). In Java, 62% of parents in one village refused to let their children be vaccinated because of fears over the safety of the vaccine and rumors that it violates Islamic law because it was produced from monkeys (Casey, 2005).

As history repeats itself, WHO has pledged it won't administer polio vaccine without consent, but it cannot escape the legacy of the smallpox campaign, which is fueling resistance. Once again, the organization is turning to education as the answer, relying on the expert power of science and on laboratory tests to assure citizens of the vaccine's purity ("Nigeria Polio Vaccine," 2003). But Western, scientific discourse is not creating a shared identity with the religious beliefs of the public, and campaign workers are encountering heavy resistance as villagers set their dogs on them (MacKenzie, 2004).

Although the political context has changed from that of the Cold War to that of West versus East, dichotomies of identity are once again contributing to campaign failure, and the lessons of the past do not seem to be informing the decisions of the present. This example demonstrates how the moment of identity is a crucial, and often overlooked, component of international public relations campaigns. Establishing identities with which both producers and consumers can resonate should be a major goal of any public relations effort.

In chapter 9 we come full circle, bringing the five moments of the circuit together to provide a more synergistic look at how they function as whole.

Case Study

9

Capturing the Synergy of the Circuit

The Cultural–Economic Model

❖ ❖ ❖

Thomas Friedman was referring to globalization, but he may as well have been talking about the circuit of culture when he said, "With a complex non-linear system you have to break it up into pieces and then study each aspect, and then study the very strong interaction between them all. Only this way can you describe the whole system" (1999, p. 24). This chapter brings together the five moments of the circuit addressed separately in the last five chapters to examine the implications of their synergy for international public relations practice.

We begin where we left off, with the smallpox eradication case, briefly examining how the five moments worked together throughout the campaign and the larger ramifications of those connections. We then apply the principles gained from using the integration of the moments to outline a new model of international public relations practice: the cultural–economic model, a label that embraces culture as the currency of the globalized information age.

❖ LESSONS FROM THE SMALLPOX
    ERADICATION CAMPAIGN

Looking back over the smallpox eradication campaign, we can see how
the moments inform each other. In fact, it's quite difficult to talk about
them separately and to parse the case into separate moments. Consider
the international regulatory environment in which the campaign took
place: the Cold War. This regulatory environment affected production
because the rivalry between the United States and the Soviets led to an
early lack of U.S. support for the campaign. Only when the campaign
was tied to U.S. Cold War political goals, such as increasing influence
in developing countries to stem communism, did campaign producers
receive from the United States the money, supplies, and personnel
necessary to achieve their objectives. In turn, although the campaign
was originally a Soviet initiative and Soviets competed with the United
States to supply the campaign, it acquired a U.S. identity when
Dr. D. A. Henderson was hired in the mid-1960s.

As the Soviets and the United States vied to use the campaign to
achieve political and economic goals, a discourse of neocolonialism
developed. The developed world created and imposed an identity of
disempowered people on residents of the developing world where
smallpox was still endemic. This identity represented an economic
threat to the developed world, not a moral duty to provide humanitarian aid. However, consumers fought the identity imposed on them by
not reporting cases, causing campaign leaders to rethink their production and representation strategies. Conversely, WHO created a representation of smallpox as a moral issue in the developing world through
the discourse of shame used to achieve compliance with eradication
efforts. WHO published case numbers by country as representations of
backwardness; the higher the number of cases, the more backward and
irresponsible the identity of the government.

As this one small example demonstrates, by pulling the Cold War
regulatory thread, we begin to unravel the entire circuit. Similarly, we
can pick apart the threads that form the web of meaning surrounding WHO's representation of smallpox as the enemy. For the mainly
Western workers producing the campaign, smallpox existed as a scientific fact, making technology the weapon of choice and scientific know-
how the winning strategy. For consumers, however, smallpox was
incorporated into their everyday lives and regulatory environments
through its numerous identities, such as a deity or inevitable fact of life.
To use technology against a deity was pointless, if not immoral. In these

instances, some producers created a new meaning, a shared identity, by blending vaccination with existing religious beliefs to achieve campaign goals. However, producers who identified consumers as ignorant because they did not subscribe to Western science justified force as a tactic of production. In turn, WHO's use of force created for some an identity of the international agency as an abusive, colonial power.

We should never forget, then, that the moments are always interrelated, always shaping each other. Their intersection defines the bounds of possible meanings that can arise at any particular point in time, that is, in any given articulation. However, they don't predetermine the particular meaning that will arise. Because meanings are variable, changing, and contextually bound, consumers adopted vaccination into their everyday lives in ways the moments couldn't predict. Although the moments provide general guidance for a campaign, then, they never determine what will emerge in any particular situation. The moments give us guiding principles, but as practitioners we must remain open to the particular circumstances of any given situation.

The Competing Discourses of Smallpox Eradication

Another insight gained from applying the circuit of culture to the smallpox eradication case is that meaning is never static or monolithic. To clarify, let's examine the competing discourses that emerged after eradication. Dr. D. A. Henderson (1998) used the word *quixotic* to describe eradication, connoting the role of luck or chance in achieving campaign objectives. Compare that perspective with the one put forth by WHO's director general: a public health miracle. By being cast as a miracle, eradication became an achievement blessed by fates or gods, lending moral superiority to it, and its complexities were reduced to a simple, singular event. A subsequent editorial in the *Washington Post* ("A Modern Miracle," 1979, p. A26) stated, "The banding together of people everywhere without regard to politics or national glory, to defeat a common enemy—is the true miracle." By reducing events in this manner, the dominant discourse wrote out of consideration many crucial conflicts that drove the campaign, such as the Cold War politics that affected production and the resistance that arose from smallpox's identity as a deity in some countries.

Nations developed their own posteradication discourses that presented narrow perspectives that rewrote history. In the official WHO account of the campaign in India, for example, an Indian health official recounts,

One of the most gratifying features of this programme is the
unified and effective way in which the Government of India and
the World Health Organisation have collaborated. At every level
national and WHO staff worked shoulder to shoulder, pursuing
their goal with technical competence, dedication and enthusiasm.
(S. Gunaratne, in Basu et al., 1979, p. v)

In actuality, many WHO officials considered India one of the most difficult countries to work with and in because of its bureaucratic healthcare system and lack of enthusiasm for a health campaign addressing
only a single issue: smallpox.

Dr. Larry Brilliant (1985) presents a competing perspective in his
memoirs of the campaign, noting that both WHO and the Indian government used each other for leverage within their own organizations to
achieve their own objectives. In Brilliant's terms, the relationship was a
marriage of necessity marked by behind-the-scenes maneuvering, not
of mutual support and transparency. However, the official version
notes that "no strong cultural or religious resistance to vaccination sufficient to have any influence on the programme was encountered"
(Basu et al., 1979, p. 112). Written out of history are a host of issues,
such as the need to change strategy and tactics to vaccinate Shitala
worshippers and the use of force to vaccinate villagers in midnight
raids and pacifist believers on holy days at pilgrimage sites.
Reinforcing this reductionist history is the photographic record, which
shows only people willingly lining up to be vaccinated or to receive
rewards for reporting a case (Photo 9.1).

U.S. discourse recast the campaign in ownership and self-congrat-
ulatory terms. Although Dr. D. A. Henderson worked hard to remove
the U.S. identity imposed on the campaign, after the campaign many in
the country claimed credit for campaign success. A *Washington Post*
article in late 1979 credited the sophistication and intelligence of the
campaign to U.S. leadership and stated that "U.S. money of course pre-
dominated" (Cohn, 1979, p. A2). A 1978 report from the U.S. Centers
for Disease Control declared that the United States could be proud that
it contributed so much to eradicating a disease that "no longer
involved our nation," concluding that "for the first time, social justice
in public health had been achieved" (Foege & Dowdle, 1997, p. 992).

The campaign as a representation of social justice became a dominant discourse in the years after the campaign. This packaging of
events wiped from collective memory the exercise of government
authority to vaccinate people against their will and the lack of rights
for developing countries to determine their own greatest health needs

All rewards were handed out in public ceremonies.

Photo 9.1   An 8-Year-Old Girl Receives Her Reward for Reporting a
Smallpox Case

SOURCE: Photo courtesy of CDC, WHO, and Stanley O. Foster, M.D., M.P.H.

and address them. For example, Dr. Lawrence Altman (1979) said the
campaign made public health doctors think more about how to apply
their work to improve the quality of life in other countries. Left unsaid
and unexamined was the need for those same doctors to work with
people in developing countries to determine just how they defined
their health needs and quality of life. Instead, the dominant narrative
established a discourse of neocolonialism and dependency, with
Western science providing aid for those deemed less fortunate,
whether they wanted it or not (Photo 9.2). Written out of consideration
were issues of national sovereignty, informed consent, and citizen
rights (Das, 1999).

A recent, far more critical counterdiscourse has emerged surrounding eradication efforts as vertical insertion campaigns, meaning
that they use dedicated personnel to address one issue only, ignoring
broader health issues. Since smallpox eradication, single-issue health
campaigns have proliferated, leading to what one critic has called
"eradicationitis" (Godlee, 1995, p. 181). One reason for the proliferation
is the desire of donor nations to control how their funds are spent. As
one European aid organization spokesperson said, "We invest in these

Photo 9.2   A Public Celebration in Ghana, Featuring U.S. Secretary
General William Stuart, Marked Rebecca Ansah Asamoah
Receiving the 25 Millionth Smallpox Vaccination
of the Campaign

SOURCE: Photo courtesy of CDC.

programmes because we have control over what we invest in. If we
don't like what happens we can vote with our cheque book" (in
Godlee, 1995, p. 179).

It's become controversial to address health issues singly, however,
particularly when a campaign involves outside interference in internal
affairs. The one vertical insertion program that has been effective—
onchocerciasis (river blindness) control—differs because it grew out of
a direct request from the peoples and governments of seven African
countries, giving them campaign ownership. Recent discourse surrounding international health campaigns focuses on the U.N.'s eight
Millennium Development Goals, which are designed to use a more
holistic approach to "meet the needs of the world's poorest" (U.N., n.d.,
¶ 1). Neocolonialism still lurks, however, with developed countries
and international development institutions, such as the World Bank,
empowered to determine appropriate assistance and technology to
meet these goals.

Bringing the Circuit Full Circle

Another lesson gleaned from examining the eradication case in its totality through the lens of the circuit of culture is that issues and narratives go through cycles that are context dependent. Although WHO officials declared smallpox officially dead in 1980, smallpox stocks remained in U.S. and Russian laboratories for scientific research purposes. However, U.S. intelligence reports released in 1999 and 2000 indicated that other countries, such as North Korea and Iraq, had obtained the virus and that Japan's Aum Shinrikyo sect and Osama bin Laden might also possess smallpox stocks (Creehan, 2001).

Ironically, the success of the smallpox eradication campaign led to new fears that with the cessation of vaccination, the world was more vulnerable than ever to smallpox. Based on these reports and fears after September 11, 2001, the U.S. government established the Office of Public Health Preparedness. To lead the new unit the government tapped the world's expert on dealing with smallpox outbreaks: Dr. D. A. Henderson.

Suddenly, smallpox was once again on the world's agenda, having gained new saliency. Figure 9.1 shows the sharp increase in the number of stories about smallpox in major papers before and after September 11. It also demonstrates Down's (1972) **issue attention cycle:** *Certain issues come into prominence through precipitating events, such as September 11, then remain on the agenda for a short period of time before dropping off, still largely unresolved as the issue loses salience.* What the graph doesn't demonstrate

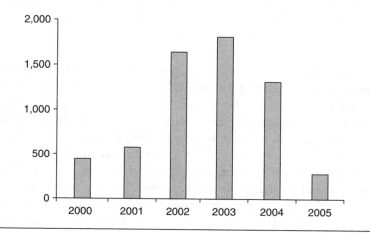

Figure 9.1   Number of Stories Concerning Smallpox Appearing in Major Papers From 2000 to 2005, as Determined by a Lexis-Nexis Search

is how dominant discourses changed over this same period, from WHO's public health miracle and model public health campaign to a tool of terrorism against the developing world.

Examining the circuit of culture as a whole, then, allows us to see how the five moments work together to construct multiple meanings around any given issue and how dominant discourses emerge and change over time. It also demonstrates how competing discourses emerge from different contexts, making it an insightful tool for international work.

❖ NEEDED: A NEW MODEL OF INTERNATIONAL PUBLIC RELATIONS PRACTICE

The insights gained by applying the circuit of culture to international public relations practice point to the need for a new, iterative model of public relations that embraces the interrelationships of culture, identity, and power. To demonstrate what a new model would entail, it helps to examine the underlying suppositions of current models of practice.

Most Western approaches to public relations practice are built on a linear communication model. The research, action and planning, communication, evaluation (RACE) model of practice, for example, delineates clear campaign beginning and end points, with consecutive steps in between. Practitioners research an issue, develop key messages, and place them in appropriate media, which are then distributed to the target audience at the end of the communication chain. To ensure that the message was clearly communicated, practitioners perform evaluative research.

The RACE model clearly privileges the producer of information as the origination point of all communication and assumes that audiences are passive receivers of information. But as we discussed in chapter 7, publics actively construct their own meanings and are, in fact, producers of messages as well. However, linear models are not dynamic enough to account for audiences as active meaning makers.

Other problems with practice standards based on a linear communication model stem from the underlying assumptions concerning the ideal political and economic environment in which such a model can function. Most Western approaches to public relations practice are based in **neoliberal political–economic thought,** *which proposes that the greatest social, political, and economic good results from the free flow of capital and a free market system.* Consequently, public relations cannot function in anything other than a democracy; without democracy you don't have public relations, you have propaganda. Within democracies, public relations contributes to the free flow of ideas and information. As the Public Relations Society of America's member statement of professional values explicitly states, "We provide a voice in the marketplace of ideas, fact, and viewpoints to aid informed public debate."

However, to link public relations to democracy privileges a Western notion of what public relations is and isn't. It ignores public relations practices in many other areas of the world, including some that dominant Western discourse labels propaganda. It also equates public relations success with contributions to the organizational bottom line. The Western literature is replete with theory and techniques for proving public relations effective in supporting organizational economic goals, such as strategic planning and management by objective, segmenting publics according to their value to the organization, and insisting that public relations be a management function.

This strong economic underpinning drives much criticism of public relations as a profession. Rejecting neoliberal political–economic thought, the **critical political–economic approach** *states that public relations contributes to structural inequalities of power, prestige, and profit in capitalist systems* (Hesmondhalgh, 2002). This perspective positions public relations as a tool of the wealthy and powerful to remain wealthy and powerful, conflating public relations and propaganda. Perhaps the most outspoken U.S. proponents of this view are John Stauber and Sheldon Rampton, founders of the Center for Media and Democracy, publishers of *PR Watch,* and authors of *Toxic Sludge Is Good for You: Lies, Damn Lies and the Public Relations Industry.* In Stauber's words, "We're the most propagandized people in history because the type of propaganda that's waged in western democracies is waged by commercial advertising, marketing, and especially public relations" (Media Education Foundation, 2002, p. 2).

We agree with Fraser Seitel (2000, ¶ 1) that "the practice of public relations is neither some sinister, surreptitious force nor the exclusive province of the rich and powerful." The leaders of the civil rights movement in the United States, for example, made masterful use of public relations techniques to draw attention to their cause and empower their constituents. And the success of MoveOn.org in organizing grassroots political action in the United States also speaks to the power of public relations practice to enable all, not just the wealthy and empowered. What is needed is a new model that accounts for public relations as a discursive practice.

❖ THE CULTURAL–ECONOMIC MODEL OF
INTERNATIONAL PUBLIC RELATIONS PRACTICE

Using the circuit of culture as an analytic lens suggests a model of international practice that neither dichotomizes nor conflates public relations and propaganda and that neither privileges nor demonizes public relations practice. It informs a model that embraces the rich variety of public relations functions and formats found throughout the world. We call this new way of thinking about international public relations practice the **cultural–economic model**, *which encompasses the notion that public relations is predicated on communicative relationships, and culture is a constitutive part of any communicative enterprise.* The model makes culture, used in the broad sense of the term, the currency of a globalized world operating within an information economy (Castells, 1996).

Whereas political–economic approaches privilege the structures of communicative enterprises such as public relations, the cultural–economic model stresses the meanings and values associated with those structures. It doesn't deny the role of the political in informing practice, but it shifts the emphasis from the structures themselves to the relationships between them and the meanings generated by and through those relationships. In other words, it's an iterative, discursive model rather than a linear one. It positions the creation of meaning not as an absolute created by producers and conveyed to audiences with varying degrees of clarity but as a contested process among producers and consumers who occupy differing positions of relative power depending on circumstance and who are both producers and consumers at any given time. The advantage of the model is that it accounts for "truth" as contested ground, allowing practitioners to successfully negotiate the competing discourses surrounding culture, identity, and power that underlie all international public relations work.

The Centrality of Culture

By using the circuit of culture as a base, the cultural–economic model places culture squarely at the center of public relations practice. As we discussed in chapter 3, we don't mean culture as the shared norms and habits of a particular place or people. We mean culture as a process and a space in which meanings are constituted and competing discourses emerge. Each moment of the circuit produces a range of meanings, with each moment constrained by the range of meanings produced in each of the other moments.

An important lesson for practice, then, is that cultural texts or artifacts, such as public relations campaigns and their related tactics, are polysemic, containing more than one possible interpretation or meaning. Meanings are always constructed within the range allowed by institutional frameworks and then reconstructed as consumers use them in their particular social situations. "The meaning that any object has at any given time is a contingent, historical achievement" (du Gay, 1996, p. 47).

By placing culture at the heart of practice, the cultural–economic model allows practitioners to balance the ethnocentric and polycentric approaches to practice, as discussed in chapter 6. Built into the model is an inherent tension between the institutional and the situational, between culture as a way of life and culture as the production and circulation of meanings. The model embraces a degree of cultural relativism, but it does so within the structured framework provided by the five moments. It allows practitioners to maintain professional standards and norms while remaining flexible and open to other perspectives and ways of seeing, an approach well demonstrated by the smallpox eradication campaign.

The cultural–economic model's emphasis on communicative relationships positions public relations as a process. The model allows practitioners not only to be open to change but to expect change, eschewing management models of practice that counsel strict adherence to preordained strategic plans. As one analyst of the smallpox eradication campaign observed, a key lesson of the campaign is the need to "insure that organization members do not begin to reify beliefs and deify conventional modes and objectives" (Hopkins, 1989, p. 127). In other words, we need to realize that effective public relations practice results more from continuous environmental monitoring and responsiveness than from strictly adhering to a strategic plan.

However, we don't want to suggest that planning has no place and all is situational. The cultural–economic model accounts for structure as well as relational flux, providing practitioners with a way to balance trends and patterns with the particular circumstances that arise in any given situation.

The Question of Identity in a Globalized World

The cultural–economic model also provides guidance to practitioners negotiating issues of identity in an increasingly globalized world marked by diaspora and hybridity. **Diaspora** *is the dispersal of ethnic groups from their homelands.* For example, a large Pakistani community calls Britain home, and the largest concentration of Japanese outside Japan is found in Brazil. Concurrent with diaspora is the notion of increasing **hybridity,** *the rise of multiple new forms of overlapping identities.* As we discussed earlier, Turkey is a hybrid of East and West, of Europe and Islam, forming a new identity that is neither European nor Islamic. At the individual level, ethnicity can no longer be viewed pragmatically as comprising mutually exclusive categories, and living in multicultural societies leads individuals to develop ethnic identities with varying salience in their lives (Jamal, 2003).

The model also accounts for another form of hybridity, that of glocalization. Diaspora and hybridity remove the West as the central, defining concept of place and culture and replace it with endless combinations of forms that have no fixed reference. In an increasingly globalized world, notions of space, including the role of the nation and of national cultures, are becoming increasingly problematic. We can no longer speak of a monolithic national culture. Practitioners must be open to myriad hybrid forms of the global and the local, which have no central defining point or location. Whereas neoliberal models of international public relations practice often simply append Hofstede's and Hall's monolithic cultural indices and constructs onto Western forms of practice, the cultural–economic model accounts for the multitudinous, shifting identities that arise in a globalized world.

The cultural–economic model of practice allows practitioners to recognize and appreciate the ways in which publics adopt and adapt aspects of other cultures and practices into their own. It cautions against forcing publics into mutually exclusive slots and defining publics or issues in dichotomized terms that reduce difference. Global publics are constantly in flux, coalescing around issues such as environmentalism and vegetarianism. In areas where technology is widely available, these publics often form in cyberspace, making proximity an increasingly less important consideration in global campaigns.

Unlike the segmentation approach endorsed by neoliberal models, the cultural–economic model of public relations practice reminds us that both as individuals and as a group, publics seldom fit any one segment, group, or category. Practitioners must use a wide range of ethnographic methods to understand the meanings created by publics and to keep abreast of their shift and flow. The smallpox eradication campaign effectively demonstrates the value of continuous field assessments for increasing the efficacy of campaign strategies.

The Micropolitics of Power

The cultural–economic model posits that public relations is predicated on communicative relationships, and inherent in relationships are issues of relative power. The model builds on Foucault's notion that power is inherent in relations themselves, not in the elements of the relationship, as we discussed in chapter 3. Depending on circumstances, then, power can shift. Which discourse will dominate in any given situation isn't preordained: "Discourse transmits and produces power; it reinforces it, but also undermines and exposes it, renders it fragile and makes it possible to thwart it" (Foucault, 1976/1978, p. 101). All the relative power of Coca-Cola couldn't make consumers accept New Coke®, and all the science and technology of the Western world couldn't convince some people of the efficacy of smallpox vaccination.

Neoliberal models of public relations practice traditionally downplay "structured forms of inequality and power . . . in favour of an implicitly optimistic notion of society as a level playing ground, where different interest groups fight for their interests" (Hesmondhalgh, 2002, p. 30). Critical political economists often charge public relations with consistently tilting the playing field in favor of those already empowered. The cultural–economic model proposes that international public relations takes place on an uneven playing field, but the field isn't consistently tilted in favor of any one particular group. The field shifts in any given articulation within the bounds supplied by the moments, meaning that the playing field is not always tilted in favor of economic power.

A good example is that of KFC in Muslim areas of Asia. In earlier chapters, we noted that KFC has been quite successful in its expansion throughout Asia. Consumers crowded the stores to enjoy an "American" experience, even though KFC had glocalized its menu offerings. With the advent of the Iraqi war, however, anti-American sentiment in Muslim areas has grown and sparked a boycott of U.S. companies, including KFC. Throughout Indonesia and Malaysia, KFC and other U.S. companies are struggling to retain market share as the dominant discourse has shifted from enjoying modernization to fighting U.S. aggression, and relative power has shifted from producers to consumers.

Also key to international public relations practice is the role of relational power within an organization. The success of the smallpox eradication campaign owed much to a flattened hierarchy and decentralized authority that empowered employees at all levels. But as one campaign observer has noted, adopting this approach "is likely to raise questions of ownership or authorship that may be organizationally disruptive, as well as problems of control and politics" (Hopkins, 1989, p. 73). How an organization is structured, then, may determine in part its ability to adopt the cultural–economic model of international public relations practice.

Practitioners as Cultural Intermediaries

In the cultural–economic model, practitioners function as **cultural intermediaries,** a term we first used and briefly described in chapter 3 as *mediators between producers and consumers who actively create meanings by establishing an identification between products or issues and publics.* Although the term was originally coined by Pierre Bourdieu (1979/1984) to refer to a specific sector of a new social class, scholars have since reappropriated it and used it more generically to refer to all those who mediate between producers and consumers, such as marketers, advertisers, and public relations practitioners. As cultural intermediaries, practitioners work at the juncture of production and consumption to create meaning by shaping and transferring information. The goal is "to create an identification between producers and consumers through their expertise in certain signifying practices" (du Gay, 1997, p. 5), work that's increasingly central to communication efforts in an era of globalization, diaspora, and hybridity.

However, this isn't to imply that international practitioners are simply translators of differing national customs and norms. This use of the term *cultural intermediaries* is creeping into general parlance, but it strays far from Bourdieu's intent. In keeping with culture in the broader sense of the term, the cultural–economic model positions practitioners as key creators of new meanings designed to establish an identification between products or issues and publics within communicative relationships. The role entails a high degree of self-reflexivity as practitioners deconstruct meanings and identities of others and of themselves and their organizations. Identities form the basis for behavior, and as we know from practice, changing or initiating behavior is a long, slow process. Creating shared identities, then, requires a long-term perspective. Practitioners must caution their organizations that international campaigns entail sustained, long-term effort. They won't yield quick results.

So what does the cultural–economic model of international public relations practice look like? It looks exactly like the diagram of the circuit of culture presented in Figure 3.1 because one cannot simply affix public relations labels to parts of the circuit without negating its explanatory power. For example, to replace *production* with *public relations practitioners* is to forget that practitioners are both producers and consumers of meaning; that they assign, assume, and adopt a variety of identities; and that they shape and are shaped by differing regulatory factors and environments. While their campaign materials form representations, they and their materials are in turn represented, packaged, and presented.

The iterative, discursive nature of the cultural–economic model defies static labels such as *practitioners, publics,* and *tactics.* In the spinning circuit of the model, there is no beginning or end point, no one voice of truth, and no fixed role or meaning. Instead of structure there is process that proceeds along lines suggested by historicity but is never preordained. It's predicated by previous meanings but not predetermined by them. The circuit of culture, then, graphically depicts the cultural–economic model, which in turn explicates how the circuit of culture informs international public relations practice.

It should also be noted that while the cultural–economic model provides us with a new way to approach international public relations practice by addressing issues of culture, identity, and power inherent in international campaigns, it also brings with it a new vocabulary. *Moments, articulations, cultural intermediaries,* and other terms we've used throughout the book don't resonate in the professional world. We caution students that at this time, using these terms in an interview won't impress anyone; being able to apply the principles of the model will, however. Chapter 10 provides guidance for applying the model to practice.

CHAPTER SUMMARY

- The dominant models of public relations practice are tied to economic goals and privilege economic wealth.

- The cultural–economic model of international public relations practice holds that public relations is predicated on communicative relationships, and culture is a constitutive part of any such relationship.

- The cultural–economic model emphasizes public relations as a discursive process, respects diversity, and does not privilege any one group.

- Functioning as a cultural intermediary requires practitioners to adopt a long-term perspective and be self-reflexive.

10

Circuiting the Globe

A Practice Matrix

❖ ❖ ❖

Contextually, the cultural–economic model reminds us that public relations is a communicative process, and the moments provide guidance for addressing a public relations challenge. This chapter uses the cultural–economic model to develop a practice matrix for public relations and demonstrates how that practice matrix can provide a roadmap for practitioners doing public relations and scholars studying public relations. The matrix is designed to promote a worldview in which both predisposing and situational factors operate concurrently.

A **worldview** *is a particular way of thinking and seeing the world.* In terms of the cultural–economic model, it's a view that recognizes the dangers of assumptions and ethnocentrism while acknowledging issues of culture, identity, and power. The practice matrix, then, represents a conceptual shift from theory to practice. However, it isn't a formula or series of steps that are the panacea for an international public relations challenge. In fact, the practice matrix ideally identifies the challenges of international public relations rather than eliminating or solving them.

The first step toward overcoming challenges is identification, which can help develop pathways that effectively negotiate the often treacherous terrain of international public relations. McDermott (1997) compared international public relations to three-dimensional chess, where practitioners are no longer playing on a two-dimensional board. To extend that idea further, we turn to the world's most popular sport, football, or soccer as it's called in the United States.

The practice matrix holds that the playing field isn't two-dimensional. Also, the matrix adds four more soccer balls to the game, each representing a moment in the circuit of culture. Lose sight of one ball, and another is coming your way. Too much time concentrating on one and you sacrifice the others. The worldview, then, is one that takes into account multiple meanings and gives public relations practitioners a skill set to play this complex game. The structure for permitting this worldview is the practice matrix presented in this chapter.

❖ ASSUMPTIONS OF INTERNATIONAL PUBLIC RELATIONS

Pulling together some of the examples discussed in this book allows us to identify some general assumptions about international public relations. Although there's an inherent danger in making assumptions, the idea is that international public relations doesn't start with a neutral playing field. Using our soccer metaphor, international public relations cannot assume that the score in the game begins at 0–0. Indeed, more often there's already a score, sometimes decidedly lopsided, before a public relations activity even begins. Some of the factors that preclude a neutral starting position are discussed in this section, beginning with the fundamental assumption that going international is a communicative act with a preordained starting point.

Existing Discourses and the Production of Meaning

Some scholars have argued that all public relations is international public relations, an issue discussed in chapter 2. Whether there's indeed a distinction between the two doesn't negate the point that a communicative process begins with the existence of an activity, cause, or organization that is international in scope. Before any formal activity is undertaken to reach an external audience, the existence of an organization carries with it the baggage of perception, some of which only tangentially relates to the organization itself, because meaning arises from discursive processes.

In chapter 3, for example, we explored how Coca-Cola is an international symbol that might be collapsed into "Americanness." The distinction between a corporate business and a country isn't necessarily a logical connection. For other countries around the world, however, Coca-Cola is a company that symbolizes Americanness and all it means to be American, from freedom and capitalism to imperialism and colonialism. These discourses can clash with local ideologies that aren't consistent with these values, creating tension before Coca-Cola even opens its doors in a new country or location.

The idea that the existence of an organization creates a discourse isn't new. Dozier and Lauzen (2000, p. 12) examine the dialectic between publics and organizations by noting "situations where mere existence of an organization is unacceptable to an activist public." Every organization, simply by existing, has relationships with publics and therefore has public relations. The lesson here is that discourse arises as soon as the idea of a cause, organization, or activity enters the public sphere. Globalization and technology accelerate the process of public scrutiny and create a vacuum of perception that precludes absolute neutrality. In other words, meaning is encoded in existence, creating what we might call an innateness that exists outside any planned communication. Public relations planning therefore must take into account that going "international" isn't a zero-sum game; anticipating the competing discourses that might arise at program conception is one step toward creating a more level field of operations.

The same problem of innateness—or what a deconstructionist such as Derrida might call historicity—also occurs in international public relations scholarship. Verĉiĉ, van Ruler, Bütschi, and Flodin (2001, p. 374) lamented the apathy of U.S. public relations scholars "for any theoretical and practical work in public relations on other continents." Furthermore, they noted that the authors of a chapter on Europe in a major book on international public relations were all Americans. Verĉiĉ et al. concluded that a discourse of U.S. public relations scholarship has generated a "mainstream" discourse, and much work is needed outside that mainstream to define the function and purpose of public relations in the global community.

Indeed, the authors of this textbook are both U.S. citizens and therefore are participants in "mainstream" public relations research. Despite our best and most noble intentions, we cannot escape the trappings of our nationality and the culture that has shaped our way of seeing. Consider the implications of the recognition that we as the authors are part of mainstream public relations scholarship:

> If mainstream public relations theory were more open to theorizing structures of power, it would also be more open to consideration

of how public relations practice could be appropriated by, and work to serve the interests of, those groups who perceive themselves as disempowered by globalization or who oppose the philosophies and/or economic effects of that globalization. (C. Weaver, 2001, p. 279)

How does the challenge of innateness fit into the circuit of culture and the practice matrix? By recognizing that organizational presence; the age, gender, class, and race of employees; and the nationality of public relations practitioners and scholars are important considerations in the domain of creating meaning, making issues of regulation the predisposing factors in the circuit of culture. Put another way, if we want to launch a public relations campaign, we must first take into account some predisposing factors. That is, what considerations do we need to have in mind from the onset of a public relations campaign? The answer comes from the moment of regulation, making it an entry point into the matrix.

Take a moment to review the moment of regulation as shown in Table 10.1. In chapter 2 we examined the "break bottle" campaigns some activist groups have waged against Coca-Cola and Pepsi in India. Such activism is an indicator of power differences and struggle. A requisite characteristic of a worldview takes into account that Coca-Cola is a global brand symbolizing global inequities in addition to its symbolic representation of the United States to Indians. By addressing the moment of regulation first, we see how the field is tilted. By applying the matrix, we see why it's tilted and how we can level it. The second point under situational factors in regulation asks about the general state of relations between the host country and the country of origin of the corporation or agency. This question and other factors from the moment of regulation help expose the problems that can sink a public relations campaign before it even begins to take form as a communicative process.

To take this idea closer to the development of the practice matrix, let's use an example. Suppose Coca-Cola were planning to open a new operation in Turkey. From chapter 8, we know that a constructed identity of Turkey in its efforts to join the EU includes a "European isn't Islamic" discourse. Following the logic of the circuit and this discussion, Coca-Cola might examine U.S.–Turkey relations for inclusion in a situation analysis of its planned operations in Turkey.

Even the most basic research, such as a few minutes using Google under the search terms "Turkey and U.S. relations," reveals more than 15 million hits. Among the more recent ones are "Some said the

(Text continues on page 222)

Table 10.1 A Practice Matrix for the Cultural–Economic Model of International Public Relations Practice

Moment	Situational Factor	Reference	Action	Reference
Regulation	What type of government exists?	Ch. 1, p. 6	If the term *propaganda* appears, consider its culture of origin and ethics surrounding its use.	
	What is the general state of relations between the host country and the organization's country of origin?	Ch. 2, p. 23	Practitioners must identify hidden cultural regulations and decode them, often through use of a key informant.	Ch. 4, p. 60 Ch. 11, p. 237
	What is the technological infrastructure of the host country?	Ch. 4, p. 57	Regulatory systems must be continuously monitored for changes in meaning.	Ch. 4, p. 60
	What structures, if any, have attempted to define or formalize the practice of public relations (e.g., country or regional professional associations)?	Ch. 1, pp. 4, 8		
	What are the semantic networks that address and define public relations?	Ch. 3, pp. 36, 40		
	In there a commensurate term for public relations in the host country?	Ch. 1, p. 5		
	What is the professional definition of public relations in the host country?	Ch. 1, p. 4		
	Is there a national or regional public relations association code of ethics for public relations practice?	Ch. 11, p. 245		

(Continued)

Table 10.1 (Continued)

Moment	Situational Factor	Reference	Action	Reference
	Are there public relations education programs in the host country? How do they discuss and define public relations?	Ch. 1, p. 10		
	How do public relations agencies in the country define what they do?	Ch. 1, p. 4		
	What is the economic profile of the country?	Ch. 4, p. 53		
	What is the political climate of the country?	Ch. 4, p. 56		
	What are some of the cultural constructs that define the host country culture?	Ch. 4, p. 60		
	What are the national and local laws that govern communication practices?	Ch. 4		
Production	What are the primary communication modalities in the host country?	Ch. 6	Research how other international interests have fared in the country and what communication problems they have faced.	
	What mass communication vehicles are used in rural and urban areas in the host country?	Ch. 2, p. 20	Remain aware of the role of power in the entire production process, including how materials are developed and where they are developed.	Ch. 6, p. 112

218

Moment	Situational Factor	Reference	Action	Reference
	Which interpersonal channels of communication are commonly used in rural and urban areas in the host country?	Ch. 1, p. 20	Identifying target audiences is as important as monitoring how those audiences change.	Ch. 6, p. 124
	Who are the opinion leaders in the host country for the issue or product your group is addressing?	Ch. 6, p. 131	Be flexible and open to change, not tied to a strategic plan.	Ch. 9, p. 207
	How might any activity by your organization contribute to local perceptions of globalization?	Ch. 6, p. 116		
	How are global brands, products, and artifacts glocalized in the host country?	Ch. 6, p. 117		
	How are target audiences defined, and how might they be imagined communities?	Ch. 6, p. 120		
Consumption	How do audiences use the product or idea?	Ch. 7, p. 137	Practitioners must monitor how audiences decode public relations actions and messages.	Ch. 7, p. 140
	What are the new meanings that arise through use?	Ch. 7, p. 137	Practitioners must continuously monitor the public opinion environment using ethnographic methods.	Ch. 7, p. 142

(Continued)

Table 10.1 (Continued)

Moment	Situational Factor	Reference	Action	Reference
	What new discourses arise surrounding the issue or product?	Ch. 8, p. 181	Practitioners must account for changing uses and meanings and adjust public relations programs as necessary.	
	What is the value to the target audiences?	Ch. 7, p. 139		
Identity	How are audiences defined, and what rationale is used?	Ch. 8, p. 168	Recognize that segmenting publics by demographics and psychographics are starting points that represent static, artificial identities.	Ch. 8, p. 170
	Can local interests be placed before global ones to decenter power and allow new identities to emerge?	Ch. 8, p. 174	Working to ascertain the identities of target audiences is an ongoing process.	Ch. 8, p. 172
	What organizational identities already exist in the host country?	Ch. 8, p. 173	The goal for practitioners is not to achieve the appearance of consensus by dominating discourse but to manage dissensus by respecting competing discourses.	Ch. 8, p. 172
	Is my organization willing to relinquish power and allow new hybrid meanings to emerge?	Ch. 8, p. 174	Continue monitoring identities assigned to target audiences, adjusting as necessary and recognizing adjustments as new opportunities for strategy and tactics.	Ch. 8

Moment	Situational Factor	Reference	Action	Reference
Representation	Have local speakers or practitioners scrutinized the messages in campaign material produced?	Ch. 5, p. 86	Identify and decode competing discourses before execution and throughout the campaign.	Ch. 5, p. 93
	What competing discourses might audiences bring to bear on campaign materials?	Ch. 5, p. 83	Research is a linchpin to campaign effectiveness. Research as many viewpoints as possible, recognizing that culture is omnipresent.	Ch. 5, p. 93
	What is the intended message encoded in campaign materials?	Ch. 5, p. 78	Develop competing discourses to support the intended meaning as needed.	Ch. 5, p. 83
	What cultural factors, including tastes, values, and beliefs, can alter the intended representation?	Ch. 5, p. 78	Serve as a strategic decoder by decoding other discourses and appropriating selected parts.	Ch. 5, p. 93
	How does the representation change or absorb the local culture?	Ch. 5, p. 87		
	How is the representation similar to or different from related campaign materials from sources outside the host country?	Ch. 5		
	Do all components of the campaign materials (i.e., text, symbols, graphics, colors) support the intended representation?	Ch. 5, p. 80		

[Turkish–U.S.] relations were 'on the brink of dying'" (TurkishPress, n.d., ¶ 1), "Turkish–US relations have cooled due to differences over Iraq" ("Turkey Defies," 2005), and a *USA Today* article covering U.S. undersecretary for public diplomacy Karen Hughes's diplomatic trip to Turkey: "Hughes—who concluded her Mideast tour Wednesday—admitted that 'obviously we have a public relations challenge here in Turkey as we do in different places throughout the world'" ("In Turkey," 2005, ¶ 3).

This information is instructive because it indicates some degree of tension between the United States and Turkey, an important consideration for Coca-Cola as a U.S. brand. The strained relations also position Turkey in a global swath of Muslim nations critical of U.S. policy, which might portend similar problems in Turkey as Coca-Cola had in India. This possibility alone situates Coca-Cola in a discourse that is, to some degree, critical of the United States.

In the parlance of the circuit it means that the identity of Coca-Cola can be encoded with desired meanings through production, but how those codes are consumed will include a perspective critical of U.S. discourse, regardless of the propitious representation Coca-Cola would like to project. Its representation therefore is a battleground of making meaning, imbued with existing discourses that surround and essentially regulate its brand in Turkey. This linkage between the moments—starting with the moment of regulation—is what the practice matrix is designed to explain.

Race, Gender, Class, Age, and Language as Discursive Productions

Another international public relations assumption is that discourses are generated, enhanced, or extended by the characteristics of the people who represent an organization. Chapter 1 discusses the example of Nu Skin assigning a man in his 30s to head the company's Malaysian operations. Despite his credentials, in the hierarchical Malaysian society he was considered too young for such responsibility. Before the manager could prove himself, establish his credibility, or illustrate his skills, he was already judged by his Malaysian cohorts based on age alone.

This example is a microcosm of the process an organization undergoes when it goes international, a process in which discourses already abound before its doors are open for business. By the same token, any activity or cause is tangible to external publics to the extent that they are aware of it. In international public relations, then, the question shouldn't include only issues of staff employment balance between the host country and country of origin but also concerns of age, gender, class, and race. These considerations are all nonverbal but produce important discourses that can be interpreted in different ways by both internal and external audiences.

The final assumption represents a change from the mere existence of an organization and staffing considerations to the importance of language. For instance, we might ask how U.S. public relations practitioners can operate when a commensurate term for public relations doesn't exist in the language of another country, an issue discussed in chapter 1. In Germany, for example, the word for public relations is *öffentlichkeitsarbeit*, which literally means "public work" and is explained as "'working in public, with the public, and for the public' . . . [which] contradicts the mainstream (U.S.) understanding of public relations" (Verĉiĉ et al., 2001, p. 376). This example and many others in chapter 1 reflect the existing cultural discourses of public relations. Idiomatic expressions often are nuanced, and small details can intensify when context is ignored.

It's also a reminder that learning another language is but a small step toward practicing public relations in a new environment. The significance of language goes beyond learning a language to learning the cultural norms that surround its use and function in a society. Layered over this process is the literal translation of public relations and the discourses associated with that translation. In simple terms, it's easy to say that public relations is practiced differently in different parts of the world. Beyond that, however, is a root cause: The term *public relations* doesn't have the same meaning in different parts of the world.

Summarizing International Public Relations Assumptions

If there's a grand conclusion we might reach from these assumptions, it's that the products of these assumptions are competing discourses. The discourses are constantly in flux, creating a composite of dissensus. Rather than fitting neatly atop or within each other, these discourses overlap and intersect in various ways, hindering consensus and symmetry. This idea is born from the assumption that international public relations cannot assume a fair, balanced starting point; to the contrary, it must take into account the competing discourses and varying power relationships that make a neutral starting point impossible.

With the recognition that international public relations is characterized by imbalance, it's possible to develop a matrix that can help level the playing field and provide ongoing guidance for a public relations activity. What that matrix looks like and how it functions are discussed in the next section.

❖ A PRACTICE MATRIX FOR
     INTERNATIONAL PUBLIC RELATIONS

The idea of using a matrix to organize theoretical perspectives and ideas about international public relations is new and takes different forms. Botan (1992) suggested that a matrix was a useful schema to organize information through an exhaustive comparative analysis of international public relations theories. Botan's public relations matrix encompassed four factors: level of international development, primary clients, legal and political context, and history of the practice. Botan believed his matrix would differ by country or culture based on these factors.

This matrix was part of a larger comparative international theory project that recognized the inherent differences of U.S. public relations theory and cultural norms vis-à-vis other nations and systems:

> Because different peoples have different histories, the relationship of public relations to government, marketing, religion and the press differs from culture to culture. Countries such as the United States, with great experience using public relations to promote products or organizations, have difficulty exchanging knowledge with countries with more experience in using it as a tool for national development or public health. (Botan, 1992, p. 158)

Sriramesh and Verĉiĉ (2003) devised a similar theoretical framework consisting of a trio of primary factors: infrastructure and international public relations, culture and international public relations, and media relations. Under each factor is a series of subcategories with questions for consideration. Zaharna (2001) developed an "in-awareness" approach to international public relations to steer practitioners around common public relations pitfalls and provide guidance. Her matrix comprises three main topical areas: a country profile, a cultural profile, and communication components. More recently, Hill and Dixon (2006) developed an information processing worldview model with a matrix for public relations practitioners that takes into account intercultural and international considerations.

Relationship of the Matrix to the Model

Of course, there are limitations to a matrix. We have continuously described public relations as a communicative process, and that process often is incongruous with the linear nature of a matrix. Visually speaking, whereas the cultural–economic model forms a circuit with indefinite starting and end points, a matrix is based on linear relationships. Rather than viewing a **practice matrix** as limiting the circuit, we view it as *a different way of organizing information into a practical structure for exploring relationships.*

For example, a strength of the circuit is its visual acuity in illustrating relationships between the moments. Conceptually, then, it's a powerful descriptive tool. The matrix transfers the conceptual power behind the cultural–economic model and its interrelationships into a format that holds more promise in identifying differences, delineating possible public relations activities, and providing a public relations worldview.

A caveat in considering the practice matrix is that it's intended to provide a roadmap for international public relations, not identify the "right" way to approach a challenge. Rarely, if ever, is there a right way in international public relations. More commonly, practitioners toil in undefined gray areas that exist on the outskirts of absolutes such as right. When those practitioners are "wrong," however, their failures might be traced to ethnocentric approaches or adhering to a symmetric, rather than world, view.

Our matrix, outlined in Table 10.1, is the lens that enables an international worldview. That worldview also recognizes the speed at which the circuit of culture operates by translating the dynamic and open-ended characteristics of the circuit into a matrix that is more responsive than reactive. The circuit is so dynamic that meaning making can occur almost immediately. The moments of the circuit can easily blur from a series of moments into a singular dynamic process of meaning making. The final lesson, then, is that meaning can evolve over time or occur so rapidly that defining single moments is impossible.

The Starting Point: Regulation

Much of this book has revolved around the process of communication and public relations. Such processes often occur as discourses surrounding and affecting all public relations activity, limiting the possibility of one true starting point. However, the practice matrix must have a defined starting point to give it form and function. As we've already suggested in this chapter, that point is the moment of regulation. Regulation provides the broad context we need to understand public relations culture and communications before we dip into the swirls of the circuit of culture. Note, however, that because the circuit has no true starting point, a practitioner could start with any of the moments and reach the same observations as if regulation were the starting point.

If we're public relations practitioners who want to start a public relations campaign in another country, we need to understand the regulatory environment of that country: the type of government, how public relations is viewed culturally, the cultural guidelines of that society, and so on. From chapter 4, you might remember that regulation affects how we view other societies and cultures, our employer, how the organization is structured, the role of management, the ethnic and gender breakdown of employees, and so on. Collectively, all of these issues fall under the moment of regulation. This moment provides a context we can use to get started.

To begin using the matrix, then, we create this context through the moment of regulation. This moment helps us understand the environment in which we are viewing public relations and our particular endeavor. Before we get to an example to put the matrix to work starting with regulation, let's translate the moments of the circuit of culture into practical public relations terms. We'll use the following as guidelines if we're public relations practitioners:

- *Regulation* addresses the limitations we have as practitioners, whether budgetary, legal, or cultural. For example, what laws or regulations apply to our work? What cultural mores or norms might affect our work? In turn, our work as practitioners contributes to the regulatory environments in which we operate.
- *Production* is what we plan to do as public relations practitioners, where strategy, planning, and research are key activities. Consumers are in turn producers, and practitioners become the consumers of the meanings they generate.
- *Consumption* is how a product or idea is used and for what ends. It is the site of production of new, competing meanings.
- *Representation* is the tangible form of production; it includes the tactics, messages, themes, product design, and informational and promotional materials and any other forms of public relations materials or activities.
- *Identity* is how we establish our organizational identity through our public relations. In other terms, who are we as an organization? How do we identify or position ourselves? This moment is also affected by how we identify, or segment, our target publics. A brand, for instance, would fit under this moment of the circuit. In turn, others form multiple identities of our organization and practices.

This is a simple way of viewing the moments, and parsimony dilutes some of the power and scope of each moment. This is where the matrix is helpful. It addresses the key considerations for each moment in one of two areas:

- **Situational factors,** which are *questions to be addressed in each moment*
- **Actions,** which *describe what a practitioner might do to guide activity in the moment*

These two areas under each moment bring together the concepts of the book by describing, guiding, and reflecting. If you don't understand a moment or part of the matrix, chapters and page numbers are provided for reference in the matrix to steer you back to the discussion in the book for clarification.

❖ APPLYING THE MATRIX

Let's try going through a couple of brief examples to put the matrix to work. The first outlines the considerations an international nongovernment organization might face when expanding its operations in South America. The second uses the matrix to demonstrate the challenges of a multinational corporation entering the British market.

Ipas and Chile

Imagine that Ipas, a women's reproductive health and rights nonprofit organization, has hired your U.S. public relations agency. Ipas is a U.S. nonprofit that wants to help reduce the deaths and injuries of women caused by unsafe abortions (see http://www.ipas.org). Although the organization has some presence in Latin America, for purposes of illustration, suppose that they're considering expanding into Chile. Following the practice matrix, we begin with the moment of regulation. We start by doing research to address each of the situational factors in the moment of regulation, such as the type of government and relations between the country and the United States.

How detailed and exhaustive that research is depends on time requirements and the scope of your project. With little effort, however, we can quickly find that Chile is a republic, a form of democracy in which elected officials, not the people, vote on legislation. By reviewing several sources, we can assess the current status of Chilean–U.S.

relations, much as we did earlier in the chapter with Coca-Cola and Turkey. Sifting through a range of scholarly and general sources, we can see that current relations between the two countries are favorable.

This research would also yield three points of possible interest. The first is that Chile elected its first female president in January 2006, which suggests a traditionally patriarchal society. The second is that Chile has had military dictatorships and coups in the past 50 years, conditions ripe for propaganda. Third, 89% of Chile's population is Roman Catholic. We'll need to take into account the strong influence of the church in this area, particularly because our client is concerned with issues of women's reproductive health, including abortion.

We might tackle the other regulators in order, jotting down notes to answer each factor. After we have some notes, we consider the actions for regulation in the matrix before we move to the next moment, production. For this moment, we would again examine each situational factor. For production, the first is, "What are the primary communication modalities in the country?" We would find that the country has more than 250 radio stations and seven television stations, less than a quarter of its population has Internet access, more than 90% of all households have at least one radio, and many also have a television set (CIA, 2005). The prevalence of these modalities provides clues we can use as insight into Ipas's expansion into Chile.

Continuing through the matrix, we move to actions, a list of statements to guide us before we move to the moment of consumption. The first action instructs us to research how other international interests have fared in the country and what communication problems they have faced. From here, international interests might be other public health initiatives, more specifically health education programs for women. This part of the matrix is asking us to identify women's health initiatives in Chile and how they are performing. Once we address this question and follow the other actions for production, we're ready to move to consumption.

For consumption, the first situational factor is "How do audiences use the product or idea?" Because our client is a women's rights organization, we need to understand what its products are. Ipas provides training, research, advocacy, distribution of equipment and supplies for reproductive healthcare, and information dissemination, which collectively form the "products" of Ipas.

Because these products are broad, this situational factor can help us identify the ways in which Chileans might use the tangible (equipment and supplies for reproductive healthcare) with the intangible (training, research, advocacy, and information dissemination). Ipas suggests that the lack of access to safe, modern abortion procedures is one reason nearly 70,000 women around the world die every year. This situational factor might instruct us to determine whether modern equipment and supplies are available in Chile and, if so, whether they are being underused or not used at all, especially given the strong Catholic presence noted earlier under regulation. Research of this sort can help us delve deep into the undercurrent of Chilean society, unlocking doors of discovery that are culturally sensitive and ethical.

We follow this process through each of the moments, taking notes and writing down our observations. When we've completed this task, we've not only considered the predisposing factors for Ipas's entry into Chile by examining the moment of regulation; we've also traveled within and around the other moments in the circuit of culture, leaving us with data we can put to use.

How we decide to use that data depends on what we're trying to accomplish. If we want to provide a situation analysis to Ipas, we have all the raw materials in place with our research. If we want to propose a full public relations plan, we have a good start, although the matrix will instruct us to include participation, observation, in-depth interviews, ethnographic studies, focus groups, and product testing. It will also tell us that research ideally is not done in a vacuum. We'll want to identify some people who can help us navigate Chilean culture, or key informants.

A second example demonstrates the global utility of the matrix and its applicability to any type of organization.

Abercrombie & Fitch Consider Great Britain

If we apply the practice matrix to a hypothetical scenario in which U.S.-based clothing company Abercrombie & Fitch is considering entry into the British market, a world of opportunities opens up for us to guide our client. As always, we begin with the moment of regulation. The first situational factor asks us what type of government is in the country. As we begin to research, we find that the United Kingdom isn't a country but a region, or nation-state, consisting of England, Scotland, Wales, and Northern Ireland. Maybe we already knew that. But research for this factor alone complicates our picture. We're not talking about a monolithic country with a singular identity; instead, there are four distinct countries in the United Kingdom, each with its own culture and history. Now we might ask Abercrombie whether it wants one launch across all four countries or whether it wants to stagger its launch, one country at a time.

From here, we might try two ways of using the matrix: Can we apply it to the United Kingdom as a whole, or do we need to do it by country? If we look at one source, *The World Factbook* (CIA, 2005), it's treated as a single entry, so the government appears to be the same in all four regions. But further research would warn us that calling all from the United Kingdom "English" is likely to get us in hot water because there's a strong sense of national identity. A person from Scotland probably will be insulted if called English.

To address various areas in the moment of regulation, let's skip a few of the situational factors and move to the sixth factor, whether there's a commensurate term for public relations. We already know English is spoken in the United Kingdom, but is the *meaning* of public relations the same as that in the United States? To answer this question, we might find public relations agencies in the United Kingdom and see how they describe their work. Or we might review international public relations resources such as the Global Alliance for Public Relations and Communication Management to see whether they can provide us with information. We might look at scholarly literature to see whether there are any case studies on public relations in the United Kingdom.

When we mine that information, patterns of the development of public relations and what it means in the United Kingdom emerge. One such observation comes from Pieczka and L'Etang (2001, p. 230): "The evolution of public relations in Britain . . . clearly shows a different pattern of development from that in the United States and, therefore, implies that the developmental model is not rigidly applicable" (see also L'Etang, 2004). This citation provides a clue that public relations in the United Kingdom doesn't follow the U.S. model. Public relations in the United Kingdom has different historical origins, which might affect the meaning of the term *public relations* in the United Kingdom.

We would then continue down the list of situational factors and actions in each moment to accumulate information we can use for our client. We'll probably find that economic development and communication modalities are similar to those of the United States. As we move into issues of culture, however, we begin to see differences that indicate that we are indeed dealing with a different culture, albeit one that speaks English. Irish playwright George Bernard Shaw reminds us what we're up against: "America and Britain are two nations divided by a common language."

The second moment in the matrix is production. We can address each of the situational factors and also look at the prescribed actions, where the first item asks us how other international interests have fared in the country and what communication problems they have faced. This means we will want to see how other brands similar to Abercrombie & Fitch have fared in the United Kingdom. We might try to find the top clothiers in the United Kingdom to see how many are American. If there aren't any, that's a clue that the United Kingdom prefers its own brands. On the other hand, if similar U.S. brands are performing well in the United Kingdom, we might look at how they position themselves.

A deeper application of the matrix would help reveal other things we might not have considered, such as the meaning of the name Abercrombie. For example, the moment of identity asks us to look at polysemy, or different meanings. According to last-names.net, Abercrombie is a Celtic and Gaelic term: "*Aber,* marshy ground, a place where two or more streams meet; and *cruime* or *crombie,* a bend or crook." We learn that the first part of our client's name, *Abercrombie,* is not American but is from the United Kingdom, where it has deeper cultural relevance. Therefore, the meaning associated with the name *Abercrombie* itself becomes part of the meaning-making process of our target audience as we recognize that the name has an existing identity in the United Kingdom.

The moment of identity also reminds us that the Abercrombie & Fitch discourse in the United States can't be completely forgotten. From the Coca-Cola example in chapter 2, we learned that multinational corporations can no longer isolate their organizational presence to parts of the world. The matrix forces us to research the predominant identity of Abercrombie & Fitch in the United States and recognize that traces of that identity will affect its launch in the United Kingdom.

Therefore, we can't overlook facts contributing to its reputation in the United States. It's more than a century old, has clothed former presidents, and, more recently, has garnered headlines for its racy catalogs (Photo 10.1). We have to keep in mind perceptions such as those mentioned by CBS News's Morley Safer (2004, ¶ 3): "The image of Abercrombie & Fitch is now party-loving jocks and barenaked ladies living fantasy lives." In 2005, the company also faced a well-publicized lawsuit charging ethnic and gender discrimination against employees and job applicants.

Abercrombie & Fitch will not begin with a clean slate in the United Kingdom; some of its reputation in the United States will creep into the United Kingdom. The cultural–economic model helps us by revealing the degree to which identity is already entrenched in the region and how we might try to build on that identity or create a new one.

Photo 10.1   President Theodore Roosevelt Often Went on African Safaris
Wearing Abercrombie & Fitch Clothing, Creating an Upscale,
Rugged Identity for the Company, Which Has Since Become
a Teen Lifestyle Brand

SOURCE: Photo by Edward Van Altena, courtesy of the U.S. Library of Congress.

CONTRIBUTIONS OF THE MATRIX

Applying the matrix to these hypothetical examples demonstrates
three things: how the matrix might be used, to what ends, and the type
of thinking it generates. Of course, a public relations practitioner might
find all the information discussed in this chapter without the matrix.
However, using the matrix gives us a defined approach to our international public relations challenges. The matrix gives us a blueprint
for moving forward by revealing cultural differences and competing
discourses.

But what if you're a student working on a paper and don't have the
time or resources to follow the circuit faithfully, painstakingly addressing each of the moments, situational factors, and actions? The more
detailed your research, the better the circuit will work for you. Even
baseline research will yield useful data, however. Using the matrix
doesn't have to be daunting. It should be a process of exploration that
gives you the insights you need to understand a situational challenge
in the world of international public relations.

The matrix should also give you a way of organizing your work and providing direction. So although you want your research to be as exhaustive as possible, even touching on a few of the situational factors and actions for each moment in the matrix will give you a sound start toward a worldview. To return to our soccer metaphor from earlier in the chapter, the matrix is the game, where preparation and practice are put to the test.

In the next chapter, we bring ethics to the forefront, which furthers our understanding of the cultural–economic model and practice matrix. The final chapter of the book incorporates the discussion of ethics to unleash the full potential of the matrix, shifting the concepts of the book from abstract to concrete, conceptual to visual, and micro to macro.

CHAPTER SUMMARY

- An international public relations worldview acknowledges assumptions based on historicity, organizational presence, age, race, class, and gender.

- The practice matrix promotes a worldview by bringing together the moments of the circuit of culture into a practical format.

- The moment of regulation includes predisposing factors and is a useful starting point for the practice matrix.

- The practice matrix is intended not to solve public relations challenges but to identify pathways to negotiate the diverse landscape of international public relations.

- Each moment in the practice matrix is divided into two areas: situational factors and actions.

- Situational factors are questions for public relations practitioners and scholars to consider for each moment; actions are signposts to guide activity in each moment.

11

Ethical Considerations in Global Practice

❖   ❖   ❖

An underlying premise of this book is that public relations practice is grounded in two related concepts: culture and power. Culture informs how we talk, think, and act; in turn, our language, thoughts, and actions are shaped by the relational flow of power. Integral to all communicative enterprises, then, are competing "truths" and power imbalances, making ethics inherent in everyday public relations practice. Although this chapter comes toward the end of the book, it's anything but an afterthought. It pulls together the ethical underpinnings that have run through the previous chapters to explore and address the ethical challenges posed by international practice.

Globalization brings to the forefront of international public relations practice two particular ethical issues resulting from the interplay of culture and power: cultural relativism (i.e., how norms and values emerge from cultural contexts) and growing power disparities between the rich and poor, resulting in what many call a new form of colonialism. In this chapter we explore these issues by drawing heavily on the interaction between two moments on the circuit, regulation and identity, to demonstrate how they inform ethical decision making and the ways in which public relations materials are produced, consumed, and represented.

❖ THE PROBLEM OF CULTURAL RELATIVISM

Although globalization has become a recent buzzword, it is not a new phenomenon. Since almost the start of recorded history, civilizations in the Mediterranean, the Indus River valley, East Asia, and other areas established trade routes that brought them into contact with different cultures. With such contact came two realizations: *Cultures develop different norms and customs, a phenomenon known as* **cultural relativism,** and successful commerce and communication depend on adjusting to those differences, a notion encapsulated in the 4th-century saying, "When in Rome, do as the Romans do." Like many old sayings, it survives today because it contains a kernel of common sense: If you respect local customs, you'll be more successful communicating and working with the local populace.

When doing business in Japan, for example, you should greet an associate by bowing and presenting your business card in both hands. The depth of the bow indicates relative status, and, if you're a foreigner, it's always good manners to bow lower to indicate respect. In much of Latin America, however, business acquaintances greet each other more informally, often with a hug and a kiss on the cheek. Although these practices may not be comfortable for everyone, they're easy to perform, and doing so indicates a knowledge and acceptance of local culture and values that does much to foster good relationships.

It's not always easy to adopt local practices, however. What if in an intercultural workplace a coworker asks you to help cover up a mistake he or she inadvertently made? A survey of business managers found that almost half of those in Singapore said they would help the coworker, whereas almost no U.S. managers would (Donalson & Dunfree, 1999). The difference is not that one culture is more ethical than the other; it's that what constitutes ethical action varies by culture—the essence of cultural relativism. In the United States, cultural norms value individualism and personal responsibility. In Singapore, cultural norms place value on social networks and support for the group.

In the United States, if organizational leaders take personal responsibility and apologize for mistakes made by the organization, the transgression usually is forgiven. For example, in 1987, Lee Iacocca, CEO of Chrysler Corp., admitted the company had made a mistake when it tampered with car odometers, and he offered restitution to affected consumers. In many Asian cultures, however, individuals often sacrifice themselves rather than bring shame to their collective organizational group. For example, in Japan the president of the Takizawa Ham Co. killed himself when the company was implicated in a food poisoning case in 2002.

In this instance, adopting local customs carries larger ethical ramifications. If you're working as a member of a Western-based international public relations firm in Asia and have a local organization as a client, should you follow local norms and help the organization cover up wrongdoing even though doing so transgresses Western public relations professional norms? This example demonstrates the tension between cultural relativism and ethical decision making. Although adapting to local customs may be good manners and foster better relations, doing so indiscriminately results in *a lack of any set, universal ethical standards, known as* **ethical relativism.**

Consider South Africa's apartheid policy, which meant that multinational organizations operating there had to segregate workers by racial group and provide better conditions and opportunities for whites. The Reverend Leon Sullivan, who joined the General Motors Board of Directors in 1971, convinced the company that complying with local norms was unethical and that they should stop doing business in South Africa. Eventually, more than 100 companies and other organizations signed on to his Sullivan Principles, guidelines for socially responsible investment in foreign countries, and pulled out of South Africa. The economic boycott was a major factor contributing to the end of apartheid.

At times, then, it may be more ethical to take an absolutist stance, steadfastly holding to home country norms and values, and in other instances it may be better to take a more relativist stance, as when greeting a business acquaintance. However, most decisions aren't so clear-cut and entail a judgment call to determine how much to adhere to home norms and how much to adapt to local norms. International practice entails continuously negotiating a position along the continuum between relativism and absolutism, a difficult process that makes cross-cultural ethics particularly challenging.

Negotiating Cultural Relativism

To work through this negotiation process, it's helpful to examine ethical conflicts in light of the cultural–economic model. Although the model doesn't provide normative values to guide ethical practice per se, using it to analyze ethical dilemmas can help you make more informed ethical decisions.

As we discussed in chapter 4, cultural norms fall under the moment of regulation. Familiarizing yourself with the regulatory environment in which you're working is a first step toward communicating effectively and negotiating potentially slippery ethical terrain. We noted that generalized cultural indices, such as those of Hofstede

(2001) and Hall (1977), can provide useful, albeit stereotypic, starting points. For example, Hofstede's individualism index and Hall's notion of high- and low-context communication predict that U.S. workers will be less likely to help a coworker cover up a mistake than will those in Singapore. (Figure 11.1 shows how Singapore and the United States compare on Hofstede's cultural dimensions.) Becoming familiar with the differing regulatory environments in which you're working not only explains why ethical conflicts develop but also may help you anticipate and possibly avoid them.

As we cautioned earlier, however, the indices presume that all members of a nation form a single, homogenized culture, even though empirical studies of ethical issues demonstrate that significant differences exist. When using the indices to unravel ethical conflict, it's

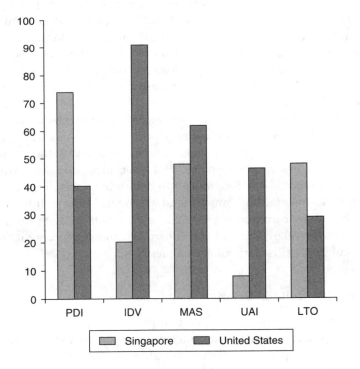

The other measures are power differential index (PDI), masculinity (MAS), uncertainty avoidance index (UAI), and long-term orientation (LTO).

Figure 11.1   A Comparison of Hofstede's Cultural Indices for Singapore and the United States Demonstrating the Large Difference Between the Two on the Individualism Scale (IDV)

important to remember that they were developed from survey averages and represent only broad national generalizations. Although we speak of broad cultural trends in this chapter to facilitate under-standing and discussion of general principles, it's necessary to obtain a more nuanced understanding to negotiate particular situations in practice. Immersing yourself in the culture and cultivating **key informants**—*people from the local culture who are willing to help you navigate it*—will help you balance cultural generalizations with situa-tional particulars. Because this process is time-consuming, interna-tional public relations firms often partner with local firms to gain comprehensive knowledge more quickly.

Although learning the form and substance of the regulatory envi-ronment in which you're working is essential to good practice, it's also helpful to learn why the regulatory environment takes the form it does. For example, the relative formality of the Japanese stems in part from Japan's high population density. To ease conflict under extremely crowded conditions, elaborate rules of interaction have developed, and conversation often is indirect to avoid confrontation. Contrast Japan with the United States and Australia. These two countries are charac-terized by large land masses and lower population densities, and their subsequent cultures are marked by relative informality and a more direct way of dealing with others.

Taking time to learn why differing cultural norms have developed as they have gives you a more complete understanding of another cul-ture and lets you avoid taking the absolutist stance that your culture is "right" and the other is "wrong," which does nothing to foster good relationships and often results in a failure to achieve public relations objectives. Informed ethical decision making along the absolutist–relativist continuum is possible only when we embrace a fuller under-standing of the competing meanings underlying cultural relativism. The following section examines a common problem for international practice—bribery—to demonstrate how the circuit can provide a more detailed understanding of cross-cultural ethical conflicts.

Laws, Norms, and Bribery

Although laws and norms are two different things, they both reg-ulate how we think and act. Cultures often pass laws against actions they consider most heinous, such as murder and theft, whereas norms are socially desirable actions, and the sanctions against disobeying them often are less codified. Whether a particular act, such as bribery, is the subject of law or norm is culturally determined.

In some East Asian countries, a small gift at the start or conclusion of a business meeting is considered good manners; to not give a gift would be rude. In many Middle Eastern and South Asian countries, such as India, *baksheesh* is a cultural norm. Its meaning is complex in that it's both a form of charitable giving to beggars and a gift to reward an official's time and effort for facilitating passage through government bureaucracy. Government officials in countries where *baksheesh* is the norm often are poorly paid, with the expectation that *baksheesh* will make up the difference. Although many citizens of these countries consider the practice unethical, it's tolerated because it's so ingrained in the culture.

In the United States, however, such practices are considered bribery, a criminal act. The 1977 Foreign Corrupt Practices Act expressly forbids any U.S. citizen to give compensation to a foreign official to achieve business objectives. In 1999, the 30 developed nations of the Organisation for Economic Co-operation approved a convention requiring each member nation to pass similar legislation. This legalistic discourse has connotations very different from the normative ones inherent in gift giving or the charity of *baksheesh*. The legalistic discourse makes bribery synonymous with illegality, which leads to reductionist, dichotomous imposed identities: Those who pay *baksheesh* are criminals, whereas those who don't are law-abiding. Closely examining how regulatory discourse shapes meaning reveals the identities we have constructed of ourselves and others—identities that affect our ethical decision making and how we regard others.

Many people outside the United States hold competing identities of U.S. business, in part because the Foreign Corrupt Practices Act is poorly enforced, as are U.S. laws concerning tax evasion and fraud. For example, a recent survey found that banking leaders in emerging nations ranked U.S. international business as more corrupt than that of most European nations (Crossette, 2002). This perspective creates an identity of the United States not as less corrupt and more law-abiding than other nations but as more sophisticated and less open in its forms of corruption (Khera, 2001).

This discussion isn't intended as a defense of bribery. Bribery of foreign officials is illegal in much of the world. But the discussion serves as a caution to look beyond simple dichotomies and not pass moral judgments based on constructed and imposed identities that reduce situational complexities to simplistic dualisms and reify cultural differences. Instead, we must step outside reductionist ways of thinking and take time to fully learn competing regulatory environments. By critically examining the identities we have constructed of ourselves and others, we open up a range of possible actions along the absolutist–relativist continuum that can lead to better relationships and help achieve public relations objectives.

For example, German multinational corporations (MNCs) operating in India often use independent consultants to determine the needs of officials and offer them gifts in kind rather than cash (Berg & Holtbrugge, 2001). In a country in which education is expensive and often unavailable, offering to build a school in a local area can build good relations, conform to law, and also satisfy the spirit of *baksheesh* and bridge cultural norms.

The issue of bribery arises from the second major ethical issue that globalization brings to the forefront of international public relations practice: the growing inequity between the rich and poor nations of the world. Concomitant with that growing economic disparity is the increase in relative power of multinational enterprises, such as MNCs and international nongovernment organizations (INGOs).

❖ GLOBALIZATION AND THE SHIFT OF POWER

Much as globalization is not a new phenomenon, neither is the multinational enterprise. The British East India Company, chartered in 1600 and granted exclusive British trading rights in the East Indies, had established a business monopoly, armed forces, and a local governance structure by the late 1600s, making it arguably a nation in its own right. What is different today is the extent to which MNCs rival nations for sovereignty. ExxonMobil's 2004 sales of almost US$300 billion were greater than the gross domestic product of all but 20 of the world's 220 nations, including Austria, Sweden, and the United Arab Emirates (CIA, 2005). Overall, 53 of the largest global economies are those of MNCs, not governments (Carroll, 2004). Increasingly, the world's power brokers are MNCs, not nations, leading BP Oil to declare on its Web site in 2000 that the MNC had become the main vehicle for global development.

Just as MNCs have increased in relative power, the gap between the rich and poor nations of the world has been growing, as shown in Figure 11.2. In 13 of the least developed nations, gross domestic product per capita declined from 1997 to 2000 (U.N., 2002). In Africa, more than 20 countries have less per capita income than they did in 1975 (Gibson, 2004). In central and Eastern Europe and the Commonwealth of Independent States, per capita income dropped 2.4% a year in the 1990s (U.N., 2002). The top fifth of the developed nations of the world control 82% of export markets and 68% of foreign direct investment, whereas the bottom fifth of nations together control just 1% of each (Mandela, 2000). This inequity has led many critics to charge that social justice and globalization are antithetical, explaining the many protesters who regularly march at the World Trade Organization, World Bank, G8, and other global economic meetings.

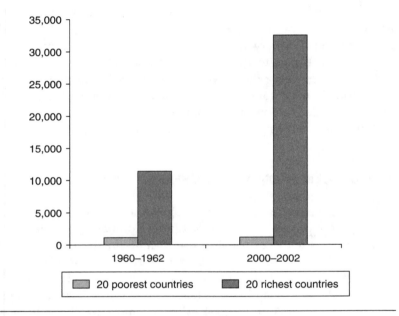

Figure 11.2   Per Capita Gross Domestic Product in the 20 Poorest and Wealthiest Countries 1960 to 1962 and 2000 to 2002 (in Constant 1995 U.S. Dollars, Simple Average)

Power differentials aren't confined to economic and government organizations. The role and scope of INGOs have increased dramatically in recent years. The 37,000 INGOs registered in 2000 represent a 20% increase from 1990 (U.N., 2002). Furthermore, most INGOs are headquartered in the developed world. Of the 738 INGOs accredited at the 1999 World Trade Organization conference, 87% were from industrialized nations. INGOs often are considered the conscience of the world, and their flow of aid from the developed to the developing world, more than US$7 billion annually, is often accompanied by a flow of values, which can raise issues of cultural relativism.

Additionally, to achieve their objectives, many INGOs create identities of target publics that contribute to a discourse of developed world moral superiority. For example, Human Rights Watch puts pressure on governments such as China's by investigating and reporting human rights abuses to international media, similar to WHO's use of the moral suasion of shame in the smallpox campaign to pressure governments in endemic areas to support eradication. Although this discourse of shame is effective, the tactics create an identity of the developed world as moral and the developing world as immoral.

Similarly, to raise support for their causes, INGOs often "humanize" their issues by showing helpless, passive victims, creating the "pornography of poverty" (Bell & Carens, 2004). Although such appeals often are effective, they disempower people in developing nations, establishing an identity of dependency that becomes divorced from the actual issues. The cover of the 2005 annual report of CARE (Photo 11.1) provides a starkly different approach. Its campaign to fight global poverty has as its tagline, "She has the power to change her world. You have the power to help her." In this approach, paternalism is avoided, and aid recipients retain dignity and control.

Even when MNCs provide much-needed employment and improved environmental standards, or when INGOs bring much-needed aid, if they impose disempowered identities on their publics, their actions devolve from well-intentioned philanthropy into paternalism. The case of Royal Dutch Shell in Nigeria illustrates this point. The Nigerian government is heavily dependent on oil income and has worked closely with oil companies to ensure uninterrupted gas production in the oil-rich Niger Delta. The area is populated by a

I am powerful

CARE is an INGO devoted to ending poverty worldwide.

Photo 11.1   The Cover of CARE's 2005 Annual Report, Presenting an Empowered Image of Developing World Peoples

SOURCE: Photo by Phil Borges, courtesy of the photographer and CARE International.

number of small ethnic minority groups who believe they have not received financial benefits from the natural resources on their lands, suffering only environmental degradation instead.

In 1995, the Nigerian government hanged nine environmental activists who were protesting oil company actions, sparking a militant reaction among the local peoples. In turn, Shell started funding and supplementing government paramilitary security forces to stop the uprisings. The incident sparked a global boycott of Shell, and a United Nations Special Report called for an investigation of Shell's activities in Nigeria (U.N., 1998). Responding to pressure, Shell launched community relations programs to build schools and hospitals, provide clean drinking water, and improve roads in the area.

But the actions proved too little, too late. Analysts charge that Shell undertook community relations actions only to reduce criticism and didn't allow local people to participate in determining what actions should be taken. As a result, environmental activists continue to disrupt production in the area, and the military's use of force to target opinion leaders and terrorize them led to an investigation by Amnesty International in late 2005. Shell's paternalistic approach hasn't resulted in improved public relations, despite the fact that it now contributes almost US$70 million yearly to human development in the region and widely publicizes its community relations efforts (see http://www .shell.com).

Contrast Shell's approach with that of IKEA. In 1992, when allegations arose that child labor was being used to manufacture IKEA carpets, management investigated the issue and worked with Save the Children, a well-respected INGO, to resolve the issue. Following this resolution, IKEA partnered with UNICEF and the International Labor Organization to address the root causes of child labor, donating US$500,000 to UNICEF in 2000 to support education and poverty reduction measures and instituting joint inspections of all suppliers with International Labor Organization representatives. When issues arose over renewable resources, a top IKEA official spent an extended period of time at Greenpeace headquarters, resulting in IKEA's donation of US$2.5 million to Greenpeace's global forest mapping project and establishing renewable resource guidelines for its manufacturers (Miller, Piore, & Theil, 2001).

By actively partnering with INGOs, delegating decision-making power to them, and not concentrating on a direct benefit to the bottom line, IKEA has avoided drawing activist fire and maintained good relations with its publics. Although the IKEA Group corporate Web site contains an "our responsibility" section, IKEA doesn't actively use the media to create an identity of itself as a responsible member of the global community. Instead, a search for IKEA in news databases reveals various identities of IKEA constructed by others, from a destination spot offered as part of a package deal by Marriott Hotels, to an informal provider of social services for the working classes in Germany, to an almost cultlike status among consumers.

This comparative example highlights some of the actions that separate philanthropy and good public relations from paternalism and poor public relations. Multinational enterprises must consider the broader and long-term ethical ramifications of their actions, not just immediate short-term gains. Identifying shared concerns and working with activists by empowering them in the decision-making process lead to better outcomes. Public relations time and efforts may be better spent on prolonged ethnographic research and organizational adherence to stated policy rather than on media and consumer relations designed to establish an image of a good global citizen.

Although the cultural–economic model doesn't tell us what constitutes ethical action, it does illustrate how the moments of regulation and identity work together when we make ethical decisions. It cautions us to avoid using reductionist, simplistic thinking when making ethical decisions and to take time to deconstruct meanings informing differing cultural norms and conflicting identities. It also demonstrates the value of being inclusive and empowering those outside the organization in organizational decision making.

How can we make this work in practice? We turn to common approaches to ethical decision making to determine how well they answer the ethical issues posed by globalization.

❖ COMMON APPROACHES TO PUBLIC RELATIONS ETHICS

Among the most commonly discussed approaches to public relations ethics are codes, stakeholder theory, and discourse ethics. We examine each in turn in terms of its ability to meet the challenges of cultural relativism and increasing power imbalances inherent in international practice.

Codes of Ethics

Most professional public relations societies have ethics codes, including the two largest international groups: the International Public

Relations Association and the International Association of Business Communicators. Codes are designed to ensure professionals' integrity and reassure the public of the profession's credibility. Because codes must serve as general guidelines applicable under any number of circumstances, they're necessarily vague.

Consider the Media Transparency Charter, adopted by the International Public Relations Association, the Institute for Public Relations, the International Communications Consultancy Organisation, and the Global Alliance for Public Relations and Communication Management. The code addresses the practice common in many areas of the world, such as Russia, for news media to charge a fee for publishing public relations materials, a practice that erodes media credibility and makes information dissemination a privilege of the wealthy. Specifically, the charter requires that any editorial content that "appears as a result of a payment in cash or kind, or barter by a third party will be clearly identified as advertising or paid promotion" (ICCO, 2006, ¶ 4).

The code provides little guidance for media relations in Ghana, however, where journalists receive a small remuneration at news conferences to cover transportation expenses. Without such payment, the poorly paid journalists wouldn't be able to attend and could miss out on legitimate news. Codes, then, may not be well suited to dealing with the conflicting meanings that emerge from differing cultural regulatory systems.

Additionally, because codes set standards and delineate punishments for their breach, codes are a form of legalistic thinking, which isn't consonant with cultural values in many parts of the world. More collectivist cultures don't readily adopt codes because they require individuals to report others for infractions (G. Weaver, 2001). In some European cultures, such as Germany, ethics often is considered a matter of private duty, outside the realm of public rules (Palazzo, 2002). In countries with a history of authoritarian or colonial leadership, rules often are perceived as something to circumvent, not follow (Husted, 2002), making adoption and enforcement difficult. Not all practitioners operate within a culture in which codes are compatible with prevailing norms.

Numerous studies demonstrate that organizational culture is a much stronger influence on ethical decision making than is a code. Where many scholars and practitioners do agree is that the process of generating a code, which entails thinking through shared general principles that should guide ethical practice, is a valuable exercise—often more valuable than the code generated.

Stakeholder Ethics

Stakeholder ethics *defines ethical action as meeting the needs and addressing the concerns of groups that hold an interest or stake in an organization,* such as shareholders, volunteers, suppliers, and media groups. Stakeholder ethics often is used as the basis for corporate social responsibility programs, although groups other than corporations often adopt the approach as well.

Although the approach sounds like a way to meet the needs of all publics, stakeholder needs often conflict, requiring organizations to choose among competing claims by prioritizing them according to their relative importance to the organization. Companies using sweatshops to manufacture goods privilege stockholders and the bottom line over employees and the supply chain. Radical environmentalist groups, such as the Earth Liberation Front, that destroy property privilege nature over property rights. Different organizational cultures, then, create different identities of stockholder groups that guide their actions and determine ethical action, imbuing this approach with ethical relativism.

Additionally, stakeholder theory doesn't address the issues raised by power differentials aggravated by globalization. As demonstrated by Royal Dutch Shell in Nigeria, a stakeholder approach may result in arguably good actions, such as providing hospitals and schools in areas of need, while still disempowering stakeholders and creating poor relationships. Numerous studies demonstrate that organizations most often adopt stakeholder ethics out of **enlightened self-interest:** *taking actions to create an identity of the organization as a good global citizen rather than out of actual altruism.*

Such an approach seldom leads to good public relations, however, because stakeholder ethics then readily devolve into shareholder ethics, causing the organization's many publics to hold competing organizational identities. When a shared identity is not established between an organization and its publics, ethical discord remains. The moment of identity in the cultural–economic model plays a crucial role in guiding ethical action.

Discourse Ethics

To negate the problems raised by trying to determine absolute ethical values, Habermas (1979, 1996) suggested *tying ethics to the communicative process,* an approach known as **discourse ethics.** Habermas proposed communication rules in which both parties must agree

- To be open and honest
- To listen to the other side rationally and without argumentation
- To be genuinely interested in reaching consensus, a goal that makes this approach compatible with the two-way symmetric model of public relations practice

Because it adopts a rule-based approach, discourse ethics depends on a process of rational negotiation.

Empirical tests demonstrate that cultures have differing negotiation styles and preferred outcomes, however. Some believe they are win–lose propositions, which precludes any chance of consensus. Recognizing the issues raised by multiculturalism, Habermas revised his procedures to include particular cultural values, but he admitted the procedure isn't applicable to all situations and can often lead to compromise and majority rule rather than rational consensus (Baumeister, 2003; Haas, 2001).

Discourse ethics also require that all parties be equally empowered, but the reality is that

- Not everyone is equally competent to present his or her views.
- Not everyone has equal access to the communicative process.
- Not everyone has the necessary desire to reach true consensus.

A case study of a community development project in Scotland demonstrates how discourse ethics often is untenable. Although the government promised the community a joint venture for community renewal, neither side in the issue could let go of long-held prejudices to form a new, unified identity from which to move forward. For example, government officials often stigmatized residents of the low-income housing area by identifying them as "the lowerarchy" and shutting them out of discussions (Gunson & Collins, 1997, p. 288). Whereas activism has been an effective strategy for community members, a dialogic approach proved strikingly ineffective.

Other studies have examined organizational efforts to establish two-way channels of communication, such as Web forums, as a means of creating meaningful dialogue. As is the case with stakeholder ethics, however, too often these efforts are geared toward deflecting true debate and simply creating an identity of a caring, ethical organization rather than actually engaging publics in negotiation. These examples demonstrate how consensus, often heralded as the goal of effective public relations, too often becomes a tool of the empowered to maintain power, and as such is not a part of ethical public relations practice (Holtzhausen, 2000).

❖ NEW ETHICAL APPROACHES AND PRACTITIONERS' ROLES

Although codes, stakeholder ethics, and discourse ethics have their particular strengths, they're not adequate to answer the challenges raised by international practice and globalization. Two newer schools of ethical thought show promise in meeting these challenges: postcolonial feminist ethics and identity ethics.

Postcolonial Feminist Ethics

Postcolonial feminist ethics *is concerned with the ongoing colonialism manifested in globalization's tendency to shift resources from the majority of the world's people and in oppression of all sorts* (e.g., gender, ethnicity, class, religion, sexual orientation). Unlike discourse ethics, postcolonial ethics holds that power differentials cannot be discounted. Instead, they form the crux of ethical thought. Relative power forms a central organizing tenet of postcolonial feminist ethics, much as it does in the cultural–economic model of practice.

Consequently, ethical action results in part from giving discursive rights to those who've been traditionally disempowered and effectively silenced. As two Ruder Finn public relations executives said of their work with the widows of the genocide in Rwanda, "It was clear to us that the ability to marshal PR expertise to highlight the critical work of women in post-conflict situations was essential to empowering them within their countries and with international audiences" (Merriam & Glauber, 2004, p. 26).

To do so, however, entails deconstructing the dominant discourse surrounding an issue to uncover how relative power is manifested. For example, deconstruction of INGO appeals reveals the pornography of poverty that disempowers peoples in developing countries. Deconstruction of stakeholder ethics reveals the paternalism underlying enlightened self-interest. By placing power differentials at the forefront of ethical thought, deconstruction forces practitioners to examine not just the ethical content of an issue but also its context.

Similar to the cultural–economic model, it provides a continuum between absolute principles and situational particulars. It entails recognition of and respect for the multiple, competing truths found in any situation and avoids treating false dichotomies as fact. It allows us to raise concern about cultural practices, such as *baksheesh*, without condemning them (Jaggar, 1998).

By avoiding dichotomies and examining a multitude of competing truths, deconstruction avoids simple right and wrong declarations. It opens up many possible courses of action consonant with home country principles yet sensitive to local customs and norms, demonstrating the false dichotomy that exists between global and local as well. The earlier example of German MNCs using consultants to determine local needs and provide gifts in kind rather than paying *baksheesh* to officials provides an example of this type of action. Postcolonial feminist ethics avoids the pitfalls of cultural relativism by providing us with a blueprint by which to negotiate between ethical universalism and pure relativism.

Self-reflexive deconstruction also forces us to examine root causes and take a long-term perspective. Refusing to use child labor because you believe it's wrong doesn't solve the problem and may even aggravate it. Child labor exists because of poverty and a lack of educational opportunities. Children in many parts of the world have to work to eat and survive. Ethical action entails not simply stopping the use of child labor, and thereby possibly contributing to child deaths, but addressing the root causes of the problem, much as IKEA has done by partnering with INGOs and trade associations.

Identity Ethics

Postcolonial feminist ethics also recognizes the crucial role played by identity in ethical decision making, which ties it to the second emerging field of ethical thought: **identity ethics,** *which is premised on the "hybridity and multiplicity of identities"* (Mack-Canty, 2004, p. 161). As we noted in chapter 9, globalization has lent two distinct aspects to identity: diaspora, the spread of cultures outside their former geographic boundaries; and hybridity, the adoption and adaptation of different cultural aspects, forming an infinite variety of cultural meldings. The multiplicity and fluidity of identities demand an acceptance of pluralism and conflict and a respect for and acknowledgment of the multitudinous perspectives of publics, particularly disenfranchised ones.

In this manner, identity ethics values diversity, not difference. Whereas difference splinters and dichotomizes, dividing "us" from "them," identity ethics embraces diversity and pluralism, along with the cacophony of voices that often ensues. What postcolonial feminist ethics and identity ethics demonstrate is the need to embrace conflict, debate, and critical inquiry, both for the insights they provide and for the process they facilitate of allowing all to be heard. The goal becomes not reaching consensus but managing dissensus.

The result is a true situation ethics but not ethical relativism. There's a large difference between saying you'll do what you feel like in any given situation and saying you must be sensitive to all situational particulars as you apply principles and examine consequences.

Practitioners as Traitorous Identities

Adopting a postcolonial feminist and identity ethics perspective is consonant with the cultural–economic model and contributes to it by delineating the ethical role of public relations practitioners. Practitioners must be open to learning as much as possible about the environment in a manner that respects other cultures and their perspectives. Practitioners must be self-reflexive, deconstructing organizational "truths" and seeking out multiple alternative viewpoints, especially from those often disempowered by dominant discourse. They must critically examine their organizations' multiple identities and those they have constructed of publics, breaking out of dichotomous modes of thought to recognize and respect the number of competing truths inherent in any situation.

Successfully adopting this perspective entails what Bailey (1998) calls establishing a **traitorous identity**—*being able to challenge and resist organizational assumptions to accept and value diversity*. Developing a traitorous identity requires that practitioners, in their professional role, step outside not only their organizations' comfort zones but also their own and be willing to try on new identities, assume new risks, and learn not just *about* other cultures but *from* them. It entails going beyond cultural indices and other reified measures of cultural difference, such as surveys and other "scientific" methods that aggregate individual data into generalizabilities, to more ethnographic methods that allow multiple perspectives to emerge. It entails more listening than talking, more being directed than leading.

Practitioners must be able to step outside organizational culture, casting a critical eye on it while remaining a valued member of that culture. In this sense, then, *traitorous* does not mean disloyal. It means being open to competing discourses and diverse voices. A current international practitioner puts it this way: "What is required of us is not merely an ability to adapt quickly, but a basic humility about ourselves combined with a fundamental curiosity about others" (Pelfrey, 2004, p. 29).

Perhaps most important, an ethical practitioner is aware that every decision is an ethical one. Planning a campaign and producing campaign materials involves establishing and privileging a particular discourse of cultural perspectives and relative power relationships. The smallpox eradication case raised some profound ethical issues that illustrate this point. When campaign leaders decided to use war imagery to represent the campaign, they established a discourse that allowed possible victims to be treated as enemies and forcefully vaccinated. When they used the moral suasion of shame as a tactic, they imposed a discourse of moral superiority that discounted the developing world's right to self-determination. Because no campaign decision or tactic is ever devoid of ethical content, development of a traitorous identity is necessary to think through the ethical ramifications of everyday actions to avoid making mistakes of ethical omission as well as commission.

That such an approach is feasible and contributes directly to organizational success is demonstrated by organizations such as IKEA. Assuming a traitorous identity isn't easy, nor is it always a comfortable role. But as one public relations scholar notes, "Public relations should facilitate making profoundly uncomfortable conversations possible" (Spicer, 2000, p. 129).

CHAPTER SUMMARY

- Ethics emerges as the confluence of the moments of regulation and identity, although ethics is inherent in all aspects of public relations practice.

- International practice must balance organizational norms with respect for local practices, negotiating a position along the continuum between ethical absolutism and cultural relativism.

- Enlightened self-interest leads to short-term measures, paternalism, and poor public relations.

- Philanthropy results from partnering with other organizations and local communities to resolve issues and address underlying root causes, leading to effective public relations.

- Commonly discussed approaches to public relations ethics don't sufficiently address the challenges posed by globalization.

- Practitioners must assume a traitorous identity, deconstructing dominant discourse, challenging organizational assumptions, and seeking out and valuing diversity and dissent.

12

The Future of International Public Relations Practice

❖ ❖ ❖

Applying the practice matrix that emerges from the cultural–economic model takes work, but so does any public relations project. The purpose of the practice matrix is to provide new ways of thinking about how public relations practitioners can serve as cultural intermediaries. We're adapting that descriptor to connote a certain type of public relations practitioner, one who's willing to work through barriers to develop a worldview. The semantic toolbox of the worldview includes terms we've used throughout the book: *dissensus, flexibility, meaning making, difference, power, culture, moments, articulations, reflexivity, flux, change, identity, representation, production, consumption,* and *regulation*. These are but a few of the terms that denote ways of seeing and doing public relations generated by the cultural–economic model.

In this chapter, we examine what these ways of seeing and doing public relations mean for the future of the field. We begin by examining the implications of practitioners and scholars embracing the cultural–economic model and how that can affect patterns of global public relations. This discussion leads into what we anticipate as future developments in the field of international public relations.

❖ IMPLICATIONS FOR PRACTITIONERS EMBRACING THE CULTURAL–ECONOMIC MODEL

In chapter 2, we grouped public relations activities into various areas that included multinational corporations, nation building, travel and tourism, nonprofits, trade associations, and sports, among others. The matrix is applicable to each of these areas and the many others that might not fall into simple categorizations—a reminder that the matrix is useful for any public relations text or activity. It's a compass that provides direction across the uneven landscape of international public relations, and its use should advance our study of public relations, helping us move forward by developing new ideas about international public relations.

By doing so, however, we must occasionally glance back to see what we're leaving behind. The circuit repeatedly teaches us that nothing is fixed, from meanings to cultural mores to targeted publics; all are changing at various rates and in various ways, all affecting how we do our work in public relations.

Along with change comes reluctance to leave the comfort zones of what we know and have come to accept. Challenging traditional discourses is a perilous task that can result in uncertainty and disillusionment but also offers great potential. In this section, we explore how the cultural–economic model can transform the traditional practice of public relations, beginning with the idea of reframing its uses in global society.

Reframing Public Relations Practice Across Borders and Cultures

We've mentioned the many criticisms organizations face in the court of public opinion. Watchdog groups and the media have blasted Coca-Cola for alleged mislabeling of its products, improper waste disposal, and its ill-fated release of New Coke®. Russia is unable to shake the vestiges of its communist past, deterring investment. Human rights groups have accused Nike of running sweatshops in developing countries. The king of Swaziland has been admonished for leading his lavish lifestyle in an impoverished country. India was blamed for slowing global efforts to eradicate smallpox.

What do all these examples have in common? They all represent problems of reputation and credibility, the most cherished possessions of any organization or individual. It's easy to imagine linking public relations to any of these situations along with pejorative terms such as *debacle, fiasco,* or *failure.* Coke's Dasani® blunder is a "public relations disaster," as we mentioned in chapter 2. Chapter 5 noted that one Russian journalist said the country has a "public relations problem" in luring foreign investment. Look at most Western media sources and skim this book, and you'll see that these types of phrases attest to the problems faced by organizations, governments, or people.

These examples demonstrate that public relations often is associated with crisis, perceived or actual wrongdoing, and criticism. The result is a discourse of public relations shrouded in suspicion and distrust. If we apply the logic of the cultural–economic model, we have a way of decoding this discourse, leaving us with new insights. The "public relations as bad news" discourse could become dominant enough to cancel out other competing discourses, such as those more favorable to the practice of public relations. Such discourses would spawn from the moment of regulation, which instructs us that cultural expectations can affect the practice of public relations.

To reframe that discourse, we need newer discourses that offer competing perspectives. The model offers the raw materials for public relations practitioners to encode their materials and campaigns with such new discourses. Through those efforts, public relations can also be about maintaining and protecting credibility, even when things are going well. To reframe international public relations, then, we need to use the cultural–economic model and its ethical guidance to develop discourses of public relations in periods of tranquility.

What does that mean? Public relations needn't always be about fixing problems and reputations. One starting point is to examine the public relations techniques of organizations that aren't in trouble or going through turbulent times. What are they doing? How are they building their reputation? What are they communicating, how are they communicating, and to whom are they communicating?

The answers to these questions can help us identify discourses of public relations that aren't predicated on strife. Notice how the cultural–economic model generates ethical signposts for practitioners and scholars through these types of questions. Think of the model as a system of checks and balances that avoids privileging Western norms or resulting in ethical relativism.

Defining Global Public Relations

We've already discussed the problems of defining public relations. The onus falls on practitioners to articulate what they do. The cultural–economic model positions practitioners to have a worldview, serve as cultural intermediaries, and expect inconsistent perspectives. Armed with that knowledge, a public relations practitioner is in a position to manage dissensus.

One way to manage dissensus is to acknowledge issues of control and power, which are at work in all forms of public relations. Understanding these issues is about stepping outside our comfort zone and into a sphere where discourses, practices, and cultures are different. This logic brings together power and identity, two of the central components of the circuit of culture and the cultural–economic model. Fine, you might say, but what does this mean? It means that public relations practitioners shouldn't try to eliminate competing discourses and create consensus but should work on formulating competing discourses to create shared meanings and identities.

There are two lessons here to globally define public relations. The first is that public relations is always occurring—good, bad, or indifferent. The idea of historicity teaches us that doing nothing is a form of public relations. The second is that if the field of public relations is seeking a global definition, it must be all-inclusive. Comparing other countries to U.S. standards of public relations and suggesting that they have a long way to go until they catch up to the United States diminishes what we can learn from other cultures and what they deem as public relations.

Scholars are also encouraged to shift their attention from comparative case studies built on Western public relations models. Such studies have contributed to our understanding of international public relations, but they also preclude the development of new theories and ideas. A case study rooted in Western models is limited by Western assumptions. For practitioners, the challenge is to seek multiple viewpoints before undertaking a public relations initiative. The matrix forces practitioners to analyze materials written not only by host nationals but also by Westerners who have traveled to foreign lands, sharing what they've learned. Together, these voices help us see cultures from the inside looking out and vice versa. The call is to examine countries according to the range of meanings they hold, as found in their respective histories, cultures, and political and economic systems.

In short, there's a need to develop and formulate new models developed by host nationals and scholars who embrace the principles of the cultural–economic model. Only then can we begin to move toward global definitions of public relations that are balanced, diverse, and inclusive.

Challenging Assumptions

A final way in which the cultural–economic model can inform international public relations is by pushing those who embrace it to challenge assumptions. The idea here isn't to unlearn or drop everything you know about public relations. You won't be surprised to find that the crux of challenging assumptions is to consider how the intersection of culture, identity, and power shapes how we see the world. That intersection also influences how we view the function of public relations. The products of this intersection form the foundation of a critical and cultural public relations perspective and a paradigm shift from the positivist theories that predominate in Western public relations scholarship.

Remember that culture provides a regulatory environment that shapes our way of seeing and interacting with the world. If we're unable to question our culture and occasionally divorce ourselves from it, we are ill equipped to experience other cultures on their own merit. Many student exchange programs encourage their students to let go of their own cultures and avoid comparisons, for instance. The Southern Cross Cultural Exchange program Web site (see http://www.scce.com) has this to say about successful exchange students: "They stopped comparing things with home, decided to tolerate the differences, find out how and why things were so different, and start living life as a local immediately."

Power is acting within and around public relations at all times. As you read this, you're in a relative position of power. Why? First, you speak English, which has been called the dominant global language. Recognizing that billions of people around the world can't speak or read English is a key consideration. Second, you're in a financial position to afford this book. Perhaps you're reading it for a class or as a public relations scholar or practitioner. Regardless, you have access to power structures, whether universities, public relations agencies, or organizations with a public relations function, and are in a position of privilege.

Finally, you have some interest in public relations; for millions of people around the world, public relations is meaningless when their very survival is at stake. As the smallpox eradication case study demonstrated, however, public relations can provide the education that can save lives.

For public relations to have impact that can save lives, eradicate disease, and ameliorate global strife, it must be viewed and understood in its proper context. Far too often that context is in relation to the world's economic powers. To only understand and recognize public relations in those dominant areas decreases the breadth of public relations as a legitimate global practice. The head of the Reserve Bank in Zimbabwe underscored this point in a recent speech. He noted that globalization is actually decreasing per capita wealth in many developing countries. The tides of globalization also destroy the public relations industries in those countries because nobody can afford it, he added.

In sum, the public relations industry is disappearing from the areas in which it may be most needed. It's following the tide of globalization, leaving uneven development, unfulfilled promise, and stunted evolution in its wake. This path is problematic because it substantiates global inequality in general. As Thomas Friedman (1999, p. 258) observed, "It seems to me that there is something inherently unstable about a world that is being knit tighter and tighter by technology, markets and telecommunications, while splitting wider and wider socially and economically."

Public relations might continue to have higher visibility in strong economies, but its practice and study shouldn't be limited to those areas. Although pundits might say public relations is growing in certain areas of the world, our position is that it's been there all along, perhaps not labeled as such and perhaps not practiced in Western terms by public relations agencies.

The third determinant in challenging assumptions is difference and identity. Practitioners unable to appreciate difference bring a preconceived notion of how public relations should be practiced. When we relinquish control, we aren't powerless; we're sensitive to difference and embrace diversity. The inability to let go and see other cultures, even if they appear quite similar to our home culture, is why many international consultants fail. Savvy consultants know they can rely on their professional experience, but they must also be open and adaptable to that which is foreign to them.

Embracing the cultural–economic model gives us access to different meanings by revealing the undercurrents of culture that exist well beneath the surface. It encompasses the familiar triad of power, culture, and identity. Inevitably, we'll want to compare other cultures to our own and wonder why they don't do things as we do. Challenging assumptions is a process that entails work and sensitivity. This is where the practice matrix comes in. If you look again at the situational moments and actions under each moment, you should see opportunities, not barriers.

Grasping those opportunities means adopting a traitorous identity, discussed in chapter 11. The fundamental idea is that it's not enough to challenge assumptions a few times. It must be part of a process of continually challenging, mirroring the communicative process that defines public relations.

Keep in mind that the cultural–economic model emphasizes communication as the currency of this information age. This emphasis on the process of communication divorces the model from dominant neoliberal models that tie public relations to economic goals. Placing communication over economics empowers publics by according them respect as dynamic entities that create and perpetuate culture. The notion that publics are active participants in the communication process of the model answers some of the criticisms commonly leveled against public relations.

❖ WHERE DO WE GO FROM HERE?

The cultural–economic model can't be used to predict the future of international public relations. By its very nature, however, it's flexible enough to keep up with the changes and remain viable as the field continues to grow and evolve. What that growth might look like is the subject of the final part of this book, starting with global meanings of public relations.

Global Processes of Meaning Making and Public Relations

The definition, role, and scope of public relations will continue to change as marginalized voices are brought to the forefront of global public relations discourse. We suggest that societal perceptions of its values and worth will continue to change, as will its scope of practice. For instance, if there's no universal definition of public relations, it is contested. The lack of a base doesn't make it immune to the global tides that will bring to bear emerging discourses of public relations.

In the future, then, we might expect to see the function of public relations expand and blur the boundaries between public relations and similar topical disciplines, such as marketing and advertising. Debates about propaganda, persuasion, information, and point of view shouldn't be discarded; they should be viewed in relation to public relations. In short, what we mean by public relations today isn't necessarily what it will mean years from now. This point encourages practitioners and scholars to stay abreast of the field by monitoring global perceptions of public relations and joining public relations associations.

However, it's important to recognize that public relations agencies and associations are generally the formalizing structures that define public relations practice around the world. And, as we noted earlier, those structures tend to cluster in countries with strong economies. That doesn't mean that public relations education and scholarship must follow the same gravitational pull toward the world's economic engines. The challenge to public relations is to widen its frame for viewing the world through a politic of inclusion. We don't have to agree with public relations practices around the world or necessarily like them. But we can learn from practices that are different from ours.

Again, the idea of difference is the stream of commonality in our discussion. Acknowledging difference and embracing diversity is difficult work, however. Ronald Steel (1996, p. D15) noted the U.S. penchant for resisting difference: "We insist that they be like us. And of course for their own good. We are the world's most relentless proselytizers. The world must be democratic. It must be capitalistic. . . . No wonder many feel threatened by what we represent."

At stake is the future of public relations and whether it continues to veer toward dominant global forces or is reflexive enough to include areas of the world that are underrepresented, economically "developing," and absent a Western heritage of public relations agencies, associations, and tradition. A first step toward broadening the scope of international public relations is to generate more studies that don't compare public relations practices around the world but consider them in their own cultural context with their own economy, political structure, and situational particulars. The result can be a much richer, broader understanding of public relations.

Along with that understanding is a need for ethnic diversity in public relations. The field must be as culturally, racially, and ethnically diverse as the audiences it seeks to reach.

Global Politics and Economy

The engines driving public relations will be political, economic, and cultural. Culture merits special attention because of its prominence in our understanding of what it means to do and practice public relations. However, economy and politics are as important. Economic growth around the world brings with it the irrepressible forces of globalization. One byproduct of globalization is an increase in institutional structures to define public relations.

We expect to see more institutions at the local, national, and international levels that seek to label their work "public relations." These institutions might include multinational corporations, trade associations, and professional public relations associations. Technology will continue to dissolve national and organizational lines, making nations and companies more transparent and less isolated.

This trend extends into economic power, as countries emerging from developing status will bring to bear more powerful discourses about public relations. It's still likely that the number of formalizing institutions will cluster around countries and regions of economic growth. This pluralism will translate to more voices vying to define the practice of public relations. The challenge for practitioners is to remain open to these new discourses and remain flexible to new interpretations and meanings of public relations.

The Cultural Engine

As we've discussed, culture is the focal point of all public relations. How culture changes our world and how we see it will continue to confound and surprise us. The cultural–economic model gives us the tools to adapt to change and, most important, to ensure that culture is at the bulls-eye of public relations campaigns. That bulls-eye will remain unfixed, moving slightly and retreating back to its original place or perhaps never returning to that spot. When we challenge our assumptions, incorporate lessons from the circuit of culture, use the practice matrix, and eschew complacency in any public relations endeavor, the groundwork for truly effective international public relations practice is firmly in place.

Instead of casting the net of scholarly inquiry repeatedly over the same regions of the world, the field of public relations must find ways to express itself as a global practice. One approach to elevate the status of public relations internationally is for practitioners to look for guidance outside the realm of public relations. For example, the WHO case study in this book came largely from medical journals. There's much for public relations to learn about itself by stepping outside of comfort zones and its traditional knowledge base, provided largely by Western scholars and global public relations enterprises.

We aren't suggesting that practitioners start reading medical journals or become generalists. What we are saying is that practitioners must be open to looking beyond traditional public relations knowledge for new insights and discoveries. This step, along with the lessons of the cultural–economic model, can better position public relations practitioners as innovative communicators who can wield influence in world affairs. How quickly practitioners respond to the challenge is of great importance: "The current state of global communication is distressing and dangerous. One thing that clearly emerge[s] . . . is a need for the communications professional to take a far greater role in world affairs" (PRSA.org, 2003, ¶ 2).

Even for practitioners who have little interest in influencing world affairs, knowledge of such affairs is a hallmark of a cultural intermediary. Knowing about the world is the first step to understanding it. Of equal importance to practitioners is a commitment to being reflexive and seeing the world around them on terms other than their own. In this regard, the cultural–economic model is more than a model. It provides ways of seeing that are also about listening to marginalized voices and other disciplines that can inform public relations practice globally.

The end result of using the cultural–economic model of international public relations is a new way of seeing what we do in public relations, how it affects others, and how it can benefit diverse groups. The model strays from many Western theories and practices by suggesting that cultural issues are the centerpiece of public relations. In broader terms, it addresses the limitations of many Western public relations theories by suggesting fresh, global views of public relations, truly a new way of seeing.

Henry Miller (1957, p. 25) reflects this new way of seeing: "One's destination is never a place, but a new way of seeing things." New ways of seeing are only part of the goal; of equal importance is the recognition that the destination has suddenly become a new starting point. By negotiating culture, identity, and power, the practice of international public relations comes full circle.

CHAPTER SUMMARY

- Public relations doesn't have to be associated with solving problems.

- Public relations is always occurring, good, bad, or indifferent, and the cultural–economic model enables new ways of studying and analyzing its global dimensions.

- The practice matrix of the cultural–economic model provides a way to analyze and develop an unlimited range of public relations activities.

- The cultural–economic model provides a broad-based critical and cultural approach to international public relations.

- The nature and definitions of public relations are likely to remain in flux.

- Public relations will continue to be driven by political, economic, and cultural factors.

- Practitioners should strive to act as cultural intermediaries who are sensitive to cultural differences.

Bibliography

Acosta-Alzuru, C., & Kreshel, P. J. (2002). "I'm an American Girl . . . whatever that means": Girls consuming Pleasant Company's American Girl identity. *Journal of Communication, 52*(1), 139–161.

Adler, C. (2003, November 24). Colonel Sanders' march on China. *Time Asia.* Retrieved July 20, 2005, from http://www.time.com/time/asia/magazine/article/0,13673,501031124-543845,00.html

African Cultural Center. (n.d.). *Languages & religion.* Retrieved June 15, 2005, from http://www.africanculturalcenter.org/5_3languages_religion.html

Alanazi, A. (1996). Public relations in the Middle East: The case of Saudi Arabia. In H. Culbertson & N. Chen (Eds.), *International public relations: A comparative analysis* (pp. 239–255). Mahwah, NJ: Lawrence Erlbaum.

Altman, L. K. (1975, September 29). Global war on smallpox expected to be won in '76. *New York Times,* pp. 1, 26.

Altman, L. K. (1976, November 18). Scientist, 2 doctors and world health agency win Lasker awards. *New York Times,* p. A30.

Altman, L. K. (1977, January 20). Smallpox outbreak in Somalia hurts eradication effort. *New York Times,* p. A25.

Altman, L. K. (1979, October 16). The doctor's world: The eradication of smallpox. *New York Times,* p. C3.

Anderson, B. (1991). *Imagined communities: Reflections on the origin and spread of nationalism* (Rev. ed.). New York: Verso.

Andersson, H. G. (1996). Interview with John Scott Porterfield: Smallpox eradication program volunteer (1971). *Biohazard News,* republished from *Outbreak.* Retrieved October 29, 2004, from http://www.biohazardnews.net/porterfield

Auclair, M. (1992). Out in Africa: Going where no communicator has gone before. *Communication World, 9*(2), 43–46.

Auerbach, S. (1977, March 23). Smallpox: A deadly disease in its death throes. *Washington Post,* p. A20.

Ayish, M., & Kruckeberg, D. (1999). Abu Dhabi National Oil Company (ADNOC). In J. Turk & L. Scanlan (Eds.), *Fifteen case studies in international public relations* (pp. 122–130). Gainesville, FL: The Institute for Public Relations.

Badler, D. (2004). 10 rules for building a successful global corporate communications organization. *Strategist, 10*(1), 18–21.

Bailey, A. (1998). Locating traitorous identities: Toward a view of privilege-cognizant white character. *Hypatia, 13*(3), 27–42.

Banks, S. P. (2000). *Multicultural public relations: A social-interpretive approach* (2nd ed.). Ames: Iowa State University Press.

Basu, R. N., Ježek, Z., & Ward, N. A. (1979). *The eradication of smallpox from India.* New Delhi: World Health Organization.

Baudrillard, J. (1988). *Selected writings* (M. Poster, Trans.). Cambridge, England: Polity.

Baudrillard, J. (1994). *Simulation and simulacra* (S. F. Glaser, Trans.). Ann Arbor: University of Michigan Press. (Original work published 1981)

Baumeister, A. T. (2003). Habermas: Discourse and cultural diversity. *Political Studies, 51*, 740–758.

Bazin, H. (2000). *The eradication of smallpox: Edward Jenner and the first and only eradication of a human infectious disease.* New York: Academic Press.

BBC World Service Trust. (2002, December 5). *Ghana: Preventing trachoma.* Retrieved April 28, 2006, from http://www.bbc.co.uk/worldservice/trust/news/story/2005/08/020306_trachoma.shtml

Bell, D. A., & Carens, J. H. (2004). The ethical dilemmas of international human rights and humanitarian NGOs: Reflections on a dialogue between practitioners and theorists. *Human Rights Quarterly, 26*, 300–329.

Berg, N., & Holtbrugge, D. (2001). Public affairs management activities of German multinational corporations in India. *Journal of Business Ethics, 30*, 105–119.

Bernays, E. L. (1923). *Crystallizing public opinion.* New York: Liveright Press.

Bernays, E. L. (1965). *Biography of an idea: Memoirs of public relations counsel Edward L. Bernays.* New York: Simon & Schuster.

Bhabha, H. K. (1996). Culture's in-between. In S. Hall & P. du Gay (Eds.), *Questions of cultural identity* (pp. 53–60). Thousand Oaks, CA: Sage.

Billig, M. (1995). *Banal nationalism.* Thousand Oaks, CA: Sage.

Black, J. (1999, November 1). Losing ground bit by bit. *BBC News.* Retrieved July 14, 2005, from http://news.bbc.co.uk/1/hi/special_report/1999/10/99/information_rich_information_poor/472621.stm

Bodeen, C. (2005, July 23). Chinese farmers in dispute with factory. *Associated Press.* Retrieved July 23, 2005, from http://news.yahoo.com

Borders, W. (1976, October 3). Battle goes on to free world from smallpox. *New York Times,* p. A17.

Boshnakova, D., & Zareva, R. (2005). *PR landscapes: Bulgaria.* Retrieved June 5, 2005, from http://www.globalpr.org/knowledge/businessguides/Profile_Bulgaria.pdf

Botan, C. (1992). International public relations: Critique and reformulation. *Public Relations Review, 18*(2), 149–159.

Botan, C. H., & Soto, F. (1998). A semiotic approach to the internal functioning of publics: Implications for strategic communication and public relations. *Public Relations Review, 24*(1), 21–44.

Boulding, K. E. (1959). National images and international systems. *The Journal of Conflict Resolution, 3*(2), 120–131.

Bourdieu, P. (1984). *Distinction: A social critique of the judgement of taste* (R. Nice, Trans.). Cambridge, MA: Harvard University Press. (Original work published 1979)

Brilliant, L. B. (1985). *The management of smallpox eradication in India.* Ann Arbor: University of Michigan Press.

Brilliant, L. B., & Brilliant, G. (1978, May–June). Death for a killer disease. *Quest,* p. 5.

Brinkerhoff, D., & Ingle, M. (1989). Integrating blueprint and process: A structured flexibility approach to development management. *Public Administration and Development, 9,* 487–500.

Brook, S., & Tryhorn, C. (2005, July 6). Long race begins for UK media. *Guardian.* Retrieved July 1, 2005, from http://media.guardian.co.uk/site/story/0,14173,1522562,00.html

Brown, S. (2003, November 19). In IKEA we trust, Swedes tell pollsters. *Reuters News Service.* Retrieved November 20, 2003, from http://news.yahoo.com

Bruning, S. D., & Ledingham, J. A. (1999). Relationships between organizations and publics: Development of a multi-dimensional organization–public relationship scale. *Public Relations Review, 25*(2), 157–170.

Burkeman, O. (2004). The miracle of Älmhult. *Guardian.* Retrieved July 6, 2005, from http://www.guardian.co.uk

Burns, B. M. (2001, October 30). *The NGO war against globalization: Implications for international public relations.* Atlanta, GA: Atlas Award Lecture on International Public Relations.

Burson, H. (2003a). *The next steps in going global: Offices in Asia and Australia.* 6th in a series of 50th Anniversary Memos. Retrieved August 4, 2005, from http://www.bm.com/pages/about/history/memos/6

Burson, H. (2003b). *The thrill of landing a new client: Two cases: General Motors and Coca-Cola.* 9th in a series of 50th Anniversary Memos. Retrieved June 18, 2005, from http://www.burson-marsteller.com/pages/about/history/memos/9

Butler, R. (2005). *World's largest cities.* Retrieved June 10, 2005, from http://www.mongabay.com/cities_pop_01.htm

Carpenter, D. (2005, June 14). McDonald's flagship aims at the hip. *Associated Press.* Retrieved June 15, 2005, from http://news.yahoo.com

Carroll, A. B. (2004). Managing ethically with global stakeholders: A present and future challenge. *Academy of Management Executive, 18*(2), 114–120.

Casey, M. (2005, August 27). Mass polio vaccination campaign in Indonesia hampered by rumors, ignorance. *Associated Press.* Retrieved October 24, 2005, from LexisNexis database.

Castells, M. (1996). *The information age: Economy, society and culture: Vol. 1. The rise of the network society.* Cambridge, MA: Blackwell.

Challenor, B. D. (1971). Cultural resistance to smallpox vaccination in West Africa. *Journal of Tropical Medicine and Hygiene, 74,* 57–59.

Chay-Németh, C. (2003). Becoming professionals: A portrait of public relations in Singapore. In K. Sriramesh & D. Verčič (Eds.), *The global public relations handbook: Theory, research, and practice* (pp. 86–105). Mahwah, NJ: Lawrence Erlbaum.

Cheney, G., & Christensen, L. T. (1997). Identity at issue: Linkages between "internal" and "external" organizational communication. In F. Jablin & L. L. Putnam (Eds.), *New handbook of organizational communication* (pp. 231–269). Thousand Oaks, CA: Sage.

Chong, A., & Valencic, J. (2001). *The image, the state and international relations.* London: The London School of Economics and Political Science.

Chow, R. (1993). *Writing diaspora.* Bloomington: Indiana University Press.

Christensen, L. T. (1997). Marketing as auto-communication. *Consumption, Markets and Culture, 1*(3), 197–228.

CIA. (2005). *The world factbook.* Retrieved January 26, 2006, from http://www.cia.gov/cia/publications/factbook/index.html

CIA. (2006). *The world factbook.* Retrieved March 21, 2006, from http://www.cia.gov/cia/publications/factbook/index.html

Clarke, I, III, Micken, K. S., & Hart, H. S. (2002). Symbols for sale . . . at least for now: Symbolic consumption in transition economies. *Advances in Consumer Research, 29,* 25–30.

Cleaver, H. M. (2003). *Zapatistas in cyberspace: A guide to analysis and resources.* Retrieved July 27, 2005, from http://www.eco.utexas.edu/homepages/faculty/Cleaver/zapsincyber.html

Clifford, J. (1988). *The predicament of culture: Twentieth century ethnography, literature and art.* Cambridge, MA: Harvard University Press.

Cockburn, A. (2005, April 13). Message in a bottle. *The Free Press.* Retrieved June 15, 2005, from http://www.freepress.org/columns/display/2/2005/1107

Cody, E. (2005, June 13). For Chinese, peasant revolt is a rare victory. *Washington Post Foreign Service.* Retrieved June 14, 2005, from http://news.yahoo.com

Cohn, V. (1979, October 26). Total victory in two-century effort is proclaimed by smallpox warriors. *Washington Post,* p. A2.

Cooper-Chen, A. (1996). Public relations practice in Japan: Beginning again for the first time. In H. M. Culbertson & N. Chen (Eds.), *International public relations: A comparative analysis* (pp. 222–237). Mahwah, NJ: Lawrence Erlbaum.

Crawford, A. P. (2004). Communicating with the Arab world. *Strategist, 19*(1), 30–32.

Creedon, P. J., Al-Khaja, W. A., & Kruckeberg, D. (1995). Women and public relations education and practice in the United Arab Emirates. *Public Relations Review, 21*(1), 59–77.

Creehan, S. (2001). A forgotten enemy: The threat of smallpox. *Harvard International Review, 23*(1), 6–7.

Crossette, B. (2002, May 17). Russia and China called top business bribers. *New York Times*, p. A10.

Croteau, D., & Hoynes, W. (2002). *Media society: Industries, images and audiences* (3rd ed.). Thousand Oaks, CA: Pine Forge Press.

Culbertson, H. M. (1996). Introduction. In H. M. Culbertson & N. Chen (Eds.), *International public relations: A comparative analysis* (pp. 1–13). Mahwah, NJ: Lawrence Erlbaum.

Culbertson, H. M., & Chen, N. (2003). Public relations in mainland China: An adolescent with growing pains. In K. Sriramesh & D. Verĉiĉ (Eds.), *The global public relations handbook: Theory, research, and practice* (pp. 23–45). Mahwah, NJ: Lawrence Erlbaum.

Das, V. (1999). Public good, ethics, and everyday life: Beyond the boundaries of bioethics. *Daedalus, 128*(4), 99–134.

Davies, M. (1980, May). A job well done. *World Health*, pp. 6–9.

de Certeau, M. (1984). *The practice of everyday life* (S. F. Rendell, Trans.). Berkeley: University of California Press.

De Launey, G. (2005, April 7). Killing fields deal hits delay. *BBC News*. Retrieved June 4, 2005, from http://news.bbc.co.uk/go/pr/fr/-/2/hi/asia-pacific/4419671.stm

Delight over KFC Tibet decision. (2004, June 26). *BBC News*. Retrieved July 19, 2005, from http://news.bbc.co.uk/2/hi/south_asia/3836927.stm

Derrida, J. (1974). *Of grammatology*. Baltimore, MD: Johns Hopkins University Press.

Doksoz, R. E. (2004). Tourism and Dracula's homeland. In D. J. Tilson & E. C. Alozie (Eds.), *Toward the common good: Perspectives in international public relations* (pp. 163–175). Boston: Pearson.

Donalson, T., & Dunfree, T. W. (1999). When ethics travel: The promise and peril of global business ethics. *California Management Review, 41*(4), 45–63.

Dougall, E. (2005). Revelations of an ecological perspective: Issues, inertia, and the public opinion environment of organizational populations. *Public Relations Review, 31*(4), 534–543.

Down, A. (1972). Up and down with ecology: The "issue attention cycle." *The Public Interest, 28*, 38–50.

Dozier, D. M., & Lauzen, M. M. (2000). Liberating the intellectual domain from the practice: Public relations, activism, and the role of the scholar. *Journal of Public Relations Research, 12*(1), 3–22.

du Gay, P. (1996). *Consumption and identity at work*. Thousand Oaks, CA: Sage.

du Gay, P. (1997). Introduction. In P. du Gay (Ed.), *Productions of culture/cultures of production* (pp. 1–10). Thousand Oaks, CA: Sage.

du Gay, P., Hall, S., Janes, L., Mackay, H., & Negus, K. (1997). *Doing cultural studies: The story of the Sony Walkman*. Thousand Oaks, CA: Sage.

Edmondson, G. (2005, June 24). Got 5,000 euros? Need a new car? *BusinessWeek Online*. Retrieved July 1, 2005, from http://news.yahoo.com

Falconi, T. M. (2003). On the worldwide public relations community. In *Public relations in Europe* (pp. 14–16). Retrieved April 8, 2003, from http://www.eprn.org/EuropeanPRnews2_1/Column1.pdf

Farooq, O. (2003, March 24). Indian rebels target US cola. *BBC News.* Retrieved May 28, 2005, from http://news.bbc.co.uk/1/hi/world/south_asia/2881191.stm

Federal Research Division of the Library of Congress. (n.d.). *Sudan: Ethnicity.* Retrieved June 15, 2005, from http://www.mongabay.com/reference/country_studies/sudan/35.html

Fenner, F., Henderson, D. A., Arita, I., Ježek, Z., & Ladnyi, I. D. (1988). *Smallpox and its eradication.* Geneva: World Health Organization.

Fish, J. (2000, January 5). Propaganda wars in Kosovo and Chechnya. *BBC News.* Retrieved June 6, 2005, from http://news.bbc.co.uk/1/hi/world/europe/591916.stm

Fobanjong, J. (2004). The quest for public relations in Africa. In D. J. Tilson & E. C. Alozie (Eds.), *Toward the common good: Perspectives in international public relations* (pp. 203–214). Boston: Pearson.

Foege, W. F., & Dowdle, W. R. (1997, October 24). Editorial note. *Morbidity and Mortality Weekly Report,* pp. 991–994.

Foley, J. (2005). Trinidad: Life on the margins. In L Chávez (Ed.), *Capitalism, God, and a good cigar* (pp. 45–61). Durham, NC: Duke University Press.

FoodService.com. (2004, January 16). *Yum! Restaurants International opens 1000th KFC in China.* Retrieved July 20, 2005, from http://www.foodservice.com/news/company_news_detail

Foucault, M. (1978). *The history of sexuality: Vol. 1. An introduction* (R. Hurley, Trans.). New York: Pantheon. (Original work published 1976)

Foucault, M. (1995). *Discipline & punish: The birth of the prison* (A. Sheridan, Trans.). New York: Vintage Books. (Original work published 1975)

Freitag, A. R. (2002). Ascending cultural competence potential: An assessment and profile of U.S. public relations practitioners' preparation for international assignments. *Journal of Public Relations Research, 14*(3), 207–227.

Friedman, T. L. (1999). *The Lexus and the olive tree.* New York: Farrar, Straus and Giroux.

Fürsich, E., & Robins, M. B. (2002). Africa.com: The self-representation of sub-Saharan African nations on the World Wide Web. *Critical Studies in Mass Communication, 19*(2), 190–211.

Fürsich, E., & Robins, M. B. (2004). Visiting Africa: Constructions of nation and identity on travel websites. *Journal of Asian and African Studies, 39*(1–2), 133–152.

GAPR. (2004). *PR landscapes: Romania.* Global Alliance for Public Relations and Communication Management. Retrieved June 7, 2005, from www.globalpr.org/knowledge/businessguides/Profile_romania.pdf

Gardner, S., & Standaert, M. (2003). *Estonia and Belarus: Branding the old bloc.* Retrieved May 19, 2006, from http://www.brandchannel.com/features_effect.asp?id=146

Gaunt, P., & Ollenburger, J. (1995). Issues management revisited: A tool that deserves another look. *Public Relations Review, 21*(3), 199–210.

Gibson, N. C. (2004). Africa and globalization: Marginalization and resistance. *Journal of Asian and African Studies, 39*(1–2), 1–28.

Gilroy, P. (1997). Diaspora and the detours of identity. In K. Woodward (Ed.), *Identity and difference* (pp. 299–343). Thousand Oaks, CA: Sage.

Gladwell, M. (1998, July 6). The spin myth. *New Yorker,* pp. 66–73.

Global Business Coalition on HIV/AIDS. (2005). *Fact sheet: New commitments to fight HIV/AIDS in China by GBC member companies.* Retrieved July 17, 2005, from http://www.businessfightsaids.org/atf/cf/%7BEE846F03-1625-4723-9A53B0CDD2195782%7D/GBC%20Company%20Commitments%20Fact%20Sheet.pdf

Global Reach. (2004). *Global Internet statistics.* Retrieved July 26, 2005, from http://global-reach.biz/globstats/index.php3

Godlee, F. (1995, January 21). WHO's special programmes: Undermining from above. *British Medical Journal,* pp. 178–182.

Greaves, D. (2001, April 1). Social dis-ease of collective irresponsibility. *The Lancet,* p. 1190.

GreenCOM Project. (2005). *South Africa: Active learning about climate change.* Retrieved May 25, 2006, from http://www.greencom.org/greencom/pdf/SouthAfrica.pdf

Greenough, P. (1995). Intimidation, coercion and resistance in the final stages of the South Asian smallpox eradication campaign, 1973–1975. *Social Science and Medicine, 41*(5), 633–645.

Greenwald, J. (1985, July 22). Coca-Cola's big fizzle: Consumer revolt forces the company to bring back the old, familiar flavor. *Time,* pp. 48–52.

Grunig, J., & Hunt, T. (1984). *Managing public relations.* New York: Holt, Rinehart and Winston.

Grunig, L. A., Grunig, J. E., & Verĉiĉ, D. (1998). Are the IABC's excellence principles generic? Comparing Slovenia and the United States, the United Kingdom, and Canada. *Journal of Communication Management, 2,* 335–356.

Gunson, D., & Collins, C. (1997). From the *I* to the *We:* Discourse ethics, identity, and the pragmatics of partnership in the west of Scotland. *Communication Theory, 7*(4), 278–300.

Haas, T. (2001). Public relations between universality and particularity: Toward a moral–philosophical conception of public relations ethics. In R. Heath (Ed.), *Handbook of public relations* (pp. 423–433). Thousand Oaks, CA: Sage.

Habermas, J. (1979). *Communication and the evolution of society* (T. McCarthy, Trans.). Boston: Beacon.

Habermas, J. (1996). *Between facts and norms* (W. Regh, Trans.). Cambridge: MIT Press.

Hall, E. T. (1977). *Beyond culture.* New York: Anchor Press/Doubleday.

Hall, E. T., & Hall, M. R. (1995). *Understanding cultural differences.* Yarmouth, ME: International Press.

Hall, S. (1980). Cultural studies: Two paradigms. *Media, Culture and Society,* 2(1), 57–72.

Hall, S. (1991). The local and the global: Globalization and ethnicities. In A. D. King (Ed.), *Culture, globalization and the world system* (pp. 19–30). London: Macmillan.

Hall, S. (1993). Encoding/decoding. In S. During (Ed.), *The cultural studies reader* (pp. 90–103). New York: Routledge.

Hall, S. (1996). Introduction: Who needs "identity"? In S. Hall & P. du Gay (Eds.), *Questions of cultural identity* (pp. 1–17). Thousand Oaks, CA: Sage.

Hall, S. (1997a). The centrality of culture: Notes on the cultural revolutions of our time. In K. Thompson (Ed.), *Media and cultural regulation* (pp. 208–236). London: Sage.

Hall, S. (1997b). Introduction. In S. Hall (Ed.), *Representation: Cultural representations and signifying practices* (pp. 1–11). Thousand Oaks, CA: Sage.

Hansen, A. (1993). Greenpeace and press coverage of environmental issues. In A. Hansen (Ed.), *The mass media and environmental issues* (pp. 150–178). Leicester, UK: Leicester University Press.

Harare embarks on major public relations campaign. (2002, February 9). *Africa News Service.* Retrieved January 6, 2006, from InfoTrac Onefile database.

Heath, R. L. (1993). A rhetorical approach to zones of meaning and organizational prerogatives. *Public Relations Review, 19*(2), 141–155.

Heath, R. L. (1997). *Strategic issues management: Organizations and public policy challenges.* Thousand Oaks, CA: Sage.

Henderson, D. A. (1980, May). A victory for all mankind. *World Health,* pp. 3–5.

Henderson, D. A. (1998). Eradication: Lessons from the past. *Bulletin of the World Health Organization, 76,* 17–21.

Hesmondhalgh, D. (2002). *The culture industries.* Thousand Oaks, CA: Sage.

Hill, L. B., & Dixon, L. D. (2006). The intercultural communication context: Preparation for international public relations. In M. Parkinson & D. Ekachai (Eds.), *International and intercultural public relations: A campaign case approach* (pp. 66–84). Boston: Allyn & Bacon.

Hill, L. N., & White, C. (2000). Public relations practitioners' perception of the World Wide Web as a communication tool. *Public Relations Review, 26*(1), 31–51.

Hofstede, G. (2001). *Culture's consequences: Comparing values, behaviors, institutions and organizations across nations* (2nd ed.). Thousand Oaks, CA: Sage.

Hofstede, G. (n.d.). *Geert Hofstede™ cultural dimensions: Brazil.* Retrieved July 15, 2005, from http://www.geert-hofstede.com/hofstede_brazil.shtml

Hollie, P. G. (1985a, July 14). Coca-Cola swallows its words. *New York Times,* p. D28.

Hollie, P. G. (1985b, July 12). Fans of "old Coke" wouldn't give up. *New York Times,* p. D15.

Hollie, P. G. (1985c, April 23). Formula for Coca-Cola is expected to change. *New York Times,* p. D1.

Holtzhausen, D. R. (2000). Postmodern values in public relations. *Journal of Public Relations Research, 12*(1), 93–114.

Hopkins, D. R. (2002). *The greatest killer: Smallpox in history.* Chicago: University of Chicago Press.

Hopkins, J. W. (1989). *The eradication of smallpox: Organizational learning and innovation in international health.* Boulder, CO: Westview Press.

Huang, Y. H. (2001). OPRA: A cross-cultural, multiple-item scale for measuring organization–public relationships. *Journal of Public Relations Research, 13*(1), 61–90.

Husted, B. W. (2002). Culture and international anti-corruption agreements in Latin America. *Journal of Business Ethics, 37,* 413–422.

Hutton, J. G. (1999). The definition, dimensions, and domain of public relations. *Public Relations Review, 25,* 199–214.

ICCO. (2004). *Introductory guidance paper on international public relations.* International Communications Consultancy Organisation. Retrieved June 20, 2005, from http://www.iccopr.com/site/content/view/130/99/

ICCO. (2006). *Media transparency charter.* International Communications Consultancy Organisation. Retrieved January 23, 2006, from http://www.iccopr.com/members/?fuseaction=MediaTransparencyCharter

IGTOA. (2005a). *International Galapagos Tour Operators Association Web site.* Retrieved July 20, 2005, from http://www.igtoa.org/news/alerts/Jan05/index.php

IGTOA. (2005b). *International Galapagos Tour Operators Association Web site.* Retrieved January 9, 2006, from http://www.igtoa.org/newsletter/2005/january05/

Ihator, A. (2001). Corporate communication: Challenges and opportunities in a digital world. *Public Relations Quarterly, 46*(4), 15–18.

Illman, P. E. (1980). *Developing overseas managers and managers overseas.* New York: AMACOM.

Imperato, P. J., & Traoré, D. (1968). Traditional beliefs about smallpox and its treatment in the Republic of Mali. *The Journal of Tropical Medicine and Hygiene, 10*(1), 224–228.

India and W.H.O. in big drive to prevent revival of smallpox. (1975, November 2). *New York Times,* p. 16.

InternationalReports.net. (2001). *Ecuador 2001.* Retrieved July 20, 2005, from http://www.internationalreports.net/theamericas/ecuador/2001/opportunites.html

In Turkey, Hughes gets an earful on Iraq. (2005, September 28). *USA Today.* Retrieved November 4, 2005, from http://www.usatoday.com/news/world/2005-09-28-turkey-hughes_x.htm

Jaggar, A. M. (1998). Globalizing feminist ethics. *Hypatia, 13*(2), 7–31.

Jamal, A. (2003). Marketing in a multicultural world: The interplay of marketing, ethnicity and consumption. *European Journal of Marketing, 37*(11–12), 1599–1620.

Joarder, A. K., Tarantola, D., & Tulloch, J. (1980). *The eradication of smallpox from Bangladesh.* New Delhi: World Health Organization.

Katz, M. (2005). Salsa criticism at the turn of the century: Identity politics and authenticity. *Popular Music and Society, 28*(1), 35–54.

Keenan, K. (2003). Public relations in Egypt: Practices, obstacles, and potentials. In K. Sriramesh & D. Verčič (Eds.), *The global public relations handbook: Theory, research, and practice* (pp. 178–198). Mahwah, NJ: Lawrence Erlbaum.

Kenyon, K. (1998, October). Church drives traffic at Philippine shopping mall. *Shopping Centers Today.* Retrieved August 5, 2005, from http://www.icsc.org/srch/sct/current/sct9810/22.htm

Kerschner, J. (2004, July 11). Ecotourism abuse. *The Borneo Post Sunday.* Retrieved July 21, 2005, from http://www.borneoecotours.com/news/details.asp?newsid=52

KFC. (2002, September 3). KFC opens China's first drive-thru restaurant. Retrieved July 19, 2005, from http://www.kfc.com/about/pr/090302.htm

Khera, I. P. (2001). Business ethics east vs. west: Myths and realities. *Journal of Business Ethics, 30,* 29–39.

Kim, W. (2003, May). *Public relations in Korea.* Panel presentation at the meeting of the International Communication Association, San Diego, CA.

King seeks 11 palaces for wives. (2004, January 12). *BBC News.* Retrieved June 12, 2005, from http://news.bbc.co.uk/1/hi/world/africa/3389211.stm

Kono, D. Y. (2002). Are free trade areas good for multilateralism? Evidence from the European Free Trade Association. *International Studies Quarterly, 46,* 507–527.

Kunczik, M. (2004). *Images of nations and transnational public relations of governments with special reference to the Kosovo.* Paper presented at the symposium Final Status for Kosovo, Chicago, IL. Retrieved June 5, 2005, from http://pbosnia.kentlaw.edu/symposium/kunczik-Images%200f%20Nations%20and%20Transnational%20Public%20Relations%20by%20Governents%20with%20SpecialReference%20to%20the%20Kosovo.htm

Lancaster, J. (1998, October 27). Barbie, "Titanic" show good side of "Great Satan." *Washington Post,* p. A1.

Lasswell, H. D. (1948). The structure and function of communication in society. In L. Bryson (Ed.), *The communication of ideas.* New York: Harper.

Lawrence, F. (2004). Things get worse with Coke. Retrieved June 20, 2005, from http://www.guardian.co.uk/uk_news/story/0,,1174014,00.html

Leitch, S., & Neilson, D. (2001). Bringing publics into public relations: New theoretical frameworks for practice. In R. Heath (Ed.), *The handbook of public relations* (pp. 127–138). Thousand Oaks, CA: Sage.

Leitch, S., & Richardson, N. (2003). Corporate branding in the new economy. *European Journal of Marketing, 37*(7–8), 1065–1079.

Lester, E. (1992). Buying the exotic "other": Reading the "Banana Republic" mail order catalogue. *Journal of Communication Inquiry, 16*(2), 74–85.

L'Etang, J. (2004). *Public relations in Britain: A history of professional practice in the 20th century.* Mahwah, NJ: Lawrence Erlbaum.

Ma, E. K. (2001). Consuming satellite modernities. *Cultural Studies, 15*(3–4), 444–463.

Mackay, H. (1997). Introduction. In H. Mackay (Ed.), *Consumption and everyday life* (pp. 1–12). Thousand Oaks, CA: Sage.

Mack-Canty, C. (2004). Third-wave feminism and the need to reweave the nature/culture duality. *NWSA Journal, 16*(3), 154–179.

MacKenzie, D. (2004, March 13). A magnificent obsession. *New Scientist,* pp. 44–47.

Maddox, R. (1993). *Cross-cultural problems in international business.* Westport, CT: Quorum Press.

Mahoney, H. (2004, December 20). Communications commissioner to battle to introduce change. *EUObserver.* Retrieved July 27, 2005, from http://ec.europa.eu/commission_barroso/wallstrom/interviews/euobserver_20041220_en.htm

Mandela, N. (2000). The challenge of the next century: The globalization of responsibility. *New Perspectives Quarterly, 17*(1), 34–35.

Mather, R. J., & John, T. J. (1973). Popular beliefs about smallpox and other common infectious diseases in south India. *Tropical and Geographical Medicine, 25*(2), 190–196.

Maynard, M. (2003). From global to glocal: How Gillette's SensorExcel accommodates to Japan. *Keio Communication Review, 25,* 57–75.

Maynard, M., & Tian, Y. (2004). Between global and glocal: Content analysis of the Chinese Web sites of the 100 top global brands. *Public Relations Review, 30,* 285–291.

McCracken, G. (1988). *Culture and consumption: New approaches to the symbolic character of consumer goods and activities.* Bloomington: University of Indiana Press.

McDermott, P. M. (1997, November 8). *Workshop on international public relations.* Annual convention of the Public Relations Society of America, Nashville, TN.

McGregor, C. (2003, June 24). Solving Russia's image problem key to attracting U.S. finance. *St. Petersburg Times.* Retrieved July 19, 2005, from http://www.sptimes.ru/index.php?action_id=2&story_id=10347

Media Education Foundation. (2002). *Toxic sludge is good for you: The public relations industry unspun.* Northampton, MA: Author.

MEPRA. (2004, December). *MEPRA plans growing role to create PR career openings.* Retrieved June 6, 2005, from http://www.mepra.org/news.php

Merriam, D., & Glauber, A. (2004). Public relations can aid peace-building efforts. *Strategist, 10*(1), 26–27.

Mickey, T. J. (1997). A postmodern view of public relations: Sign and reality. *Public Relations Review, 23*(3), 271–284.

Miller, D. (1997). Consumption and its consequences. In H. Mackay (Ed.), *Consumption and everyday life* (pp. 13–50). Thousand Oaks, CA: Sage.

Miller, H. (1957). *Big Sur and the oranges of Hieronymus Bosch.* New York: New Directions.

Miller, K. L., Piore, A., & Theil, S. (2001, March 12). The Teflon shield. *Newsweek International,* p. 26.

A modern miracle. (1979, October 29). *Washington Post*, p. A26.

Moffitt, M. A. (1994). Collapsing and integrating concepts of "public" and "image" into a new theory. *Public Relations Review, 20*(2), 159–170.

Molleda, J., Connolly-Ahern, C., & Quinn, C. (2005). Cross-national conflict shifting: Expanding a theory of global public relations management through quantitative content analysis. *Journalism Studies, 6*(1), 87–102.

Montenegro, S. L. (2004). Public relations in Latin America: A survey of professional practice of multinational firms. In D. J. Tilson & E. C. Alozie (Eds.), *Toward the common good: Perspectives in international public relations* (pp. 102–126). Boston: Pearson.

Moores, S. (1997). Broadcasting and its audiences. In H. Mackay (Ed.), *Consumption and everyday life* (pp. 213–246). Thousand Oaks, CA: Sage.

Morgan, R. (1969). Attitudes towards smallpox and measles in Nigeria. *International Journal of Health Education, 12*(2), 77–85.

Morganthau, T. (1985, June 24). Saying "no" to New Coke. *Newsweek*, pp. 32–33.

Morinis, E. A. (1978). Two pathways in understanding disease: Traditional and scientific. *WHO Chronicle, 32*(2), 57–59.

Morley, D., & Chen, K.-H. (1996). Introduction. In D. Morley & K.-H. Chen (Eds.), *Stuart Hall: Critical dialogues in cultural studies* (pp. 1–24). London: Routledge.

Morley, D., & Robins, K. (1995). *Spaces of identity: Global media, electronic landscapes and cultural boundaries*. New York: Routledge.

Morley, M. (2004). Anatomy of a global corporate brand. *Strategist, 10*(1), 14–17.

Morosini, P. (2002). Competing on social capabilities: A defining strategic challenge of the new millennium. In L. Mohn (Ed.), *A cultural forum: Vol. 3. Corporate cultures in global interaction* (pp. 28–32). Retrieved January 5, 2006, from http://www.bertelsmann-stiftung.de/bst/media/Cultural-Forum-III-FINAL.pdf

Morris, B. (1987, June 3). Coke vs. Pepsi. *Wall Street Journal*, p. 1.

Motion, J., Leitch, S. (2002). The technologies of corporate identity. *International Studies of Management & Organization, 32*(3), 45–64.

Motion, J., Leitch, S., & Brodie, R. J. (2003). Equity in corporate co-branding: The case of Adidas and the All Blacks. *European Journal of Marketing, 37*(7–8), 1080–1094.

Nair, V. V. (2002, October 16). There's more to Russia. *The Hindu Business Line.* Retrieved July 19, 2005, from http://www.blonnet.com/ew/2002/10/16/stories/2002101600020100.htm

Nelson, C. (1985). The smallpox eradication campaign. In *Collaborative research on tropical diseases* (p. 9). Retrieved April 19, 2004, from http://www.developmentstrategies.org/Archives/1985NASTropDiseases/1985Trop12.htm

Newport, F. (2003). Accounting's image recovers: Computer, restaurant, and grocery industries have most positive images. *Gallup Poll News Service.* Retrieved June 7, 2005, from http://www.gallup.com/poll/content

Nigeria polio vaccine passes test. (2003, November 20). *BBC News.* Retrieved February 23, 2004, from http://news.bbc.co.uk/go/pr/fr/-/2/hi/africa/3223874.stm

Ohmae, K. (1989, May–June). Managing in a borderless world. *Harvard Business Review, 67*(3), 152–161.

Oliver, T. (1985). *The real Coke, the real story.* New York: Random House.

Overby, J. W., Woodruff, R. B., & Gardial, S. F. (2004). French versus American consumers' attachment of value to a product in a common consumption context: A cross-national comparison. *Journal of the Academy of Marketing Science, 32*(4), 437–460.

Palazzo, B. (2002). U.S.–American and German business ethics: An intercultural comparison. *Journal of Business Ethics, 41,* 195–216.

Pelfrey, D. (2004). Changing frames: The American effect. *Strategist, 10*(1), 28– 29.

Pentagon hires public relations firm to reverse opposition in Islamic world. (2001, October 19). *Knight Ridder.* Retrieved June 20, 2005, from http://www.prfirms.org/resources/news/pentagon101901.asp

Pieczka, M., & L'Etang, J. (2001). Public relations and the question of professionalism. In R. Heath (Ed.), *Handbook of public relations* (pp. 223–235). Thousand Oaks, CA: Sage.

Prada, P. (2005, April 8). Catholicism challenged in Brazil. *The Boston Globe.* Retrieved August 5, 2005, from http://www.boston.com/news/world/latinamerica/articles/2005/04/08/catholicism_challenged_in_brazil?mode=PF

PRSA.org. (2003, November 25). *Communicators discuss their roles in global decision making.* Public Relations Society of America. Retrieved January 31, 2006, from http://prsa.org/_news/press/pr112503.asp

Ragan Communications. (2001, May). *Cyber-attack against Starbucks shows what to do when a crisis brews.* Ragan Communications, Inc. Retrieved June 11, 2005, from http://www.organicconsumers.org/starbucks/pr.cfm

RBC. (2003, November 26). Expert estimates corporate PR market. *RosBusinessConsulting News Online.* Retrieved April 26, 2006, from http://www.rbcnews.com/free/20031126181526.shtml

The real story of New Coke®. (n.d.). Retrieved August 1, 2006, from http://www2.coca-cola.com/heritage/cokelore_newcoke.html

Reber, B. H., & Harriss, C. (2003, August). *Building public relations definitions: Identifying definitional typologies among practitioners and educators.* Paper presented at the annual meeting of the Association for Education in Journalism and Mass Communication, Kansas City, MO.

Reed, J. D. (2002). Virus vanquisher. *Smithsonian, 32*(11), 28.

Rhee, Y. (2002). Global public relations: A cross-cultural study of the excellence theory in South Korea. *Journal of Public Relations Research, 14*(3), 159–184.

Riley, M. (1991, May). *Indigenous resources in a Ghanaian town: Potential for health education.* Paper presented at the annual meeting of the International Communication Association, Chicago, IL.

Roy, A. (1997). *The God of small things.* New York: Random House.

Rushdie, S. (1991). The riddle of midnight: India, August 1987. In S. Rushdie, *Imaginary homelands: Essays and criticism 1981–1991* (pp. 26–36). London: Granta.

Safer, M. (2004, November 24). The look of Abercrombie & Fitch. *CBS News Worldwide.* Retrieved January 24, 2006, from http://www.cbsnews.com/stories/2003/12/05/60minutes/main587099.shtml

Said, E. W. (1979). *Orientalism.* New York: Vintage.

Said, E. W. (1981). *Covering Islam: How the media and experts determine how we see the rest of the world.* New York: Pantheon.

Salaman, G. (1997). Culturing production. In P. du Gay (Ed.), *Production of culture/cultures of production.* London: Sage.

Salcedo, R. (2003). When the global meets the local at the mall. *The American Behaviorist, 46*(8), 1084–2004.

Save the North Sea. (2004). *Reduce marine litter: Save the North Sea project results.* Retrieved June 11, 2005, from http://savethenorthsea.com

Schmeck, H. M., Jr. (1978, May 21). The last case of smallpox: An old story, told again. *New York Times,* p. E9.

Schreiner, B. (2005, January 15). China licking its fingers. *Washington Times.* Retrieved January 20, 2006, from http://washingtontimes.com/business/20050114-095939-7816r.htm

Seitel, F. P. (2000, July 31). *Relax Mr. Stauber, public relations ain't that dangerous.* Retrieved January 29, 2006, from http://mediachannel.org/views/oped/seitel.shtml

Sereg, R. (n.d.). *Media and public relations strategy for nongovernmental organizations.* Freedom House. Retrieved January 30, 2006, from http://216.239.51.104/search?q=cache:liBDCSPTPkJ:www.freedomhouse.org/reports/ngopr.html+ronald+sereg&hl=en&gl=us&ct=clnk&cd=3

Shanahan, W. M., & Prabhaker, P. (2003, January). *Establishing a category brand in the United States: A case study of marble from Greece.* Paper presented at the Seventh Annual International Conference on Global Business and Economic Development, Bangkok, Thailand.

Spicer, C. H. (2000). Public relations in a democratic society: Value and values. *Journal of Public Relations Research, 12*(1), 115–130.

Sriramesh, K. (1992). Societal cultural and public relations: Ethnographic evidence from India. *Public Relations Review, 18*(2), 201–211.

Sriramesh, K. (2003). Introduction. In K. Sriramesh & D. Verčič (Eds.), *The global public relations handbook: Theory, research, and practice* (pp. xxv–xxxvi). Mahwah, NJ: Lawrence Erlbaum.

Sriramesh, K., & Verčič, D. (2003). A theoretical framework for global public relations research and practice. In K. Sriramesh & D. Verčič (Eds.), *The global public relations handbook: Theory, research, and practice* (pp. 1–22). Mahwah, NJ: Lawrence Erlbaum.

Srivastava, A. (2003). *Communities reject Coca-Cola in India.* Retrieved June 15, 2005, from http://www.corpwatch.org/article.php?id=7508

Steel, R. (1996, July 21). When worlds collide. *New York Times,* p. D15.

Sveshnikoff, A. (2005, April). The slow-death of "black" PR. *International Public Relations Association.* Retrieved June 10, 2005, from http://www.ipra.org/membersfrontline/frontlineapr2005/1.htm (article has moved to http://www.webershandwick.co.uk/outcomes/issue7/topstory.html).

Taghi Beigi, Y. (2002, January 5). Tehran dishes out satellite crackdown. *Asia Times Online*. Retrieved July 13, 2005, from http://atimes.com/c-asia/DA05Ag02.html

Thaung, U., & Ko Ko, U. (2002). The eradication of smallpox. In U. Ko Ko, K. Lwin, & U. U. Thaung (Eds.), *Conquest of scourges in Myanmar* (pp. 47–119). Yangon, Myanmar: Academy of Medical Science.

Tilson, D. J. (2004). Privatization and government campaigning in Ecuador. In D. J. Tilson & E. C. Alozie (Eds.), *Toward the common good: Perspectives in international public relations* (pp. 63–82). Boston: Pearson.

Tilson, D. J., & Alozie, E. C. (2004). *Toward the common good: Perspectives in international public relations*. Boston: Pearson.

Tkalac, A., & Pavicic, J. (2003). Nongovernmental organizations and international public relations. In K. Sriramesh & D. Verčič (Eds.), *The global public relations handbook: Theory, research, and practice* (pp. 490–504). Mahwah, NJ: Lawrence Erlbaum.

Treanor, J. (1999, July 14). Coca-Cola loses some of its fizz. *Guardian*. Retrieved June 20, 2005, from http://www.guardian.co.uk/food/Story/0,205743,00.html

Tsetsura, K. (2003). Theoretical development of public relations in Russia. In K. Sriramesh & D. Verčič (Eds.), *The global public relations handbook: Theory, research, and practice* (pp. 301–319). Mahwah, NJ: Lawrence Erlbaum.

Tsetsura, K., & Kruckeberg, D. (2004). Theoretical development of public relations in Russia. In D. J. Tilson & E. C. Alozie (Eds.), *Toward the common good: Perspectives in international public relations* (pp. 176–192). Boston: Pearson.

Tucker, J. B. (2001). *The once and future threat of smallpox*. New York: Grove.

Tuli, J. (1980, May). India's "war plan." *World Health*, pp. 12–13.

Turkey defies U.S. with Syria visit. (2005, April 13). *BBC News*. Retrieved November 4, 2005, from http://news.bbc.co.uk/2/hi/middle_east/4440183.stm

TurkishPress. (n.d.). *Turkish–U.S. relations in 2003*. Retrieved November 4, 2005, from http://www.turkishpress.com/specials/2003/yir/usa.asp

Tutor, L. (2002, December). Keeper of the flame. *QSR Magazine*. Retrieved July 20, 2005, from http://www.qsrmagazine.com/issue/interview/cheryl_bachelder_print.phtml

2003 PR agency of the year. (2003, May). *Adweek Magazines' Technology Marketing, 23*, 26–27.

Tyler, J. (2002, December 10). Savvy-traveler: Eco-tourism in the Galapagos. *CNN.com*. Retrieved July 20, 2005, from http://archives.cnn.com/2002/TRAVEL/DESTINATIONS/12/10/savvyt.galapagos.tourism/index.html

Uganda hires PR agency to buff up its image. (2005, May 21). *Mail & Guardian Online*. Retrieved January 13, 2006, from http://www.mg.co.za/articlePage.aspx?articleid=241278&area=/breaking_news/breaking_news_africa/

U.N. (1998, April 15). *United Nations Special Rapporteur's report on Nigeria*. New York: Author.

U.N. (2002). *Escaping the poverty trap: The least developed countries report 2002*. New York: United Nations Conference on Trade and Development.

U.N. (n.d.). *UN millennium development goals*. Retrieved May 26, 2006, from http://www.un.org/millenniumgoals/

UNESCO. (2003). *Criteria for appraisal of teaching/learning material for HIV/AIDS prevention in school settings*. Retrieved January 30, 2006, from http://portal.unesco.org/education/en/file_download.php/35faf8620c749b455 5542be4de3bfdebUNICEF+Teacher+Guide.pdf

UNEXWorld. (2003, February 28). *Government to allocate $1.97m for foreign exhibitions*. Retrieved July 19, 2005, from http://www.unex.ru/exponews/1/11_1.html

Valin, J. (2004, October). *Overview of public relations around the world and principles of modern practice*. Remarks made to the Conselho Federal de Profissionais de Relações Publicas conference, Brasilia, Brazil.

van Ham, P. (2001). The rise of the brand state: The postmodern politics of image and reputation. *Foreign Affairs, 80*(5), 2–6.

Van Hook, S. R. (n.d.). *PR business is booming*. Retrieved April 6, 2003, from http://aboutpublicrelations.net/aa042901a.htm

Van Leuven, J. K., & Pratt, C. B. (1996). Public relations' role: Realities in Asia and in Africa south of the Sahara. In H. M. Culbertson & N. Chen (Eds.), *International public relations: A comparative analysis* (pp. 93–107). Mahwah, NJ: Lawrence Erlbaum.

van Ruler, B. (2003). Public relations in the Polder: The case of the Netherlands. In K. Sriramesh & D. Verčič (Eds.), *The global public relations handbook: Theory, research, and practice* (pp. 222–243). Mahwah, NJ: Lawrence Erlbaum.

Verčič, D., Grunig, L. A., & Grunig, J. E. (1996). Global and specific principles of public relations: Evidence from Slovenia. In H. M. Culbertson & N. Chen (Eds.), *International public relations: A comparative analysis* (pp. 31–66). Mahwah, NJ: Lawrence Erlbaum.

Verčič, D., van Ruler, B., Bütschi, G., & Flodin, B. (2001). On the definition of public relations: A European view. *Public Relations Review, 27*(4), 373–387.

Von Bormann, T. (2003, May 6). Polishing the rainbow. *Africa News Service*. Retrieved July 15, 2005, from Expanded Academic ASAP database.

Wakefield, R. I. (1999). Public relations in new market development: The influence of converging multi-cultural factors. In J. Turk & L. Scanlan (Eds.), *Fifteen case studies in international public relations* (pp. 99–112). Gainesville, FL: The Institute for Public Relations.

Weaver, C. K. (2001). Dressing for battle in the new global economy: Putting power, identity, and discourse into public relations theory. *Management Communication Quarterly, 15*(2), 279–288.

Weaver, G. R. (2001). Ethics programs in global businesses: Culture's role in managing ethics. *Journal of Business Ethics, 30*, 3–15.

We can re-brand and sell Nigeria: Adeoya. (2004, April 8). *Africa News Service*. Retrieved July 15, 2005, from Expanded Academic ASAP database.

Welcome to bankruptcyland: Theme parks in Japan. (2003, April 5). *The Economist, 367*, 69.

WHO. (1964). *WHO expert committee on smallpox* (Technical Report Series No. 283). Geneva: World Health Organization.

WHO. (1968). *Smallpox eradication: Report of a WHO scientific group* (Technical Report Series No. 393). Geneva: World Health Organization.

WHO. (1972). *WHO expert committee on smallpox eradication: Second report* (Technical Report Series No. 493). Geneva: World Health Organization.

WHO. (1980). *The global eradication of smallpox: Final report of the global commission for the certification of smallpox eradication.* Geneva: World Health Organization.

Wilcox, D. L., Ault, P. H., Agee, W. K., & Cameron, G. T. (2001). *Essentials of public relations.* New York: Allyn & Bacon.

Williams, H. (2001, March 30). Russia faces up to global challenge: The PR industry faces a huge perception problem in post-communist Russia. *PR Week,* p. 9.

Williams, R. (1961). *The long revolution.* London: Chatto and Windus.

Williams, R. (1981). *Culture.* London: Fontana Press.

Wood, J. (2005). *PR landscapes: China.* Retrieved June 5, 2005, from http://www.globalpr.org/knowledge/businessguides/Profile-China.pdf

Woodward, K. (1997a). Concepts of identity and difference. In K. Woodward (Ed.), *Identity and difference* (pp. 7–50). Thousand Oaks, CA: Sage.

Woodward, K. (1997b). Introduction. In K. Woodward (Ed.), *Identity and difference* (pp. 1–6). Thousand Oaks, CA: Sage.

Wordsworth, A. (2005, September 13). It really is a small world after all: Disney by the numbers. *National Post,* p. A2.

WTO. (2005, July 20). International tourism receipts grew by 36 billion euros in 2004. *World Trade Organization news release.* Retrieved July 27, 2005, from http://www.world-tourism.org/newsroom/Releases/2005/july/prwto_34.htm

WTO tarnished by Seattle failure. (1999, December 4). *BBC News.* Retrieved January 13, 2006, from http://news.bbc.co.uk/1/hi/special_report/1999/11/99/battle_for_free_trade/549794.stm

Würtz, E. (2005). A cross-cultural analysis of websites from high-context cultures and low-context cultures. *Journal of Computer-Mediated Communication, 11*(1), article 13.

Yanshuo, N. (2004). Bird bug brings lessons. *Beijing Review.* Retrieved July 19, 2005, from http://www.bjreview.com.cn/200411/World-200411(E).htm

Year of the Mouse: Disneyland. (2005, September 10). *The Economist,* p. 64.

Yoo, J.-W. (2005, February 19). Dynamic Korea image goes global. *Korea Times.* Retrieved June 10, 2005, from http://www.korea.net/pda/newsView.asp?serial_no=20050218015&part=111

Zaharna, R. S. (1995). Understanding cultural preferences of Arab communication patterns. *Public Relations Review, 21*(3), 241–255.

Zaharna, R. S. (2001). "In-awareness" approach to international public relations. *Public Relations Review, 27*(2), 135–148.

Zinser, L. (2005, July 6). Olympic bidding turns into a 5-ring circus. *International Herald Tribune,* p. 1.

Zukin, S., & Maguire, J. S. (2004). Consumers and consumption. *Annual Review of Sociology, 30,* 173–197.

Index

About the Authors

Patricia A. Curtin is professor and SOJC endowed chair in public relations in the School of Journalism and Communication at the University of Oregon, Eugene. Previously, she was associate professor and director of the Ph.D. program at the University of North Carolina–Chapel Hill. She earned her master's and doctoral degrees from the University of Georgia after 13 years of corporate and agency work. Curtin serves on the editorial boards of two public relations journals and as book review editor for *Journalism & Mass Communication Quarterly*. A past head of the Public Relations Division of the Association for Education in Journalism and Mass Communication, she is the author of more than 50 refereed research papers. She has given numerous professional seminars and presentations on public relations and intercultural communication topics. An avid traveler, she recently sailed around the world as a faculty member on the spring 2005 voyage of Semester at Sea, a shipboard experiential learning program.

T. Kenn Gaither is an assistant professor at the Elon University School of Communications, where he teaches courses in international public relations, public relations, and mass communication. He has more than 9 years of professional public relations experience and was part of a team that won a Hyundai MicroElectronics of America Excellence in Service Award for public relations work associated with its $4.5-billion merger with LG Semicon in 1999. Gaither is fluent in Portuguese and has lived in Brazil, Ghana, and China. As a staff member on the University of Virginia's Semester at Sea program, he has sailed on seven voyages and visited more than 25 countries. Most recently he served as assistant dean on the spring 2005 voyage. This extensive time abroad has spurred his research interest in international public relations, particularly in developing countries. He has written or co-authored articles in several public relations journals and presented more than 15 papers at national and international conferences.

Cambria Press will publish his dissertation, "Nation Branding, Propaganda, and Public Relations: An Analysis of English-Language Developing Country Head of State Web Sites," in 2007. Gaither earned his Ph.D. from the University of North Carolina–Chapel Hill, where he was a Park Doctoral Fellow and outstanding graduating Ph.D. student. He has an M.F.A. in literary journalism from the University of Pittsburgh.